# Iron Ore Deposits and Banded Iron Formations of India

# Iron Ore Deposits and Banded Iron Formations of India

G.S. Roonwal

2012
DAYA PUBLISHING HOUSE®
New Delhi – 110 002

ISBN 978-81-7035-761-2



*Published by* : **Daya Publishing House®**
4760-61/23, Ansari Road, Darya Ganj,
New Delhi - 110 002
Phone: 23245578, 23244987
Fax: (011) 23260116
e-mail : dayabooks@vsnl.com
website : www.dayabooks.com

*Laser Typesetting* : **Classic Computer Services**
Delhi - 110 035

*Printed at* : **Chawla Offset Printers**
Delhi - 110 052

PRINTED IN INDIA

*my wife*
*Veena*
*in heaven*

# Acknowledgement

This book is a result of support from colleagues especially Professors S. Acharya, J. Mukhopadhaya, D. Beura, A.B. Panigrahi, Dr. E.R. Ramanaidou, and Dr. K.P. Ghosh, the Geological Survey of India. I thank them for permitting me to use their published material. The Department of Science and Technology, Government of India supported this study (vide letter No. HR/UR/OP/2006). The Federation of Indian Mineral Industries, New Delhi provided me space during one year of this study.

*G.S. Roonwal*

# Preface

Iron is one of the oldest metals used in the Indian steel industry. Iron is ubiquitous in the lithosphere both as a major and trace amounts. In abundance iron ranks fourth, the other three being oxygen, silicon and aluminium. The most important use of iron is in the making of steel, which essentially is an alloy of iron, with carbon and other elements depending on the end use.

India's iron industry is one of the oldest in the world. Two types of iron ores are present-hematite and magnetite. Further, at present, India is fourth in the production of iron ore and third in the production of crude steel.

Total resources of iron ore are estimated at 25 billion tonnes, and our production is about 220 million tonnes of iron ore, and about 56 million tonnes of steel (2008–2009 level).

Precambrian-banded iron formations is an extremely variable rock type that was deposited over a long span of early history of the earth. Because the BIFs is variable and was deposited in a wide variety of environments, there are differing views. Infact not many may agree on a common definition of the iron formation. Some restrict the definition to chert bearing rock, some include pyritic shells, and others include sulfide rich tuff or greywacke. This can partly be attributed to because individual author groups have different backgrounds and orientation, some are sedimentologists other are stratigraphers, some are geochemists, others microbiologist while other again economic geologists.

Massive Iron Ore deposits and the banded iron formations (BIF) occur in the Precambrians of the Indian shield. They occupy large area of the order of several thousand km$^2$ in the State of Jharkhand, Orissa, Chhattisgarh, Karnataka, Maharashtra and Goa. Although the BIF formations occur in the metamorphosed country rocks, they are largely unmetamorphosed or very feebly metamorphosed so that shales have the feature of phyllites.

One of the major unresolved problems of Banded Iron Formation or the Iron Formation in true way is their original mineralogy, especially in those which are magnetite bearing. While Precambrian Iron Formations containing laminoidas the predominant oxide mineral have been widely described (Klein, 1973) and compared, information on magnetite quadrate Iron Formation is relatively few. The latter, as they occur often within metamorphosed terrain, are considered by many as metamorphosed hematite and schente iron formation (La Barge 1964), but precipitation of primary magnetite in such formation has also been largely advocated (Goodwin 1973). The problem regarding mineralogy becomes even more difficult in view of observation that the type of iron mineralogy or the degree / level or metamorphism do not influence or significantly effect the banding/and or bedding parameters of iron formations. In a few accounts of Arachean magnetite questions, the mineral hematite, on the other hand has been considered "secondary".

The BIFs in India were geologically mapped in the beginning by the officers of the Geological Survey of India. Largely these base maps are accurate accounts and hold good to this day. Some opinions were expressed on the origin of these formations - as sedimentary deposits, later enriched by bacterial activity. However, detailed study on the environments of their depositional history and the provenance have been conducted on the BIF deposits. The prominent being by Acharya, 1964–2008; Mazumdar and Chakraborty, 1977; Mukhopadhaya *et al.*, 2004–2008).

It is my belief that such an integrated synthesis on the Precambrian BIFs of India would help understand the environment of their deposition, to enable to correlate similar occurrences in the different regions in India, as well as in the other continents. In this respect their synthesis should have both regional and global significance, fulfill the gaps, and would be of use to colleagues. When it receives their attention, my objective would be largely fulfilled. In the absence of details on the pattern of sedimentation, the tectonic set-up of the basins of deposition, and the geochemical, biological parameters, it is clear that no proper modelling on their environment of deposition and genesis is available.

In the other parts of the once the super-continent of Gondwanaland, where similar Banded Iron Formation rocks occur, such as in Brazil, and Australia, some studies have been conducted, which indicate a modeling of the environmental pattern of the deposition of the Banded Iron Formations. The Banded Iron Formation rocks including the associated phyllites show well-preserved sedimentary structures. There are also associated igneous rocks - lava, the plutonic basic (mafic) and ultramafic rocks associated with the BIFs or the Iron Ore Formation known in the Singhbhum, Orissa region. Associated with the large basinal environments of the BIFs are the marginal shallow basinal environment such as the Kolhan Basin in the same region, which shows the changing land - sea relationship in the Singhbhum - Orissa region. Since a very large areas are covered by BIFs in India, and iron ore is an important resource of the nation, it is necessary to undertake a synthesis and compendium study, and thus need no justification. In certain regions, again to cite Singhbhum -

Orissa, where the geology is already well known through long time efforts (Dunn, Dunn and Dey, Sarkar and Saha and the publications of the Geological Survey of India).

During my tenure as a member (2007–2010) of Environmental Impact Assessment Committee for Mining Project, in the Ministry of Environment and Forests, Government of India. I realized that there is definite need to emphasise and adopt beneficiation of low grade iron ores because by mining only high grade (more than 65 per cent), we have been waste of the useful non renewable resource. This is in my view of priority of better utilisation of iron ore reserves. I am glad this has been adopted in some measure due to my intervention.

*G.S. Roonwal*

# Contents

# Chapter 1
# Introduction

Iron has been mined from a variety of kinds of deposits, but production is now almost entirely from two types: banded iron-formations and oolitic ironstones. Banded iron-formations are rocks of mostly Precambrian age that are composed of interlaminated quartz and iron minerals. They can be subdivided into two varieties (Gross 1980): Algoma deposits, which are relatively small with an obvious volcanic association, and Lake Superior, which are much larger and have a shallow-shelf, orthoquartzite-carbonate association. The Algoma type is abundant in the Archean, but an Ordovician example is found at Bathurst, New Brunswick and there is a possible analogue associated with the Carboniferous Pb-Zn deposit at Tynagh, Ireland. Lake Superior- type ores, by contrast, are confined to a particular time interval at around 2 billion years before the present. Oolitic ironstones have a more clastic association than the iron-formations, and are higher in Al. Instead of banding, their most prominent sedimentary structure is ooliths made up of hematite or chamosite. Chert is rare, and they are found in rocks of a variety of ages from Proterozoic to Pliocene.

As of date, these two types constituted more than 90 per cent of the world's iron production, with Lake Superior ores accounting for about 65 percent (Gross 1970). At that time, ironstones made up about 20 per cent of the production, but this proportion has been decreasing: the last iron mines in Great Britain, which are in Jurassic oolitic ironstones. The extensive Lake Superior-type deposits of Australia are now coming into production, displacing smaller deposits, so that Lake Superior-type ores probably make up 75 per cent or more of production today. One reason for their predominance is a change in the nature of the feed for blast furnaces. Formerly, only ores that had been naturally enriched by the leaching of most of their $SiO_2$ (the "direct shipping ores") could be used. Since the introduction of pelletized feeds in 1955, there has been a shift to artificially concentrated cherty taconites because of lower shipping costs and lower energy costs for blast furnace operation (Kakela 1978).

Iron is the third most abundant metal, after Si and Al. Therefore, it is a major constituent of most rocks (Table 1.1), and its ores are actually rock types in their own right. The formation of these iron rocks depends on changes in oxidation state: Fe is mobilized under reducing conditions, precipitated under oxidizing. Thus, it will migrate from areas low in oxygen towards areas high in it, provided a pathway exists. Note, in Table 1.1, that igneous rocks, although varying in total iron, have about the same proportion of $Fe^3$ to $Fe^2$. Sedimentary rocks, in contrast, show a wide range of oxidation states, indicative of the presence of environments of differing oxidation potential. Therefore, it is in sediments that the greatest potential for iron enrichment exists, and almost all iron ores are sedimentary.

**Table 1.1: Abundance of Iron in Common Rock Types**

| | *FeO (Per cent)* | *$Fe_2O_3$ (Per cent)* | $\frac{Fe_2O_3}{FeO + Fe_2O_3}$ |
|---|---|---|---|
| Igneous Rocks | | | |
| alkali-olivine basalts | 7.9 | 4.2 | 0.35 |
| tholeiitic basalts | 9.5 | 3.2 | 0.25 |
| granodiorites | 2.6 | 1.3 | 0.33 |
| granites | 1.5 | 0.8 | 0.35 |
| Sedimentary Rocks | | | |
| Sandstones: | | | |
| quartz arenite | 0.2 | 0.4 | 0.67 |
| lithic arenite | 1.4 | 3.8 | 0.73 |
| graywacke | 3.5 | 1.6 | 0.31 |
| arkose | 0.7 | 1.5 | 0.68 |
| Shales and slates | | | |
| red | 1.26 | 5.36 | 0.81 |
| green | 1.42 | 3.48 | 0.71 |
| black | 4.88 | 0.52 | 0.10 |
| Seawater (as Fe) | | 0.007 ppm | |

*Source:* Wedepohl 1969 and 1971.

Iron has been known since antiquity. Iron is ubiquitous in the earth's lithosphere as either a major element or in trace amounts. In abandons or Clarke Value it ranks fourth behind oxygen, silicon and aluminum.

The most important use of iron is in the making of steel, which is essentialiy an alloy of iron with carbon and other elements depending upon the end use.

India is one of the earliest manufacturers and users of iron and steel in the world. Survey of many documentary evidence such as making of various surgical instruments in the 3rd and 4th century B.C. prove this. Till 18th Century iron and steel making in India was at par with that of Europe in the form of village crafts. This situation changed with introduction of Bessemer process in 1865 and the basic open Hearth Furnace process in 1878. These developments led to significant increase in the world steel production from about 0.5 MT in 1870 to 28 MT in 1900.

The present annual capacity of primary steel production from the integrated steel plants is placed at about 26 MT from the main producers and about 70 MT in the secondary sector by various processes.

## History of Iron and Steel Industry in India

Iron ore and steel are the crux for industrial development in a country. The vitality of the iron ore and steel industry largely influences the economic status of a country. The level of per capita consumption of steel is treated as one of the important indicators of socio-economic development and living standard of the people in any country. Iron and steel making in India dates back 480 BC when Indian archers used arrows tipped with Indian steel. Iron pillar of Dhar near Indore in Madhya Pradesh (about 321 AD), iron pillar of Qutab Minar near Delhi (about 400 AD), iron beams of Sun temple of Konark in Orissa (13th century AD) are some of the examples in ancient India. A suspension bridge in Kashmir used iron manufactured in the state of Madhya Pradesh in 1830. The first notable attempt to revive steel industry in India was made in 1874 when the Bengal Iron Works (BIW) came into being at Kulti, near Asanol in West Bengal. However, forty-four years before that, in 1830, a european, named Joshua Marshall Heath, had set up a small plant at Porto Novo on Madras Coast. Heath produced in his plant pig iron at the rate of forty tones a week. His method of iron-making needed approximately four tonnes of charcoal to produce one tonne of low quality pig iron which proved to be too expensive for Heath to carry on in the face of stiff competition from the British steel industry. The BIW made considerable improvement in the process of iron and steel making. It used coke as the fuel instead of charcoal. But the plant fell sick as the source of funds dried up. It was taken over by the Bengal Government and was rechristened as Barakar Iron Works. In 1889 the Bengal Iron and Steel Company acquired the plant and by the turn of the century the Kulti plant became a success story. It produced 40,000 tonnes of pig iron in 1900 and continued to produce the metal until it was taken over by Indian Iron and Steel Co. (IISCO) in 1936.

For modern India's Iron and Steel Industry August 27, 1907 was a red-letter day when the Tata Iron and Steel Company (TISCO) was formed as a Swadeshi venture to produce 120,000 tonnes of pig iron. The TISCO plant at Sakchi (renamed Jamshedpur) in Bihar (now Jharkhand), started pig iron production in December 1908 and rolled out its first steel the following year. In 1918, soon after the World war, Indian Iron and Steel Company (IISCO) was formed. Then Mysore government also decided to start an Iron works at Bhadravati. While IISCO started producing pig iron at Burnpur in 1922, the Mysore Iron and Steel Works took about 18 years to start its plant. Meanwhile, the Bengal Iron Works went into liquidation and merged with IISCO. The Steel

Corporation of Bengal (SCOB) formed in 1937, started making steel in its Asansol plant. Later in 1953, SCOB merged with IISCO. TISCO expanded its production capacity to one million tones ingot by the time the country achieved freedom.

The three largest iron ore companies, Vale, Rio Tinto and BHP Billiton increased their control over global iron ore production to 35.4 per cent in 2009 (34 per cent in 2008). The "Big Three" control 61 per cent of the world seaborne trade of iron ore worldwide. New iron ore mining capacity taken into operation in 2009, reached almost 75 million tonnes. Globally iron ore production is widely spread occurring in almost fifty countries, the bulk of world production came from just five countries. The five largest producers Brazil, Australia, China, India and the former Soviet Union (CIS) account for almost 80% of the world total production.

India has large reserves of good quality iron ore which can meet the growing demand of domestic iron and steel industry and can also sustain considerable external trade. Hematite and magnetite are the most prominent of the iron ores found in India. Indian deposits of hematite belong to Precambrian iron ore series and the ore is within banded iron ore formations occurring as massive, laminated, friable and also in powdery form.

About 60 per cent of hematite ore deposits are found in the eastern sector and about 80 per cent magnetite ore deposits occur in southern sector, especially in Karnataka. The total iron ore resources are estimated 25.25 billion tonnes, of which hematite ore resources stand at the order of 14.63 billion tonnes and the remaining 10.61 billion tonnes are magnetite as on 1-4-2005 (*Source*: IBM, Nagpur).

## Regional Geologic Distribution

The banded iron-formations are confined to Precambrian shield areas. They are comparable by their significant features on both the Northern Hemisphere and the Southern Hemisphere continents and, in fact, there is no major cratonic area which lacks iron-formations as prominent members of its stratigraphical column.

As most, but not all, iron-formations are metamorphosed and are parts of the regionally metamorphosed and often strongly folded sedimentary sequences that build up the consolidated masses of the Precambrian shields, they occur frequently as resistent erosional remnants of folded ancient sedimentary basins. In many cases, they can be traced as parts of synclinal or anticlinal structures over hundreds or even more than a thousand kilometres in lateral extent, forming prominent iron ranges.

Apparently, oxide-facies iron-formations represent the bulk of all economically significant iron-formations. Hence, most of the geological literature on the subject is based on this type which is the host rock of the largest and best-studied iron ore mines, at present being worked predominently on the Southern Hemisphere continents - South America, Africa, India and Australia. In these areas of subtropical climates, many of the originally low-grade iron-formations have been enriched under favourable conditions by supergene weathering processes to high-grade iron ores with 60-69 per cent iron content (*e.g.*, Dorr, 1973), which is described in India as float ore.

In Figure 1.1 and Table 1.2 is shown the distribution of the most important occurrences of iron-formations on the Precambrian shield areas of the world, It is obvious that many of them lie close to the borders of the continents or on the margins of the cratonic masses now surrounded by younger fold belts and platform sediments. As Gross (1973) has pointed out, this distribution may lead to the supposition that the margins of the old continental masses have been favourable areas for the development of depositional basins with sedimentation of iron-formations. Gross suggested that some of the iron-formations now on the borders of different continents may have formed parts of the same sedimentary basins and fold belts of consistent shield areas as they may have appeared prior to continental drift.

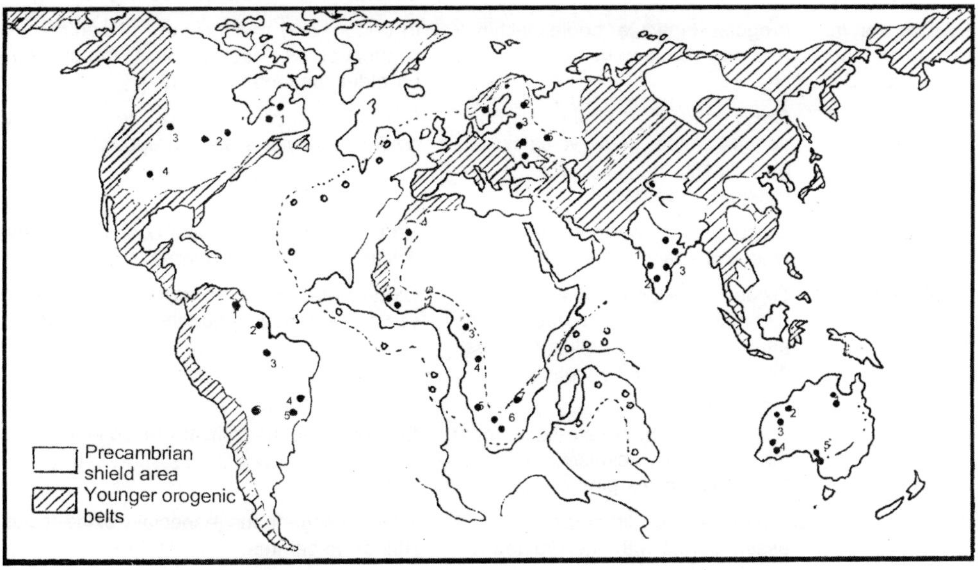


**Figure 1.1: Distribution of Prominent Precambrian Banded Iron-formations and Reconstruction of Probable Situation Prior to Continental Drift (Proterozoic iron-formation belts)**

**North America: 1 = Labrador-Ungava; 2 Lake Superior region; 3 = northern Rocky Mts.; 4 = southwest U.S.**
**South America: 1 = Irnataca Series, Venezuela; 2 Amap, Brazil; 3 Serra dos Carajs, Par 4 Bahia; 5 = Minas Gerais, ironore quadrangle; 6 = Urucum, Mato Grosso.**
**Africa: 1 = Mauritania, Ford Gouraud; 2 = Sierra Leone, Liberia; 3 = Gabon, Mekambo; 4 Angola, Cassinga and Cassala; 5 Damarã, S.W. Africa; 6 = South Africa, Witwatersrand and Transvaal Super- groups; 7 = Limpopo metamorphic belt.**
**India: I = Goa; 2 Karnataka; 3 = Andhra Pradesh; 4 Jharkhand and Orissa.**
**Australia: 1 = McArthur Basin:2 = Pilbara Block; 3 Hamersley Group; 4= Yilgarn Block 5 = Middle- back Range.**
**Europa and Aria: I Scandinavian Shield; 2 = Karelia; 3 Bielorussia; 4 = KMA, Krivoy Rog and Ukrainian Shield; S Urals; 6 = Tuva, Sayan, Baykal, South Yakutia; 7 Anshan.**
**Morphic event at 1,800 m.y. and underwent deformation by folding, symmetrical to a central crest zone.**

**Table 1.2: Major Iron Ore Distribution (After Eichler, 1976)**

| | *Algoma-type (Archean-type)* | *Superior-type (Animikie-type)* |
|---|---|---|
| Age | Pre-2,600 my. (also Proterozoic and Phanerozoic) | Pre-l,800 m.y. |
| Sedimentary environment | Eugeosynclinal tectonic basins of several 100 km diameter; iron-formation in marginal parts in connection with greenstone belts | Miogeosynclinal; iron-formation along margins of stable continental shelves; shallow water; restricted intra-cratonic basins |
| Extent | commonly lenticular bodies of a few km | Extensive formations persistent over some 100 km to more than 1,000 km |
| Thickness | 0.1 m to some 10 m | Several m to more than 100 m (1,000m) |
| Location in sedimentary sequence | Irregular, lenticular bodies within Archean "basement" rocks | In bottom and middle parts of sedimentary sequences as sheet-deposits, transgressive on older "basement" rocks |
| Associated rocks | Graywackes and shales; carbon-aceous slates; mafic volcanis; felsic pyro-clastic; ryolitic flows; pillowed andesites. | Coarse clastics; quartzite, conglomerates dolomites, black sliales (graphitic) |
| Volcanics | Close association to volcanism in time and space | No direct association with contemporaneous volcanism; volcanics normally absent |
| Sedimentary facies | Oxide-facies predominant; carbonate- and sulfide-facies thin and discontinuous; silicate-facies; all facics frequently closely associated | Oxide-fades most abundant: silicate- and carbonate-facies frequently intergradational. |
| | Sulfide- and carbonate-facies near the center of volcanism; oxide-facies on the margins | Sulfide-facies insignificant or absent |
| | Heterogeneous lithological assemblages with fine grained clastic beds. | More homogeneous (especially oxide-facies); little or no detritus. |
| | Granular and oolitic textures | Granular and oolitic textures |
| Examples | Canada: Archean basins (*e.g.* Michipicten) | Labrador Trough |
| | U.S.A.: Vermilion District, Minnesota | Lake Superior Region |
| | S. Africa: greenstone belts, Kaapvaal and Rhodesia Cratons | Transvaal and Witwatersrand Super-groups |
| | Brazil: Rio das Velhas Series | Minas Series (itabirites); Carajas/Para |
| | India: Karnataka | Jharkhand, Orissa, Goa, Karnataka |
| | Australia: Yilgarn and Pilbara Blocks | Hamersley Group |
| | U.S.S.R.: Taratash/Urals | Krivoy Rog, Kursk; Ukrainian Shield |

This regional distribution of iron-formations near and along the coastal parts of the continents is clearly seen in South America and Africa as well as in Australia and India.

Where the general geological setting has been studied in more detail, a comparison of iron-formations on opposite continents fits fairly well with the assumption of originally coherent iron-formation belts. This is the case for iron-formations on the Guayana and Liberian shields, as Gross (1973) has shown, comparing the occurrences of the Imataca Series of Venezuela with those of Liberia and Sierra Leone. The type and depositional environment of these iron-formations with their associated rocks are similar, if not identical, and so are their ages and their orogenic and metamorphic histories.

It is most interesting to note that the iron-formations of Venezuela and Western Africa, both deposited 2,500 - 3,000 m.y. ago, were affected by the same younger metamorphic events at 1,800 m.y. and under went deformation by folding, symmetrical to a central crust zone.

This would mean that the segmentation and continental drift of the Gondwana landmass, supposed to have started in many places during the Early Cretaceous, has followed a latent and much older Precambrian fault and tectonic pattern of worldwide dimensions, which may have controlled the suitable conditions for the depositional environments of iron-formations.

It is a most remarkable fact that the distribution of Precambrian iron-formations in several great cycles coincides fairly well with the ages of profound magmatic and metamorphic events during the evolution of the earth's crust.

Runcorn (1962) advocated a repeated continental drift and delivered a theory of Precambrian continental drift, caused by changes in the convection mechanism of the earth's mantle by periodical growth of the core. Such changes, as Runcorn presumes, occurred in the intervals between 2,750 and 2,450 m.y.; 1,900-1,600 m.y.; and 1,150-900 m.y. ago, thus corresponding in time with the main epochs of deposition of iron-formations many of which lie inside the worldwide fold belts of the "Superior Regime" (2,750–1,950 m.y.) as plotted by Dearnley (1965) on the presumed preGondwana landmass.

Thus, the fundamental reasons for the regional distribution of such huge accumulations of iron and silica seem to be basically connected with certain universal principles in the behaviour of the sialic crust. It is almost certain that any attempt to decipher the final reasons for the deposition of the Precambrian iron-formation has to consider not only detailed studies of single iron-formation environments but relies heavily on more knowledge of the superimposing basic factors of worldwide significance.

## Ages of Precambrian Banded Iron-Formations

Due to the lack of minerals within the iron-formations suitable for radiometric age determinations, a precise dating of these rocks has been possible only in rare cases. However, the progress in radiometric dating techniques and the great number of samples determined in recent years from associated metasedimentary and volcanic rocks makes it possible at least to mark the age limits of many prominent iron-formations of all parts of the world. Compilations of age determinations have been given by Lepp and Goldich (1964), Govett (1966), James (1966) and by Goldich (1973). The review in this chapter is essentially based on these papers.

Though banded iron-formations occur during a period of at least 3,000 m.y. through out the Precambrian, their prevailing development is confined to a single epoch between 2,600 and 1,800 m.y. ago (Goldich, 1973). As Bayley and James (1973) have shown, this interval was clearly the principal time of deposition in North America, far outweighing by their extent and iron content the more limited older and younger iron-formations. The. same is the case for many major iron-formations on other continents such as those of Russia (Krivoy Rog, Kursk), South Africa, Brazil and Western Australia, all of which seem to have been deposited approximately contemporaneously between 2,600-1,800 m.y. ago. In all these shield areas apparently, there is a progressive decrease in the abundance of iron-formations, in size as well as in quantity, in the post-1,800 m.y. period just as in the pre-2,600 m.y. epoch.

Following the framework classification given by Goldich (1973), the iron-formations should be grouped, according to their ages, in the categories: (1) older than 3,000 m.y.; (2) 3,000 - 2,600 m.y.; (3) 2,600–1,800 m.y.; and (4) younger than 1,800 m.y.

1. With few but notable exceptions, the bulk of the Early Precambrian, Archean iron-formations, though not restricted to the pre-2,600 m.y. period, belong to the Algoma-type as defined by Gross (1965). They are closely related to greenstone belts and form relatively small lenticular bodies. (The oldest known iron-formations, close to or older than 3,000 m.y., are found in the Swaziland System of South Africa (3,000-3,400 m.y.), in the Pilbara and Yilgarn Blocks of Western Australia (2,670-3,000 m.y.), in the Imatacu Complex of Venezuela (3,000-3,400 m.y.) and in the Ukrainian Shield in the Greater Krivoy Rog area (3,100-3,500 m.y.)
2. In the range from 3,000 - 2,600 m.y. numerous occurrences are known on the Canadian Shield, most of them closely associated with greenstone belts. A great number of them were deposited in the remarkably brief interval from 2,750 - 2,700 m.y. ago (Sims and Morey, 1972). In South Africa iron-formations in the Sebakvian, Bulavayan and Shamvayan Systems, stratigraphically associated with volcanic rocks, were dated at more than 2,700 m.y. (see Beukes, 1973). The same ages of >2,700 m.y. are found in some small Algoma-type occurrences in the Rio das Veihas-Series of Brazil, in India in Karnataka and in the "Iron Ore Series" of Jharkhand - Orissa and also in eastern Karelia on the Baltic Shield (for references see Goldich, 1973). Thus, it appears that the span of time between 3,000 and 2,600 m.y., especially around 2,700 m.y., marks a significant epoch, very favourable for the deposition of iron-formations.
3. The most abundant development of iron-formations in the world is found in the interval between 2,600 and 1,800 m.y. On the Canadian shield the ages of the major iron-formations of Labrador and the Lake Superior region range between 2,200 and 1,900 m.y. The interval of the main deposition was probably much less, since for the iron-formations in Minnesota, thought

to be largely contemporaneous with others in North America, a minimum age of 2,000 m.y. has been determined. In Australia the Brockrnan Iron Formation of the Hamersley Group is bracketed between 2,200 and 2,000 m.y. Similar ages are given for Krivoy Rog/Ukrainia (2,200–1,900 m.y.), for the Brazilian itabirites in Minas Gerais and in the Serra dos Carajás–Par (about 2,000 m.y.) and also for iron-formations of the Svecofennian of the Baltic Shield (minimum age of 1,900 m.y.) and of the Aldan Shield on the southeastern margin of the Siberian platform (2,000–2,750 m.y.). In South Africa iron-formations in association with clastic rocks are predominantly developed during the interval from 2,300–3,000 m.y., whereas the shelf-carbonate and carbonate–manganese associations belong to the period prior to 2,300 m.y.

4. The post-1800 m.y. banded iron-formations known in the world are quantitatively much less important; compared with the overwhelming concentration in the Lower Proteiozoic and Archean they should rather be considered as exceptions. If a clear definition of "iron-formation" should exist, it most probably would not fit the characteristics of "iron-formation", principally of the problematic younger iron-formations, described by O'Rourke (1961). Examples for these are occurrences in Nepal and in Mato Grosso/Brazil (Dorr II, 1973a). These Late Proterozoic or Early Cambrian cherty iron-formations are also typically banded but, averaging about 56 per cent Fe, they are much richer in iron than the older types. Their origin is still enigmatic.

In North America only a few minor occurrences of Late Precambrian age are known.

In the Rapitan Group of the Yukon and Northwest Territories the age of an iron-formation is correlated with that of the Windermere Group (800-600 m.y.). The iron-formation in the Yavapai Series of central Arizona was metamorphosed between 1,820 and 1,760 m.y. ago and may be coeval with those of the Lake Superior region. The iron-formation in the lower part of the Damara Supergroup of South West Africa has been deposited between 1,000 and 620 m.y. ago (see Beukes, 1973).

It is a most remarkable fact that major iron-formations all over the world can be fairly well grouped in several time intervals of the Precambrian, between 3,400 and 3,000 m.y., about 2,700 m.y. and outstandingly in one period between 2,600 and 1,800 m.y. ago with an accumulation at about 2,000 m.y. This last statement has been also made for the major iron-formations of the CIS and Russia (Alexandrov, 1973). Many of them have metamorphic ages of about 2,000 m.y. Younger ages are thought to correspond to the age of the final orogeny in the evolution of the geosyncline, which went across the Russian platform so that they do not reflect the time of deposition. The iron-formations of the Algoma-type generally are limited in size, but occur over a greater span of time, from the earliest Precambrian through the Phanerozoic, whereas the Superior-type is strictly confined to the Precambrian, the bulk of it most probably to the period prior to about 2,000 m.y. ago.

It must be pointed out that the data for single iron-formations should be used with caution as many of them might represent not the true age of deposition but mixed ages from subsequent metamorphic or orogenic events which have overprinted the old craton areas, for instance, the 500 m.y. "Panafrican Thermal Event" advocated by Kennedy (1964). Nevertheless, these factors as well as uncertainties in the use of decay constants in the different laboratories should not affect the general statement that the deposition of many major iron-formations of the world was synchronous in certain epochs of the Precambrian.

Figure 1.2 suggests that the development of iron-formations fell into relatively stable epochs precursory to and partly overlapping with the initial stages of major magmatic and metamorphic cycles during the Precambrian.

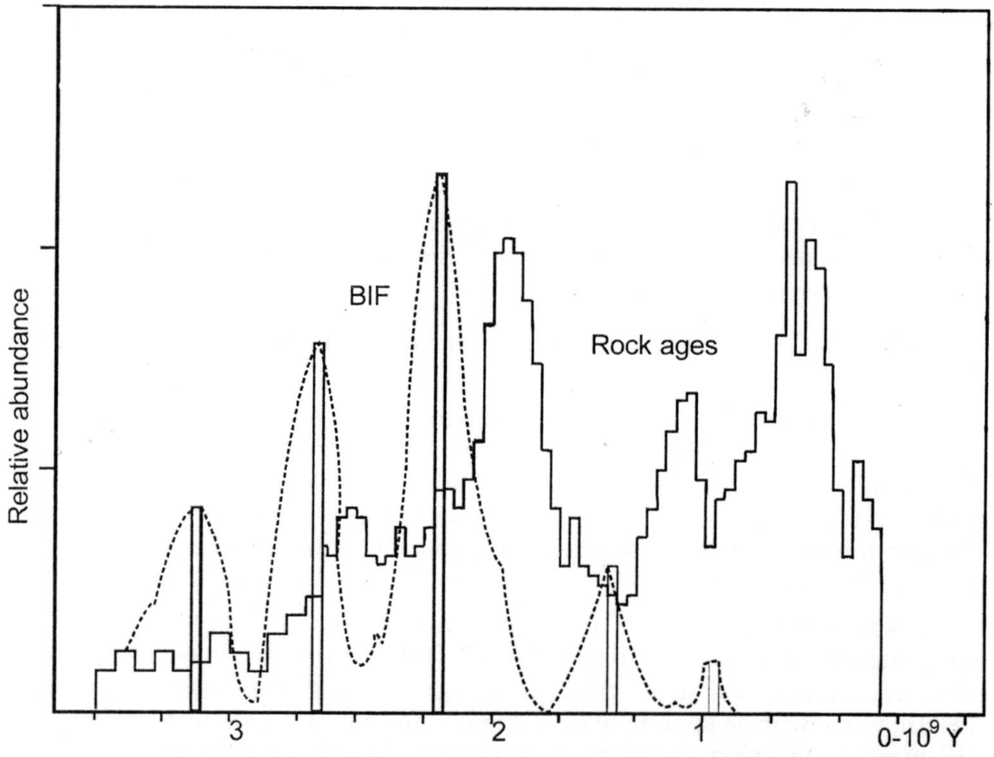


**Figure 1.2: Ages of Major Magmatic and Metamorphic Events in Earth's History (funeral and rock ages compiled from Dearnley (1965); 3,400 age determinations) and Relative Abundance of Iron-formations on the Time Scale**

Unequivocally, as it is also pointed out by Cloud (1973), the epoch between about 2,600 and 2,000 m.y. ago marks a profound change of conditions in the earth's evolution, terminating the vigorous growth of procaryotic organisms and giving rise to a development under increasingly oxidizing conditions.

## Commercial and Specifications

Iron ore is used mainly for making pig iron, sponge iron and steel. Iron and steel together form the largest manufactured products in the world and each of these centers into every brand of industry and it is a necessary factor in every part of our present day lifestyle. Pure iron use has been relatively few and has been mostly used for specialized uses. Ingot iron is galvanized for roofing, siding and tanks. In the form of corrugated pipes it is used for end-vents because of its relatively high purity it is used for oxy-acetylene welding, both as material to be welded and as welding rod. It is used in vitreous enameling. Its good ductility makes iron suitable for deep drawing operations as in the manufacturing of appliance parts *e.g.* washing machine tube. Relatively low electrical resistance and high magnetic permeability gives to its use in many types of electrical equipment, generator field, magnetic parts of relays, magnetic brakes and clutches. Iron ore is used also in ferrous alloys, cement foundry, *vanaspati* and glass factories.

The typical compositions of cast iron are given in the Table 1.3. The different grade of pig iron depends upon their contents of silicon, sulphur, phosphorous and manganese.

**Table 1.3: Typical Composition of Cast Iron**

| *Composition* | *White Iron* | *Malleable Iron* | *Grey Iron* | *Ductile Iron* |
|---|---|---|---|---|
| Carbon Wt % | 1.8–3.6 | 2.0–3.0 | 2.5–3.8 | 3.2–4.2 |
| Silicon Wt. % | 0.5–2.0 | 0.6–1.3 | 1.1 –2.8 | 1.1 –3.5 |
| Manganese Wt. % | 0.2–0.8 | 0.2–0.6 | 0.4–1.0 | 03–0.8 |
| Phosphorous % | 0.18 | 0.15 | 0.15 | 0.08 |
| Sulphur % | 0.1 | 0.1 | 0.1 | 0.02 |

*Sources*: Indian Bureau of Mines (IBM) Monograph on Iron Ores (1998).

**Table 1.4: Price of Iron Ore (Domestic Market) 1999—2004 per tone**

| *Grade* | *Market* | *1999-2000* | *2000-2001* | *2001-2002* | *2002-2003* | *2003-2004* |
|---|---|---|---|---|---|---|
| Lumps 63% Fe | FOBT Marmango Berth Goa | 15.39 | 16.28 | 16.18 | 15.97 | 17.39 |
| Lumps 60–59% Fe | –do– | 12.99 | 13.74 | 14.18 | 14.37 | 14.67 |
| Fines 63% Fe | –do– | 13.11 | 13.68 | 14.27 | 13.93 | 15.18 |
| Fines 62% Fe | –do– | 12.73 | 13.28 | 13.85 | 13.52 | 14.74 |
| Lumps Average | FOBT Noamandi Jharkhand | Rs. 327 | 314 | 313 | 335 | 335 |

US$ = US dollar; ₹ = Indian Rupee; ₹ 45 = 1 US$.

Prices are influenced not only by the intrinsic prices of the ore (base price) but also by freight expenses. Freight expenses demonstrate a more relatable behavior to the basic price of the ore. The price of the iron ores of different grade during 1999 – 2004 are given in the Table 1.4.

# Chapter 2

# Banded Iron Formations and Iron Ore Resources of the World

Estimated iron ore resources in the world by the end of 2008 are about over 8,00,000 MT. (MCS, 2008). Iron ore deposits are distributed in different regions of the world under varied geological conditions and in different geological formations. The largest concentration of iron ores is formed in banded sedimentary iron formations in the Precambrian age. These formations constitute the bulk of world's iron ore resources. The top ten countries in the world as per their iron ore deposits are the Commonwealth of Independent States (CIS), who belonged to the former Soviet Union, China, Brazil, Australia, USA, India, Sweden, Canada, South Africa and Venezuela.

Among the identified resources about 15 per cent are classified as Economic Demonstrated Resources (EDR) by the US Bureau of Mines. The EDR though small, when compared with the total identified resources are sufficient to sustain present products for more than 160 years.

The Precambrian iron-formations, of which banded ferruginous or iron cherts and jaspilites are the most important component, are known on all the continents. The rocks constituting these formations are very diverse in lithologic composition and origin: from typical volcanic (both basic and acid) to purely sedimentary (clastic, chemogenic). These iron-formations are usually related to complexly deformed geosynclinal complexes -eugeosynclinal or miogeosynclinal - although they are also encountered in slightly altered sediments on all platforms.

The largest areas where Precambrian iron-formations are developed are the East European platform: (*e.g.* Krivoy Rog, Kremenchug, Belozerka, and other districts of the Ukrainian shield, the Voronezh, Baltic, and Central Kazakhstan shields, the Lake Superior area on the North American platform, Minas Gerais in Brazil, Hamersley in Australia, Singhbum–Orissa and Dharwar Region in India, etc.

**Table 2.1: Global Iron Ore and Steel Scenario**
**World Resources of Iron Ore (Principal Countries) Million Tonnes**

| *Country* | *Crude Ore* | *Iron Content* |
|---|---|---|
| World: Total (rounded) | 340000 | 160000 |
| Australia | 45000 | 28000 |
| Brazil | 27000 | 14000 |
| Canada | 3900 | 2500 |
| China | 46000 | 15000 |
| India* | 9800 | 6200 |
| Iran | 2500 | 1500 |
| Kazakhstan | 19000 | 7400 |
| Mauritania | 1500 | 1000 |
| Mexico | 1500 | 900 |
| Russia | 56000 | 31000 |
| South Africa | 2300 | 1500 |
| Sweden | 7800 | 5000 |
| Ukraine | 68000 | 20000 |
| USA | 15000 | 4600 |
| Venezuela | 6000 | 3600 |
| Other Countries | 30000 | 17000 |

*Source*: Mineral Commodity Summaries, 2008.

*India's resources of iron ore as per UNFC system as on 1-4-2005 are estimated at 25 billion tonnes.

BIF have been located in the Precambrians beginning with the oldest strata, 3,500 m.y. old. The rocks of the Konka-Belozerka zone of the Ukrainian shield and of the Pilbara Block of the Australian platform have an age of 2,700-3,500 m.y. An age of 2,000 m.y. has been established for the iron cherts of the Bazaviuk zone of the Ukrainian shield, the Olenogorsk deposit on the Baltic shield, the Singhbum, Orissa deposit in India, and the Algoma-type BIF of the Lake Superior area.

The rocks of the Krivoy Rog - Kremenchug zone, of the Kursk group in the Kursk Magnetic Anomaly (KMA), of the Animikie group of Lake Superior, and of the Hamersley formation in Australia are dated to 1,700-2,000 m.y. Younger BIF are also known, including post-Precambrian ones, related chiefly to volcanogenic rocks.

There exist no accepted classification based on lithologic association of these rocks, though four types of geosynclinal cherty iron-formations were identified Semenenko *et al.*, (1967). Gross (1961, 1965, 1973) distinguishes a sedimentary cherty iron-formation of Lake Superior type and a volcanogenic cherty iron-formation of Algoma type which includes the keratophyre, metabasic, and ultrabasic formations.

## Geologic Setting and Depositional Environments of Banded Iron-Formations

An examination of the main areas of occurrences Precambrian BIF of different formational types has been summarized in the following keeping the general regularities of distribution of the iron-form and to their age, spatial, and genetic relationships.

Despite many common features such as banding, mineral assemblages, sedimentary facies and chemical composition, iron-formations occur in quite different sedimentary environments.

Most of the Algoma-type iron-formations are found in Archean eugeosynclinal basins, whereas most of the Middle Precambrian Superior-type iron-formations are found most commonly on the margins of stable continental shelves in miogeosynclinal environments of intercratonic and cratonic basins.

Archean basins. The most complete description of Archean tectonic basins of the Canadian Shield is given by Goodwin and Shklanka (1967) and Goodwin (1973). Ten major Archean basins have been recognized in the Superior and Churchill provinces and, to a more limited extent, also in the Slave Province of the Canadian Shield, mainly identified on the basis of iron-formations, which are typically associated with greenstone belts within the Archean basins. The elliptical basins are, in their present structurally deformed state, about 350–700 km long and are thought to represent remnants of originally quasi-circular structures in the tectonically mobile Archean crust, with diameters of between 800 and 1100 km (Goodwin, 1973).

Similar large basins have been recognized on shield areas elsewhere in the world, in Australia and in the Rhodesian and Kaapvaal Cratons of South Africa (Beukes, 1973).

Earlier Kloostennan (1973) has described several giant "ring volcanoes", with diameters of between 300 and 900 km, from the Amazon part of the Guiana Shield, which, however, have a younger age and were emplaced between 1,900 and 1,800 m.y. ago. The relationship of some known iron-formation deposits with these structures is not yet clear.

It was proposed by Goodwin (1973) that Archean basins of the Canadian Shield represent centres of crustal speading in areas where vertical thermal streams ("thermal plumes" or "hot spots") have been particularly active in the thin Archean crust. A meteorite impact scar theory is considered unlikely. The wide distribution of basins of this type in outcropping and uneroded Archean shield areas suggests that Archean basins have to be considered as first-order features of the crustal evolution in Early Precambrian time and perhaps as the ancient counterparts of modern oceans. The development of the present oceans could well have originated from zones of fragility in the Precambrian crust, indicated by the distribution of many of the major iron-formation bearing old geosynclines, now broken apart by "continental drift" in the course of younger plate-tectonic movements.

The Michipicoten area of north-central Ontario was quoted by Goodwin (1973) as a typical example of such volcano-tectonic Archean basins. It encompasses several greenstone belts and intervening batholithic complexes. Arc-type volcanics with effusions and felsic pyroclastics, coarse-grained clastics, including graywackes and thick conglomerates, and iron-formations from oxide to sulfide stains are the most important lithologic associations of the marginal parts of such basins.

The distribution of iron-formations within the ambient volcanic sequences in the greenstone belts follows the normal depositional pattern, with oxide-, carbonate- and sulfide-facies in that order from the marginal to the inner parts of a basin. Oxide-facies is by far the most common facies. Carbonate- and sulfide-facies iron-formations are equally widely developed but, in general, form only thin and discontinuous lenticular bodies of lesser significance. Commonly, iron-formations of this type are closely related to pyroclastic members of mafic to felsic volcanic sequences and shale-graywacke successions. Thus, there is common agreement to attribute the derivation of these iron-formations to volcanic activities.

Figures 2.1 and 2.2 taken from Goodwin (1973), demonstrate with a stratigraphic section of the Michipicoten basin, Ontario, the facies transitions from the shelf to the inner parts in a typical Archean basin.

Contrary to the Archean iron-formations, which are closely associated with volcanic successions in giant interarc basins of the Archean basement, the bulk of the major Middle to Early Proterozoic iron-formations was deposited in miogeosynclinal or epicontinental environments, together with clastic sequences, transgressive on the older basement. Oxide facies is the most abundant type and it is commonly not associated with volcanic rocks. These iron-formations of the Superior-type are enormous sheet deposits with thicknesses of up to several hundred metres. They are persistent over many hundreds of kilometres to more than a thousand kilometres in extent and several hundreds of kilometres in width. The major iron-formations with an age bracketed between 2,600 and 1,800 m.y., many of them probably coeval at about 2,000 m.y., are prominent rock units of the shelf parts of elongated, large miogeosynclinal or intercratonic basins along the Archean shield areas, which they commonly overlie with profound angular and erosional unconformity. The dimensions of these Proterozoic troughs, with extents of not much less than 1,000 km to more than 1,000 km, widths in the order of 100 km to several hundreds of kilometres and sedimentary thicknesses of several thousand metres, are comparable worldwide as Pflug (1967) has pointed out in his comparison of Precambrian miogeosynclines. Thus, it appears that this-kind of depositional environment for iron-formations represents a characteristic feature of the Precambrian evolution about 2,100-2,000 m.y. ago.

Prominent examples of the wide lateral distribution of continuous iron-formations are the Labrador Trough and the occurrences of the Lake Superior region, which correspond in age and other features and which can be followed over a distance

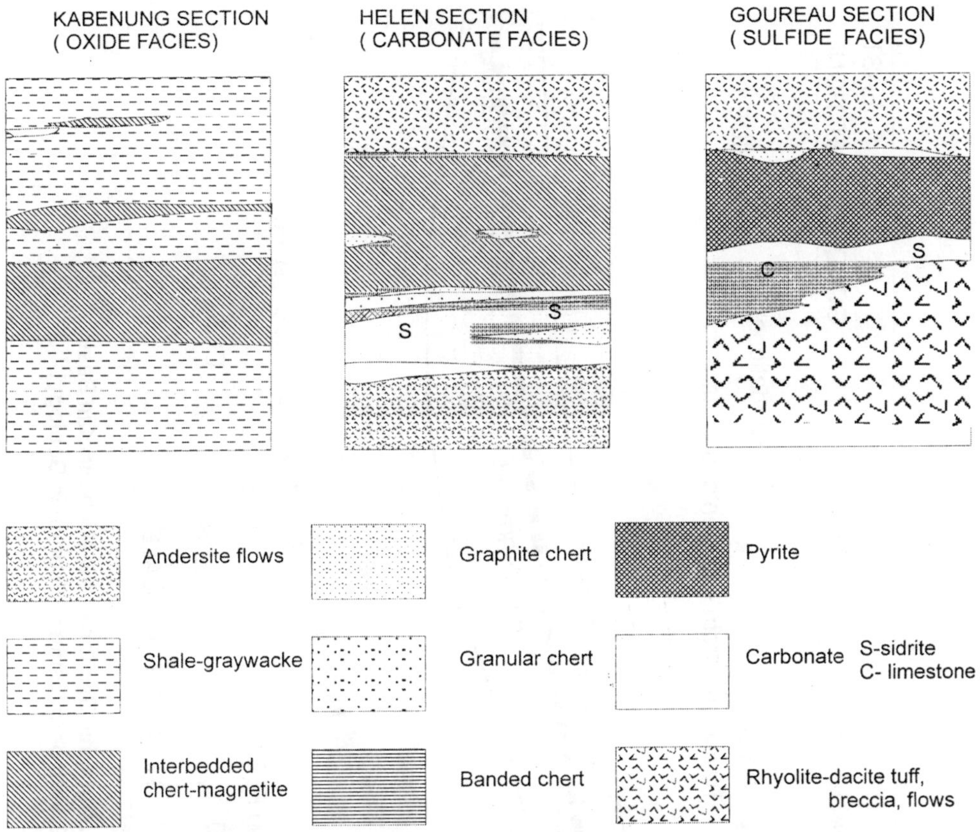


**Figure 2.1: Typical Stratigraphic Sections of Oxide, Carbonate and Suiphide Facies of Iron-Formation in the Michipicoten Basin (from Goodwin, 1973, p. 30, with permission of Economic Geology)**

of about 3,200 km along an old shoreline bordering the Canadian Shield (Gross, 1965).

The sedimentary basin of the itabirites in Minas Gerais, Brazil, had a minimum extent of 500 km and a minimum width of 160 km.

Iron-formations of the Superior-type are, however, not restricted to miogeosynclinal or platform environments in sedimentary troughs between older cratons. They are also frequently found in younger depressions on Archean cratons (intracratonic basins) such as the Witwatersrand, Transvaal and other iron-formations as described by Beukes (1973) from South Africa. Many of these basins, generally, but not always, are lacking contemporaneous volcanism. They reflect conditions of restricted basins with deposition of iron-formation in shallow and quiet water, sometimes under highly saline conditions. This is indicated, for example, in the Kuruman and Penge Iron-Formations by locally high sodium concentrations. The deposition of the iron-formation in the Hamersley basin, Western Australia, an

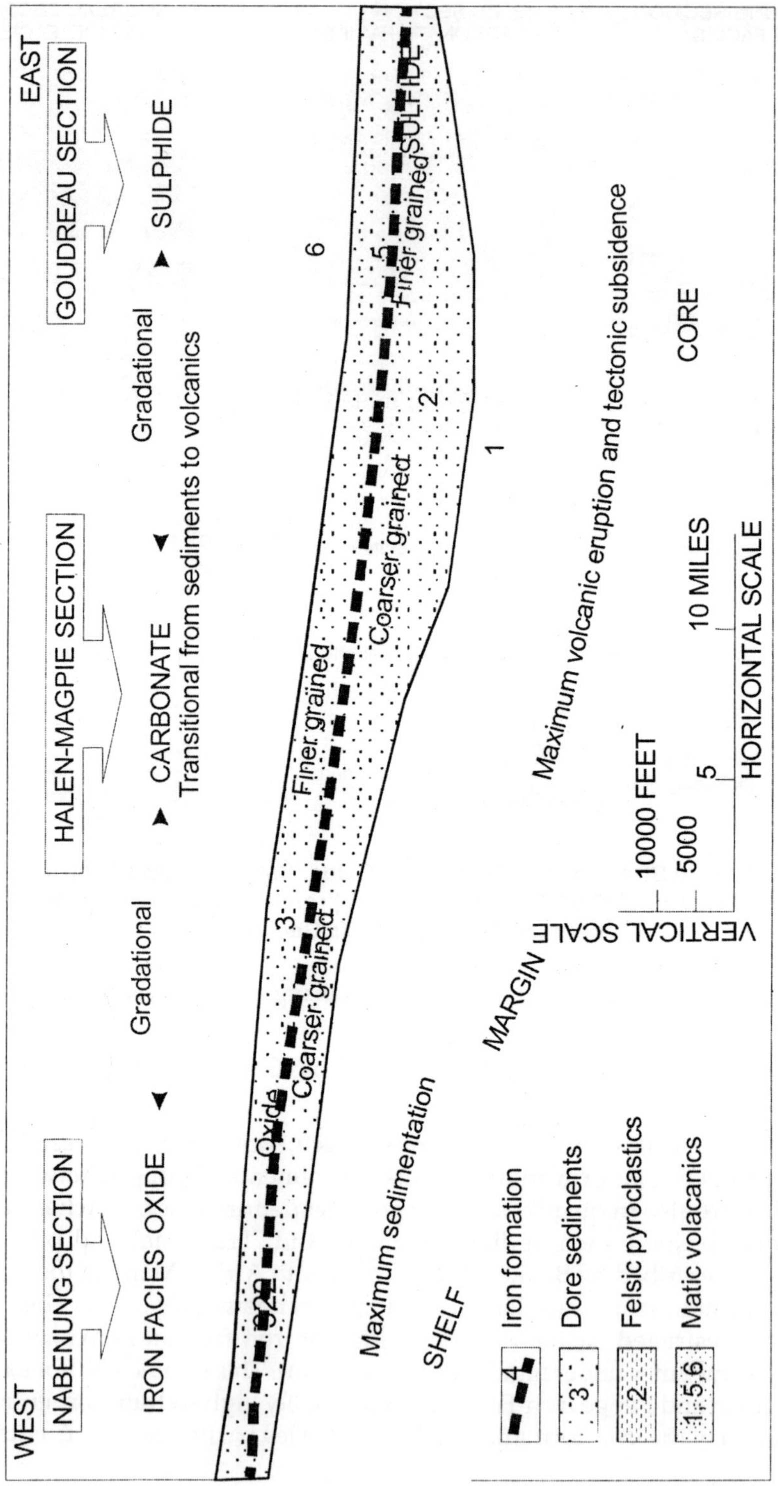


**Figure 2.2: Reconstructed Stratigraphic Section of the Michipicotan Basin (from Goodwin, 1973, p. 29, with permission of Economic Geology)**

originally ovoid basin of 500 by 250 km, is believed by Trendall (1973a) to have taken place under essentially quiescent sedimentary conditions in water depths of 50–200 m. The remarkable continuity of microbanding over almost 300 km for single bands resembles strongly younger evaporite deposits and suggests deposition in a restricted basin free from currents and wave activity, similar to evaporitic formations. In detailed studies of iron-formations of the Labrador trough, Quebec, Dimroth (1972) recognizes two main depositional facies: a lagoonal platform facies of thin-bedded oolitic, granular and conglomerate alternations with chert, deposited in water probably less than 10-15 m deep and a basin facies deposited at less than 100 in (perhaps less than 50 m) depth. Presumable pseudomorphs of chalcedony after gypsum suggest local evaporitic conditions and deposition in a probably warm and dry climate.

In opposition to this, some other Late Proterozoic iron-formations appear to have been deposited under cold-climate conditions. In the Northern Hemisphere the iron-formation of the Rapitan Group in the Mackenzie District of northwest Canada, deposited between 800-600 m.y. ago (Gabrielse, 1972), alternates with clastics of probably glacial origin. In the Southern Hemisphere, similarly, Martin (1965) described glacio-marine associations with iron-formations in both miogeosynclinal and eugeosynclinal environments of the Dainara Supergroup of South West Africa, the age of which is bracketed between 620-1,000 m.y. ago (cf. Beukes, 1973). It is of interest that these two roughly contemporaneous iron-formations on opposite sides of the globe reflect similar glacial depositional conditions. (The conclusion arises that they have been located in the pen-glacial outskirts of extensive continental glaciers or perhaps of the then polar ice caps of the ancient globe).

However, cold-climate sedimentary conditions for deposition of iron-formations in general cannot be considered as a crucial factor, since most of the major Superior-type iron-formations, grouped in the interval between 2,600-1,800 m.y. ago, have been deposited contemporaneously around the world, including the equatorial zones. Hence, different climatic factors appear to be of basically little significance for the deposition of iron-formation.

Iron-formations in Proterozoic miogeosynclines and post-orogenic intracratonic basins are major and extensive rock units. They represent a characteristic facies laid down during a certain phase in the evolution of Proterozoic geosynclines under relatively shallow-water epicontinental or shelf conditions. The typical lithofacies associations of these miogeosynclinal rock sequences are essentially thick coarse- to fine-grained quartzites with conglomerates and pelitic interruptions in the marginal and bottom parts of the transgressive sequence and predominantly pelitic rocks, sometimes graphitic shales, with local intercalations of quartaites, limestones or dolomitic rocks in the higher parts. Iron-formation, frequently in several horizons interrupted by shales and/or quartzites, was normally laid down in the lower and middle parts of the section. With thicknesses of several hundreds of metres, it may make up as much as 10 per cent of the total basin filling. In general, these clastic-chemical sequences are devoid of any volcanic associations, in opposition to Archean banded iron-formations. However, volcanic activity contemporaneous with deposition of iron-formation may also be observed, presumably merely parallelling the clastic-chemical deposition in the course of the structural development of the basin and without any direct connection with the origin of the iron-formation.

In many major iron areas, for example, the Lake Superior region (Bayley and James, 1973) or in the "Quadrilatero Ferrifero" of Brazil (Dorr II, 1973), it can be observed that the main iron-formation of the miogeosynclinal sequence was laid down in the lower part, underlain and overlain by non-volcanic clastic rocks.

Figure 2.3 gives an example of the progressive evolution of the Minas geosyncline from Minas Gerais, Brazil. The section is compiled from the data of several authors:

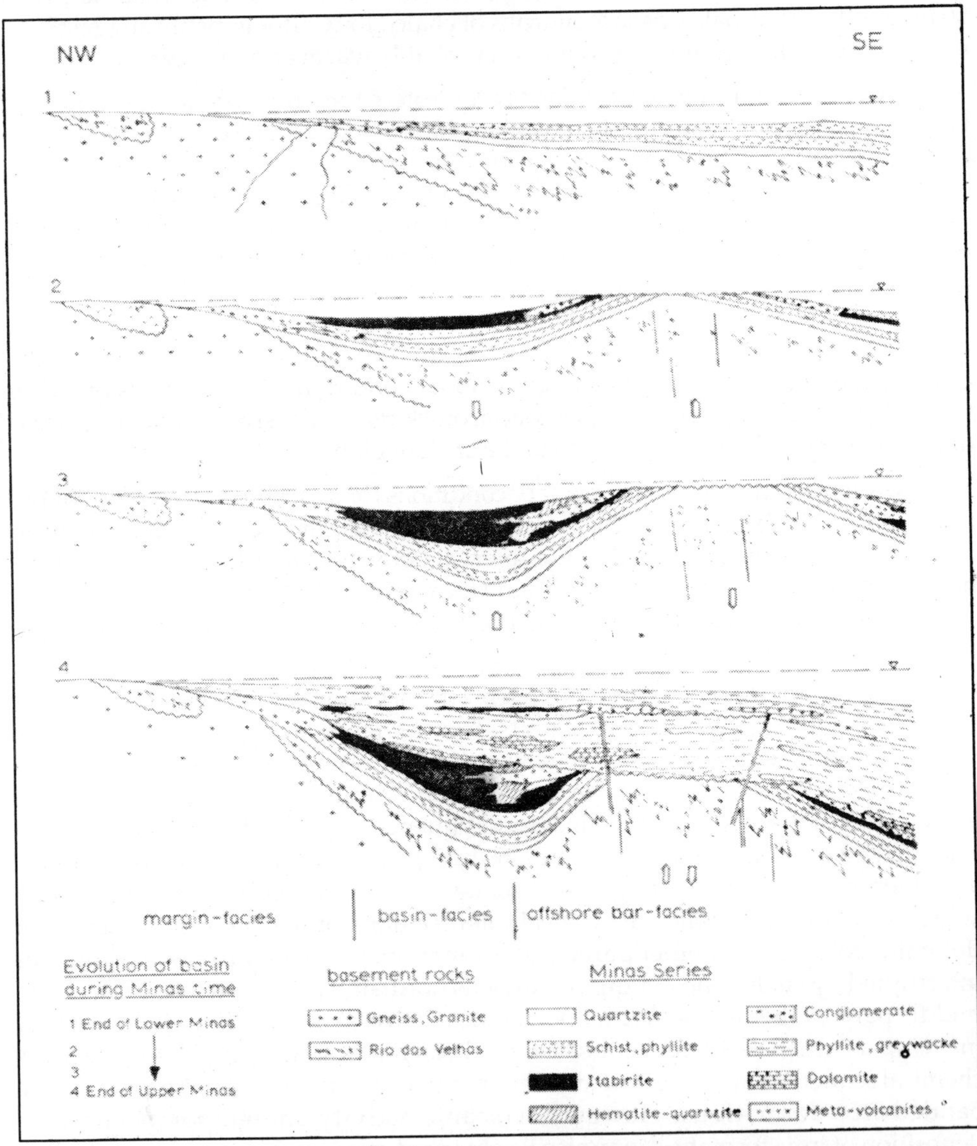


**Figure 2.3: Structural and Stratigraphic Development of the Minas Geosyncline, Minas Gerais, Brazil (modified after Gross, 1980)**

Pflug (1965) who studied the marginal parts in the Diamantina area, Dorr II (1973) in the central area of the basin investigations in the southeastern part of the "Iron Ore Quadrangle", where several features indicate an offshore uplift zone, which can be traced further to the north, parallel to the old "So Francisco Craton", as an island-arc zone restricting the miogeosynclinal basin (Kehrer, 1972).

The thickness of the Caue Itabirite varies from about 50 m to more than 600 m with an average of about 250 m. The principal iron-formation covers an area of about 160 km lateral width and can be traced over an extent of at least 500 km in a NNE - SSW direction.

The diagrammatic section shows a transgressive overlap of lower Minas Series quartzites and phyllites on the pre-Minas basement (Rio das Velhas Series; plus 2,700 m.y.) and the successive deposition of the Caua-Itabirite in an at least partly barred and continuously subsiding basin. Increasing subsidence stopped deposition of itabirite and led subsequently to eugeosynclinal sedimentary conditions with thick sequences of shales (phyllites) and graywackes with local quartzite wedges and dolomite lenses. Conglomerates and clastic hematite quartzites, probably reworked itabirites, are locally interfingering with the itabirites.

Thin and insignificant iron-formations of commonly lenticular shape may locally follow in the higher parts of the sections, embedded in eugeosynclinal sediments with or without adjacent rocks of volcanic origin. It is here suggested that these minor successive horizons represent stragglers of the vanishing stages of iron-formation deposition incidentally conflicting with volcanic material when volcanic activity started in the progressively subsiding basin. It is likely that major depositional troughs have been divided into several separate shallow basins. This may be supposed when lithologic associations of single correlative iron-formations differ considerably from one to another in the same district as it is the case in the Menominee, Marquette, Gogebic, Mesabi and Gunflint ranges of the Lake Superior District (Figure 2.4 from Gair, 1973 and Figure 2.5 from James, 1954).

Summary of depositional types of iron-formations. Relative to the principal environments of deposition, a grouping into two main types of banded iron-formation has been explicitly established by Gross (1965): the Algorna-type and the Lake Superior type. A comparison of the characteristic features of these two types is shown in Table 2.2.

The late Proterozoic iron-formations with an age of less than 1,600 m.y. show many features common with the bulk of the older iron-formations. However, there are some notable differences in their general geological setting. First of all, their regional distribution is much less abundant in time and in space and they are also less prominent units in the associated rock sequences. The mineralogical and chemical composition seems to be more variable. Chert is normally observed but may also be lacking. In the silicate-facies, high-aluminous chamosite is more common than low-aluminous greenalite. In some deposits essentially higher contents of iron, far exceeding the normal range in banded iron-formations is present. Thus, Gabrielse (1972) mentioned from the Snake River iron-formation, at the base of the coarse clastic

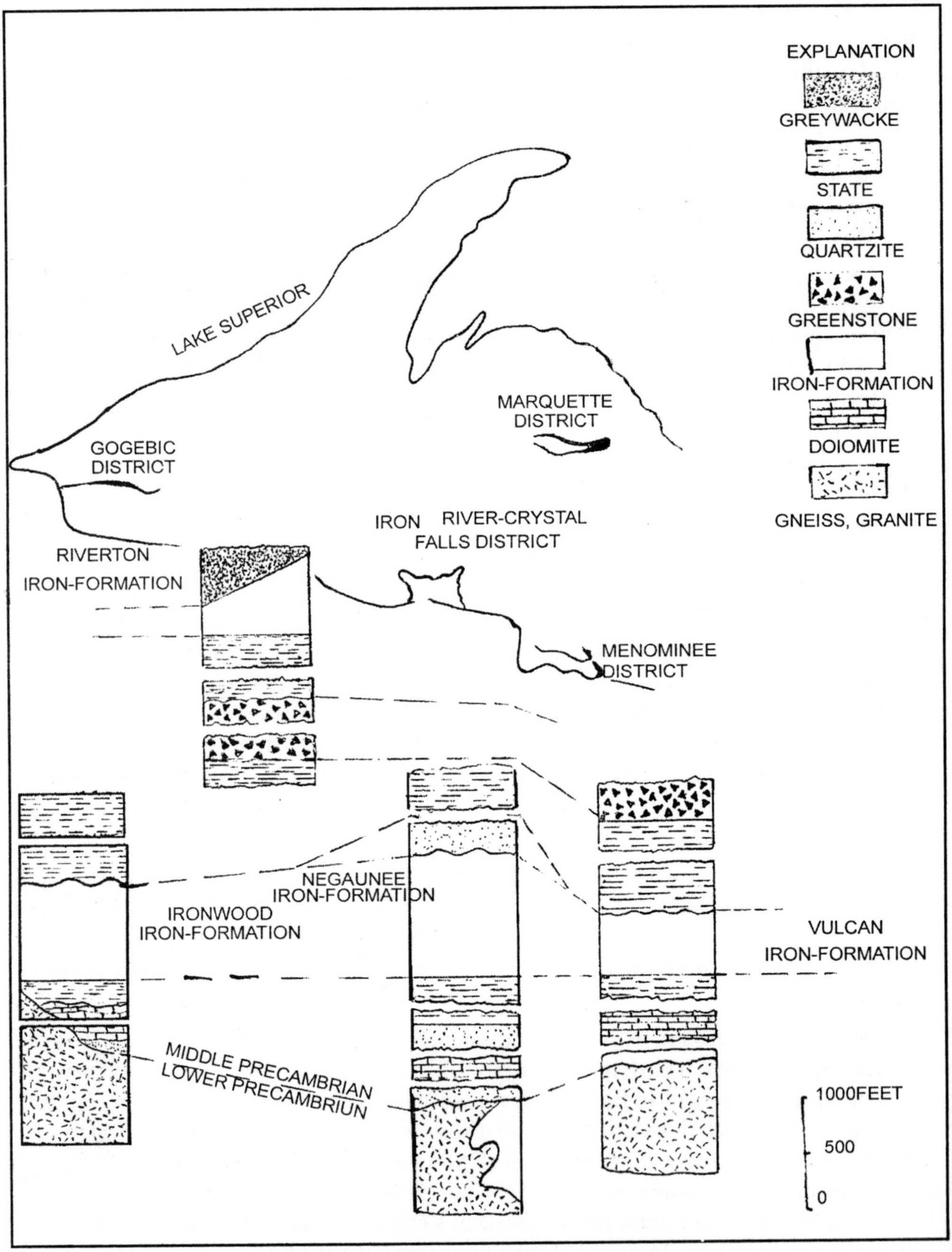


**Figure 2.4: Correlation of Major Lithologies in Iron-Formations of the Lake Superior District (from Gair, 1973, p. 367)**

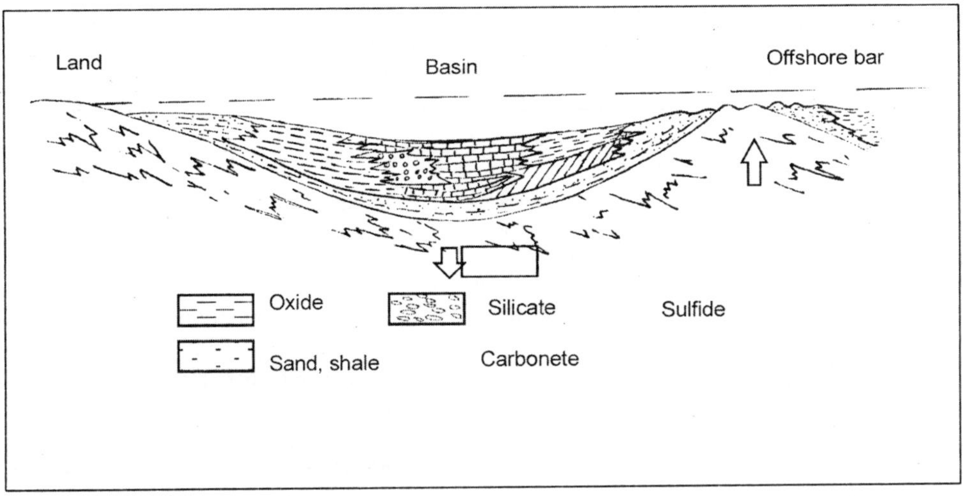


**Figure 2.5: Schematic Section Showing the Lateral and Vertical Distribution of Different Facies of Iron-Formation in a Barred Depositional Basin (Slightly modified from James, 1954)**

Rapitan Group in northwest Canada, an average content of 46 per cent iron in the hematite-jasper. Dorr II (1973a) describes from the Mato Grosso, Brazil the jaspilitic banded hematite deposit of Urucum, which has an average iron content of 56.9 per cent (range 48.7–62.1 per cent Fe) and is one of the highest grade sedimentary iron-formations in the world. The deposit is interbedded with detrital clastic material and, abnormally, with horizons of high-grade sedimentary manganese oxides.

Occurrences of Palaeozoic banded hematite jaspers with an average iron content of 56.5 per cent are known in the Himalayas of Nepal (O'Rourke, 1961). The origin of these deposits, as well as those of most of the younger Phanerozoic banded iron-formations summarized by O'Rourke (1961), is in many respects not comparable with the older iron-formations and remains enigmatic.

## Sedimentary Facies of Iron-Formations

The development of different facies of iron-formation dependent on depositional environments is similar to that of Phanerozoic marine-sedimentary iron deposits of the Minette-type explicitly defined by Borchert (1960). As is commonly known, iron occurs in nature in different oxidation states, depending mainly on the environment of deposition. The kind of chemically precipitated iron minerals is dependent principally on the pH and Eh conditions as the chief controlling factors of kind and amount of the precipitate, as has been demonstrated by Krumbein and Garrels (1952). Concentrations as well as changes of P/T conditions have no significant influence on the kind of the precipitates. As stressed by Krumbein and Garrels (1952), the pH and Eh values in normal marine environments show only slight variations between pH 8.4/Eh + 0.4 near the surface and pH 7.5/Eh + 0.1 near the bottom. For iron-formation facies reflecting reducing depositional conditions, James (1954)

**Table 2.2: Characteristic Features of Algoma- and Superior-Type Banded Iron-formations**

| | *Algoma-type (Archean-type)* | *Superior-type (Animikie-type)* |
|---|---|---|
| Age | Pre-2,600 m.y. (also Proteorozoic and Phancrozoic) | Pre-1,800 m.y. |
| Sedimentary environment | Eugeosynclinal tectonic basins of several 100 km diameter; iron-formation in marginal parts in connection with greenstone belts | Miogeosynclinal; iron-formation along margins if stable continental shelves; shallow water; restricted intra-cratonic basins |
| Extent | Commonly lenticular bodies of a few km | Extensive formations persistent over some 100 km to more than 1,000 km |
| Thickness | 0.1 m to some 10 m | Several m to more than 100 m (1,000 m) |
| Location in sedimentary sequence | Irregular, lenticular bodies within Archean "basement" rocks | In bottom and middle parts of sedimentary sequences as sheet-deposits, transgressive on older "basement" rocks |
| Associated rocks | Graywackes and shales; carbonaceous slates; mafic volcanis; felsic pyroclastics; ryolithic flows; pillowed andesites. | Coarse clastics; quartzites, conglomerates dolomites; volcanics normally absent |
| Sedimentary facies | Oxide-facies predominant, carbonate- and sulfide-facies thin and discontinous; silicate-facies; all facies frequently closely associated | Oxide-facies most abundant; silicate- and carbonate-facies frequently integradational. |
| | Sulfide- and carbonate-facies near the centre of volcanism; oxide-facies on the margins | Sulfide-facies insignificant or absent |
| | Heterogenous lithological assemblages with fine grained clastic beds. | More homogenous (especially oxide-facies); little or no detritus. |
| | Granular and oolitic textures | Granular and oolitic textures |
| Examples | Canada: Archean basins (*e.g.* Michipicoten) | Labrador Trought |
| | U.S.A.: Vermilion District, Minnesota | Lake Superior region |
| | S. Africa: Greenhouse belts, Kaapvaal and Rhodesia Cratons | Transvaal and Witwatersrand Supergroups |
| | Brazil: Rio das Velhas Series | Minas Series (itabirites); Carajas/Para |
| | India: Southern Karnataka | Jharkhand, Chhattisgarh, Orissa, Goa, Karnataka |
| | Australia: Yilgarn and Pilbara Blocks | Hamersley Group |
| | U.S.S.R.: Taratash/Urals | Krivoy Rog, Kursk; Ukrainian Shield |

consequently suggested that iron-formations containing sulfide-facies have been deposited in basins which were partly cut off from the open sea by bars, thus allowing the formation of restricted conditions with strongly negative Eh for the deposition of iron-sulfides. James (1954) and later Gross (1965) stressed the close relationship between composition, mineralogy and the oxidation state of chemically precipitated sediments and depositional environment, which allows a classification of distinctive facies types related to controlling physico-chemical factors. Thus, James (1954) separated four distinctive facies of iron-formation, namely oxide, silicate, carbonate and sulfide facies, which were deposited in that order from shallow to deep water within the basin, in chemical environments with relatively high Eh (oxide facies) to strongly negative Eh (sulfide-facies) and intermediate Eh values in the carbonate and silicate facies. This concept can be applied worldwide to all types of banded iron-formation, to the Algoma-type as well as to the Superior-type. Figure 2.7 illustrates the relative position of iron-formation facies in a restricted sedimentary basin. It has to be noted that the facies are commonly intergradational and a complete successive pattern is, not developed in nature. Associations of carbonate–sulfide facies have already been described from the Michipicoten basin (Goodwin, 1973). Sulfide facies is practically absent in all major iron-formations and apparently confined to the Archean type. Dorr II (1973b, p. 1021) mentions only a thin one in Gabon, Africa. There is a remarkable difference between the great iron-formations of the Northern and the Southern Hemispheres as to their homogeneity and facies association as Dorr II (1973a) has pointed out. Contrary to many major deposits in North America and Russia, in the iron-formations of the Southern Hemisphere, the carbonate and silicate facies are rare exceptions and oxide facies is by far the dominant type.

Transitions between hematite - magnetite and silicate - carbonate facies have been described by Gastil and Knowles (1960) from the Labrador trough. From the Gunflint Iron Formation, Minnesota, Goodwin (1956) describes lateral transitions between magnetite - silicate and carbonate facies.

## Europe

On the East European platform. BIF occur in the western part, in the Ukrainian, Baltic, and Voronezh shields, and in the eastern part of the platform in Kazakhstan.

### Iron-formations of the Ukrainian Shield

In the Ukrainian shield, BIF are developed in a number of synclinorium zones in different structural levels of the Precambrian. They are spatially unconnected, which makes it difficult to correlate them and establish their common genetic regularities. Usually several zones of development of BIF are distinguished (Semenenko, 1973).

The Konka - Belozerka synclinorium, which was stabilized in the first Precambrian cycle 2,700 m.y. ago, is considered to be the first and oldest zone. Rocks with an absolute age of 3,500 m.y. have been established in here. The cherty iron-metabasite and cherty iron-ultrabasic formations of the Lower Konka group were developed essentially at that time. In the final stages of development of the zone, basic volcanism was superseded by acid volcanism and the rocks of the cherty iron-keratophyre formation of the Upper Konka group were deposited. According to Semenenko (1973) the rocks of this zone were metamorphosed to schists and hornstones and reach the rank of gneiss only in the marginal parts of the zone at the contact with granitoids.

The second zone in the Bazaviuk synclinorium, which began to develop in the period of 2,700-2,800 m.y. and stabilized 2,300 m.y. ago. In this zone the cherty iron deposits consist of a cherty iron-metabasite formation in the Lower Bazaviuk group and a cherty iron-keratophyre formation in the Upper Bazaviuk group. The rocks of this zone are diverse in degree of metamorphism: from phyllite to pyroxene-gneiss.

The thid zone is confined to the Orekhov - Pavlograd synclinorium developed 2,300-1,800 m.y. ago. Semenenko (1973) correlates the Korsak and Mangush zones of the Pri-Azo area with this zone. Both cherty iron metabasite and cherty iron-gneiss formations are present in the Orekhov- Paviograd synclinorium, the former being limited stratigraphically to the lower part of the section and the latter of it. A feature of the iron cherts of this zone is more intensive metamorphism under amphibolite and granulite facies conditions (Kalyayev *et al.*, 1968; Glevasskiy *et al.*, 1971). Less metamorphosed rocks occur only in individual synclines, for instance the Gulyaypole.

The fourth and main zone is the Krivoy Rog - Kremenchug, developed 1,800 - 2,000 m.y. ago. The accumulation of rocks began here, as in the other zones, with the eruption of metabasic and ultrabasic rocks, which then probably were locally succeeded by rocks of the keratophyre series. Most of the iron cherts, however, are not related to the initial but rather to the middle stage of development of the zone, when the sedimentary cherty iron-formation of the Middle suite of the Krivoy Rog group was formed. Maximum development of iron cherts is characteristic of the Saksagan and Kremenchug basins.

No meta-igneous rocks have seen definitely established in the sections of the Middle suite, a fact which makes one to attribute the cherty iron strata to the remote type of formation (Semenenko, 1973) or even to believe that the original material of the sediments was the product of subaerial weathering. Depending on the typical paragenetic associations of the rocks, Semenenko (1973) distinguishes these types of cherty iron-formations on the Ukrainian shield: cherty iron-schist (sedimentary), cherty iron-keratophyre (orjaspilite-leptite), cherty iron-metabasite and cherty iron-ultrabasite.

The cherty iron (sedimentary,) formation (CIS) is the most uniform in facies. The cherty iron beds are traced for 10-20 km; their thickness reaches 100 - 300 m and their iron content reaches 30-35 per cent. According to Semenenko *et al.* (1959) these rocks were formed under conditions of prolonged hydrothermal activity of submarine volcanoes, with limited introduction of ashy material and widespread development of chemogenic deposits. On the Ukrainian shield the Krivoy Rog - Kremenchug cherty iron strata of the Middle suite and also the rocks of the Upper suite of the Upper Konka group of the Belozerka syncline are of this type.

The cherty iron-keratophyre formation (CIK) is characterized by the paragenetic association of acid dacite-rhyolite lavas, tuff-keratophyres, and cherty iron deposits. The formation is more uniform in facies. It is believed that the cherty iron sediments were formed near volcanic centers at times when volcanism was ending.

The cherty iron-metabasite (CIM) formation was formed in regions of submarine basaltic volcanism. The iron cherts in the formation are not uniform in facies and amount to 10-30 per cent of the total thickness of the sequence. The formation is extensively developed in the lower metabasic series of the Konka. Belozerka, Verkhovtsevo, and Sura synclines.

The cherty iron-ultrabasite formation (CIU) is not widespread; occurs in the Konka syncline and in the Kudashev sector of the Verkhovtsevo syncline are low-grade banded cherty iron intercalations of no great thickness interbedded with ultrabasic schists.

Other views are concerning the genetic classification of the cherty iron-formations of the Ukrainian shield and their spatial and temporal relationships. Kalyayev (1965) distinguishes three types of cherty iron-formation: sedimentary, volcanogenic-sedimentary, and the jaspilite situation within the spilite-diabase formation.

The sedimentary jaspilite formation, analogue which is the Krivoy Rog iron-ore sequence, is characterized by an association with jespilitic and psammitic sedimentary rocks whose sources were products of subaerial weathering. The sediments of this formation were deposited in the Krivoy Rog- Kremenchug marginal depression and also in individual parageosynclinal zones.

The volcanogenic-sedimentary jaspilite formation was formed in intra-geosynclinal synclinorium zones; its equivalent is the cherty iron-formation of the Belozerka syncline.

The jaspilite sub-formation developed in the spilite-diabase formation is known both in intrageosynclinal synclinorium zones and in the inner zones of the Krivoy Rog-Kremenchug marginal depression.

The interrelationships of these types of jaspilite formations are represented on the composite diagram and in the scheme of development of the Greater Krivoy Rog geosyncline, which suggest that the sedimentary-volcanogenic and sedimentary jaspilite formations are temporal analogs but were formed in different structural zones of the Greater Krivoy geosyncline: the former in the inner zones (Verkhovtsevo, Sura, Konka) and the latter in the outer zones of the marginal depressions. The sources of the material in these types of formations also are different in the former the products of volcanism predominate, in the latter, the products of subaerial weathering, forming a Precambrian geosynclinal flysch. Thus all the cherty iron-formations belong the same geosynclinal cycle, to its pre-orogenic half, and the sedimentary and sedimentary-volcanogenic jaspilite formations were formed after deposition of the Jaspilite sub-formation of the diabase-spilite formation.

## Iron-formations of the Voronezh Shield

BIF occur in stratigraphic sequences of Voronezh shield. Layers of highly metamorphosed iron-rich rocks, have been established in the old gneisses and migmatites of the Oboyan group, which is assign to the Archean (Figure 2.6).

In the Mikhaylonka group, which is correlated with the Verkhovtsevo series of the Ukrainian shield (Semenenko, 1973), iron cherts are interbedded with keratophyres and their tuffs and orthoamphibolites.

BIF are very extensively developed in the deposits of the Lower Proterozoic Kursk group, mainly in the middle suite. The iron formations are associated with

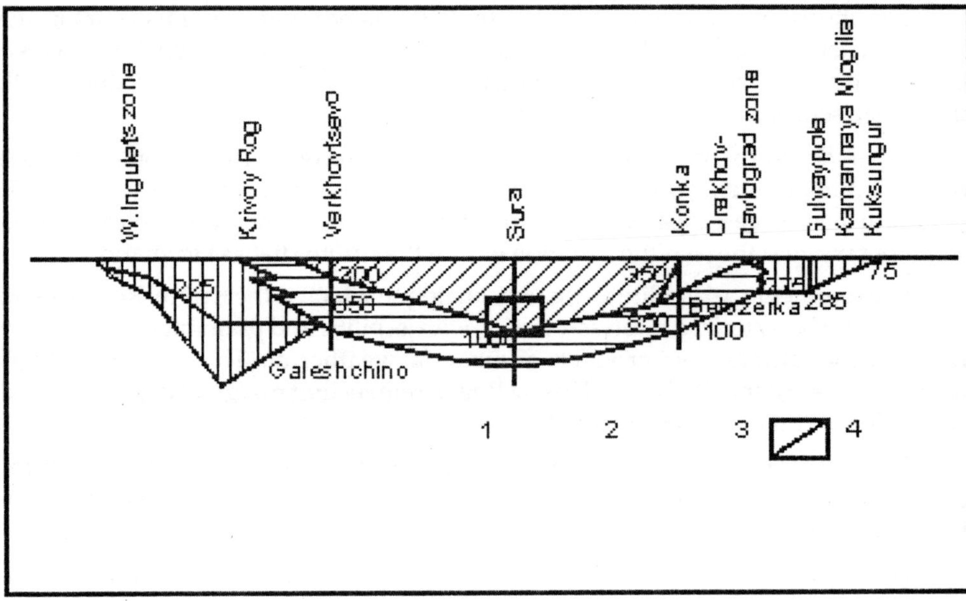


**Figure 2.6: Compensation Diagram of the Jaspilitc Formation (after Kalyayev). 1 jaspilite formation of sedimentary type in border zones; 2 = jaspilite formation of volcanogenic-sedimentary type in interior zones; 3 = overlying volcanogenic-clastic subformation in interior zones; 4 = thickness of jaspilite formation in Galeshchino and Belozerka synclinoria. Numerals on illustration- total thicknesses of formation.**

metasediments-phyllites. The iron cherts of the well studied Mikhaylovka area of constitute several discontinuous layers forming two belts: a northeastern one 450-500 km long and a northwestern one 600 km long. These belts skirt the arch uplift of the crystalline basement, as it were. The total thickness of the iron cherts of the Kursk group is of the order of 100-1200m (Illarionov, 1965). Iron cherts consisting of heavily landed and concretionary martite-hematite quartzites are also known among the rocks of the upper suite.

Plaksenko (1969) distinguishes these cherty iron-formations: cherty iron gneiss (Oboyan group), cherty iron-metabasite (Mikhaylovka group and lower suite of the Kursk group), cherty iron-schist (middle suite of the Kursk group and cherty iron-clastogenic (upper suite of the Kursk group). A volcanic source is assumed for the material of the cherty iron-metabasite formation; the formation of the cherty iron-schist formation is not connected with volcanism, but is explained by the arrival of material from the weathered layer on Archean iron-bearing rocks.

## Iron-formations of the Baltic Shield

On the Baltic shield (Melnik, 1982), BIF are known in three major structural-facies zones: the Karelian zone of the Karelides the Kola-Norwegian zone of the Karelides, and the vast zone of the Svecofennides in the southwestern part of the shield. The first two zones are separated by the Belomorides, which most investigators consider to be older than the Karelides. The question of the age relationships of the Svecofen nides of Sweden and Finland to the Karelides is not settled yet.

In the Karelian zone of the Karelides, BIF are known in northern Finland in the spilite-diabase formation and are associated with basic volcanic rocks - pyroclastics, basaltic lavas and agglomerates - in northern Norway: graphite schists and limestones are occasionally encountered in the sections.

In the Kola - Norwegian zone of the Karelides, situated in the central part of the Kola peninsula and extending into northern Norway, iron cherts are associated with gneisses, schists of basic composition, amphibolites, and paracharnockites of the Kola group. In this sequence, which can be assigned to the volcanogenic-sedimentary formation of the spilite-diabase series, both metasedimentary and meta-igneous rocks occur. In the Lake Imandra area the cherty iron-formations of the Kola group are associated with volcanic rocks of more acid composition, similar to the rocks of the porphyry-leptite formation of central Sweden. In the West Karelian zone iron cherts are restricted mainly to the Gimoly group of Lower Proterozoic age: 2,000–2,600 m.y.. The Gimoly group lies on the Archean basement of the Karelides and is overlain by the Parandovo and Bol'shoye Ozero group, where iron cherts also are known. The largest deposits of iron-formation-the Kosv and Mezhozero - are restricted to large synclinal structures preserved in the Proterozoic granites and migmatites. The iron cherts of the upper sedimentary cycle are associated with the products of acid volcanism: lavas, tuffs.

In the Syecofennides, BIF are known in central and northern Sweden (Kiruna area) and in southern Finland, also associated with volcanogenic rocks. Formational group of the same type, similar to the Proterozoic formations of Karelia, are found in all these areas. Acid volcanic rocks of the porphyry-leptite formation, and sometimes carbonate rocks, are noted in paragenesis with iron cherts; there are no typical primary clastic formations. In the Kiruna area the largest deposits of iron-formation and apatite-bearing iron ores occur in paragneisses with volcanic rocks of syenitic and rhyolitic composition and belong to the cherty iron-leptite porphyry formation correlate this formation at Kiruna with sequence of basic volcanics and iron cherts of the Bol' Ozero group, which lies with angular unconformity on the leptite-porphyry chertv iron- formation of the Ginioly group and constitutes the upper part of the Lower Proterozoic section of Karelia.

Despite the diversity of the BIF and the complexity of their interrelationships with the enclosing rocks, some general features have been established. In a detailed formational analysis. Chernov showed that the cherty iron- formations constitute the lower parts of the sections both in the Karelides and in the Svecofennides, and that their formation reflects the initial stages of geosynclinal development of the Baltic shield. In many areas the BIF are underlain by thick piles of conglomerates which rest on an old basement more than 2,600 m.y. old. The BIF are overlain by volcanic rocks of the spilite-diabase series or by clastic flyschoid formations formed in the final stages of geosynclinal development.

## Iron-formations of Central Kazakhstan

Precambrian iron occupy large structures of the area - the Karsakpay and Betpak-Dala belts, the west limb of the Maytyube anticlinorium, etc.

In the Karsakpay synclinorium the BIF are restricted to the Karsakpay group of Early Proterozoic age. The rocks of the Karsakpay group constitute a narrow north-south belt extending almost uninterruptedly for 200 km. Four macrorhythms, united into individual suites, are distinguished in this series. These macrorhythms reflect cyclicity in the manifestation of basaltic volcanism: in each rhythm the lower part of the suite consists of porphyritoids after tuffs and lavas of basaltic, less often of andesitic, composition, and the upper part consists of quartz-sericite schists, marbles, and iron-rich rocks.

In the Maytyube anticlinorium iron cherts are known among the deposits of the Satan suite, which consists mainly of clastic formations: mica schists, phyllites, conglomerates. The Satan suite lies stratigraphically above the Karsakpay series and belongs to the Upper Riphean or Lower Vendian.

Among the iron cherts of the Karsakpay synclinorium, three types of sequences and correspondingly three types of formations are identified.

The association of BIF with basic volcanic rocks is typical of the first type; it can be correlated with the jaspilite formation of the Algoma series in the Lake Superior district, which was formed in the greenstone formation. The rocks of the Verkhovtsevo group of the Ukrainian shield are also considered analogs.

The second type is distinguished by the association BIF with metasedimentary rocks–the analog of the jaspilite formation of the Saksagan group of the Krivoy Rog and the group of Canada; this formation follows the greenstone and jaspilite formations of Keewatin type in time.

The third type is characterized by the association of thin and rapidly- pinching-out iron cherts with clastic sediments, carbonate rocks and carbonaceous shales. These deposits belong to the remote jaspilite formation, developed either at the same time as the jaspilite formation of Krivoy Rog type or after it (analog of the rocks of the upper suite of the Saksagan district).

## North America

The main regions where Precambrian cherty iron-formations occur are on the Canadian shield, chiefly in the southwestern part of it.

The oldest iron cherts (2,300-2,700 m.y., Kenoran orogeny) are spatially and genetically related to the volcanogeñic greenstones of the Algoma group. On this basis Gross (1973) distinguished the volcanogenic cherty iron- formation of Algorna type. The rocks of this formation are extensively developed in the Michipicoten region (Churchill, Helen, and other districts).

In the Churchill district iron cherts are associated with metadiorites, andesites, dacite breccias and tuffs, carbonate rocks, and graywackes (Goodwin, 1973). Also typical of the Helen district is the relationship of the cherty iron sediments to volcanism, and a relationship has been established between the composition of the sediments, their location in the sedimentary basin, and the amount of volcanic products (Figure 2.2). The facies details shown in the sketch reflect the regularities of deep deposition of volcanic derivatives on the slopes of the original sedimentary basin (Goodwin, 1961; Goodwin and Ridler, 1970). The BIF which occur in the volcanic rocks are a combination of three facies-banded chert, a sulfide member, and a carbonate member (Figure 2.7, Helen section and Goudreau section). The banded chert member consists of alternating bands of cherty material and iron minerals, chiefly siderite with magnetite, pyrite, and pyrrhotite. It gradually grades into lenticular sulfide members which in turn also are gradually replaced by the underlying carbonate member. In the western part of the district a sedimentary association is developed, consisting of alternating bands of chert, magnetite, and jasper, which occur in graywackes and argillites. Thus the thick oxide facies of the western part of the district, rich in cherty material, gradually changes eastward into a thick carbonate facies containing cherty material in the center, and then into a thin sulfide facies poor in cherty material.

An interesting BIF of Algoma type is found in northwestern Canada on the Yukon–Mackenzie divide (Gross, 1972). Traces of mud flows, tuffs, ash, conglomerates, and syngenetic breccias *i.e.*, products testifying to deposition in a tectonically active

**Figure 2.7a: Geology of the Mesabi, Gunflint, and Cuyuna Districts in Minnesota (after Morey, 1973)**

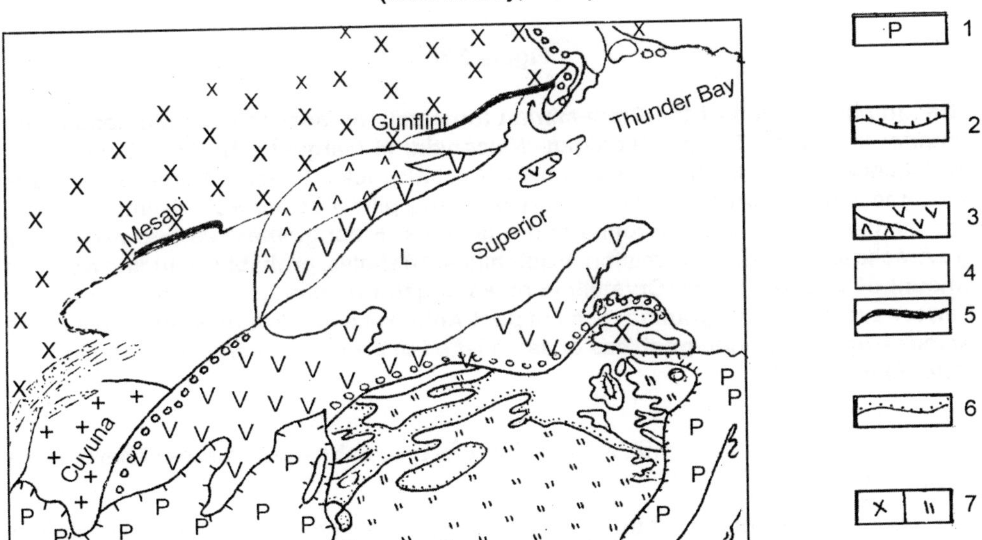


**Geologic map of the western part of the Lake Superior area: I = Phanerozoic cover; 2 = unconformity; 3 = Keweenawan rocks (above), Duluth gabbro (below); 4 = unconformity; 5 = Animikie series or group (iron-formation); 6 = unconformity; 7 = Lower Precambrian rocks (left); rocks subjected to Penokean orogeny (right).**

*Contd...*

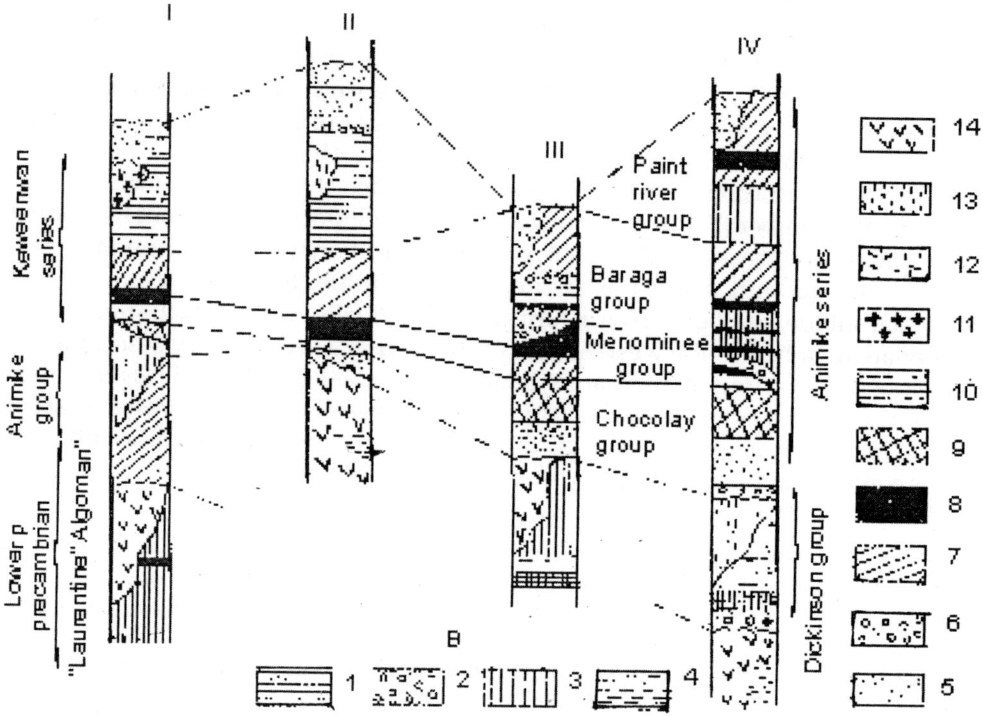


**Figure 2.7b**

**Stratigraphic section of the Precambrian (numerals on sections): J: Minnesota and Ontario; Ii Gogebic Range, Michigan–Wisconsin; III Marquette Range, Michigan; IV Menominee system, Michigan–Wisconsin. Volcanic rocks. 1 basalt; 2 greenschist tuffs and breccias; 3 = greenstones, in part retaining pillow structures; 4 amphibolites. Sedimentary rocks: 5 sandstones and quartzites; 6 conglomerates and arkoses; 7 graywacke shales; 8 iron-formation; 9 dolomites; 10 shales. probably including a certain amount of volcanic rocks. Crystalline rocks: II gabbros and granites of post-Middle Keweenawan age; 12 = granitic rocks of post-Animikie age; 13 gneisso-granites of pre Animikie age; 14 granite-gneisses of established or presumed early pre-Animikie age (After Morey, 1973).**

basin with explosive volcanic activity have been established in these cherty iron-formations.

The iron cherts of the Animikie group, extensively developed in the Lake Superior district (Figures 2.7a & b) in the states of Minnesota (Cuyuna, Mesabi, and Gunflint belts), Michigan and Wisconsin (Marquette, Gogebic, Menominee, and other belts), are younger (Huronian orogeny, consolidation 1,700-1,900 m.y. ago) (Gundersen and Schwartz, 1962; Gair, 1973). The rocks of the Anirnikie group lie on rocks of the Algoma group and are overlain by quartzites and grc:nstones of the Keweenawan group (see Figure 2.7a&b). Within the Anirnikie group itself, iron-rich and barren quartzites, paraschists. tuffs, breccias. and dolomites are interbedded and succeed one another in facies. Besides the Lake Superior district, analogous rock associations occur in the Labrador trough, in the eastern part of the Canadian shield. Gross assigned these iron cherts to the Superior type, characterized by the development of unstratified cherty and iron-rich deposits with granular or oolitic texture. Sediments of Superior type were formed in the late Precambrian in miogeosynclinal conditions of a continental shelf, succeeding a volcanogenic cherty iron-formation of Algoma type, deposited in a eugeosynclinal setting.

## South America

Deposits of Precambrian BIF, rich in iron ores of Cerro Bolivar in Venezuela (Ruckmick, 1963) and in the states of Pará and Minas Gerais in Brazil (Dorr, 1969; Tolbert *et al.*, 1973), are known. In the Sierra das Carajás area in Para, iron cherts were found not long ago in the rather inaccessible forests of the Amazon basin, and are not well known.

In Minas Gerais there is a large deposit; the iron cherts form a 500 km belt on the edge of the Brazilian shield. The Rio das Velhas group, the age of which is older than 2,800–3,000 m.y., and the Minas Gerais group, 1,800–1,300 m.y. old and lying unconformably on the gneisses of the Rio das Veihas group, are distinguished.

In the Rio das Veihas group iron cherts form thin lenticular bodies in Archean gneisses. The association with metavolcanic rocks and graywackes is typical of them.

The Minas Gerais group is divided into the lower and upper clastic strata, and also the middle chemogenic Itabira strata (Dorr, 1969). The BIF are traced for a distance of about 200 km and fill a deep symmetrical syncii which plunges to the northeast. The iron-formations consist of unbanded ferruginous varieties and thin-banded hematite-carbonate itabirites.

## Indian Platform

On the Indian platform, iron cherts constitute part of the Dharwar system, 2000–2700 m.y. old, which forms extensive synclinal zones and belts on the periphery of the Indian shield.

The iron cherts are of two main types (Krishnan, 1982) - thin-banded hematitic jaspilites and banded magnetitic cherts. Jaspilites constitute the thick Singhbhum strata (Jharkhand and Orissa), the Drug, Bastar (Chhattisgarh) and Goa, Karnataka deposits. In the Singhbhum deposit the banded hematite rocks are underlain by shales, calcareous sandstones, conglomerates, and phyllites, beneath which lie tuffs and basic lavas. The total thickness of the formation is 2,000-2,500m, up to 1,000m of which is jaspilite. A very low degree of metamorphism is typical of the ore minerals, hematite predominates, magnetite is rare, and silica is sometimes represented by opal. The age and genetic relationships of the hematite and magnetite rocks found in Goa, Chhattisgarh, and other areas are unknown. Krishnan (1982) considers the magnetite rocks to be the more metamorphosed analogs of the hematite rocks and unites them both into the Dharwar formation. However, ideas exist that the magnetitic rocks are older. Volcanism presumably is the source of the iron of the Precambrian B1F of India. Details are discusses in later chapters.

## Africa

On the African platform, iron cherts are known in several structural positions which, however, are not unequivocally distinguished. The oldest iron-formations (2900–3400 m.y.) are restricted to greenstone belts and consist of banded chert, banded ferruginous chert, and BIF proper (Beukcs, 1973). These rocks are intimately associated with cycles of volcanic activity and are constituent of them. In ultrabasic rocks of the greenstone belt, the BIF may interfinger along the strike with various types of rocks in one and the same cycle. Under these conditions the cherts and BIF consist of lenticular bodies, and several lenses may be restricted to one stratigraphic zone. Analogous structure is observed in basic and acid rocks, but the cycles are more completely developed.

The younger Kuruman and Penge iron-formations are component parts of a more prolonged (between 1,950 and 2,300 m and more important period of chemical deposition in the basin of the Transvaal system. The BIF are underlain by dolomites in the transition zone there are interbedded carbonaceous limestones, banded ferruginous cherts, and carbonaceous- argillaceous shales with pyrite, that is, typical carbonate shelf deposits.

## Australia

Iron cherts are known in three structural positions on the Australian platform. The oldest are in Western Australia in the Pilbara and Yilgarn Blocks, which were stabilized 2,700–3,000 m.y. ago. The iron cherts are not spatially persistent and not very thick.

The second group (1,700–2,000 m.y.) constitutes the Hamersley BIF in Western Australia, which occur in a syncline between old blocks. The thick strata of the formation (about 2700m) consist of iron-rich rocks interbedded with clay shales, dolomites, lavas, and tuffs. The iron-formation is underlain by conglomerates, metabasites, pyroclastics, and pillow lavas, and is overlain by quartzites, conglomerates. graywackes, and dolomites. Slight metamorphism, the temperature of which corresponds to the normal geothermal gradient, is typical of the cherty iron-formations (Trendall, 1973).

The third group consists of the BIF of the Cleve Metamorphics (South Australia). with an age of about 1,780 m.y.

A direct relationship to volcanic processes has not been established for the cherty iron-formations of Australia, but Trendall (1973a) suggests that the source of the ore material was rhythmic volcanism.

# Chapter 3

# Iron Ores Resources and Banded Iron Formation of India

Iron ores occur in different geological formations in India but the largest occurrences of economic deposits are located in sedimentary formations of the Precambrian age. Figure 3.1 shows a general geology of India and Figures 3.2 and 3.3 major iron ore depsits of India. These formations are referred to as Banded Iron Formations (BIF). The oldest magnetite-dominant deposits with bands of magnetite ore generally of Algoma type associated with banded magnetite quartzite, but the younger dominant deposits are similar to Lake Superior types, which are associated with banded hematite quartzite (BHQ) and banded hematite jasper (BHJ).

Major iron ore deposits in India could be grouped into five zones, which have been designated as Zone 1 to Zone 5. These are the main iron ore deposits of India which have real economic value. (Figure 3.2 shows these spread out location in the country).

The following are the zonal configurations of them :

Zone 1: Groups of iron ore deposits occur in the Bonai Iron Ore Ranges of Jharkhand, Orissa and some adjoining areas in the east.

Zone 2: This Group comprises the iron ore deposits lying in the 225km long north south trend in the linear belt of Central India comprising the states of Chhattisgarh and Maharashtra, especially in the eastern part of state.

Zone 3: Deposits seen in Bellary – Hospet regions of Karnataka.

Zone 4: Deposits comprising the rich magnetite deposits of Bababudan – Kudermukh area of Karnataka state.

Zone 5: Iron ore deposits of Goa state.

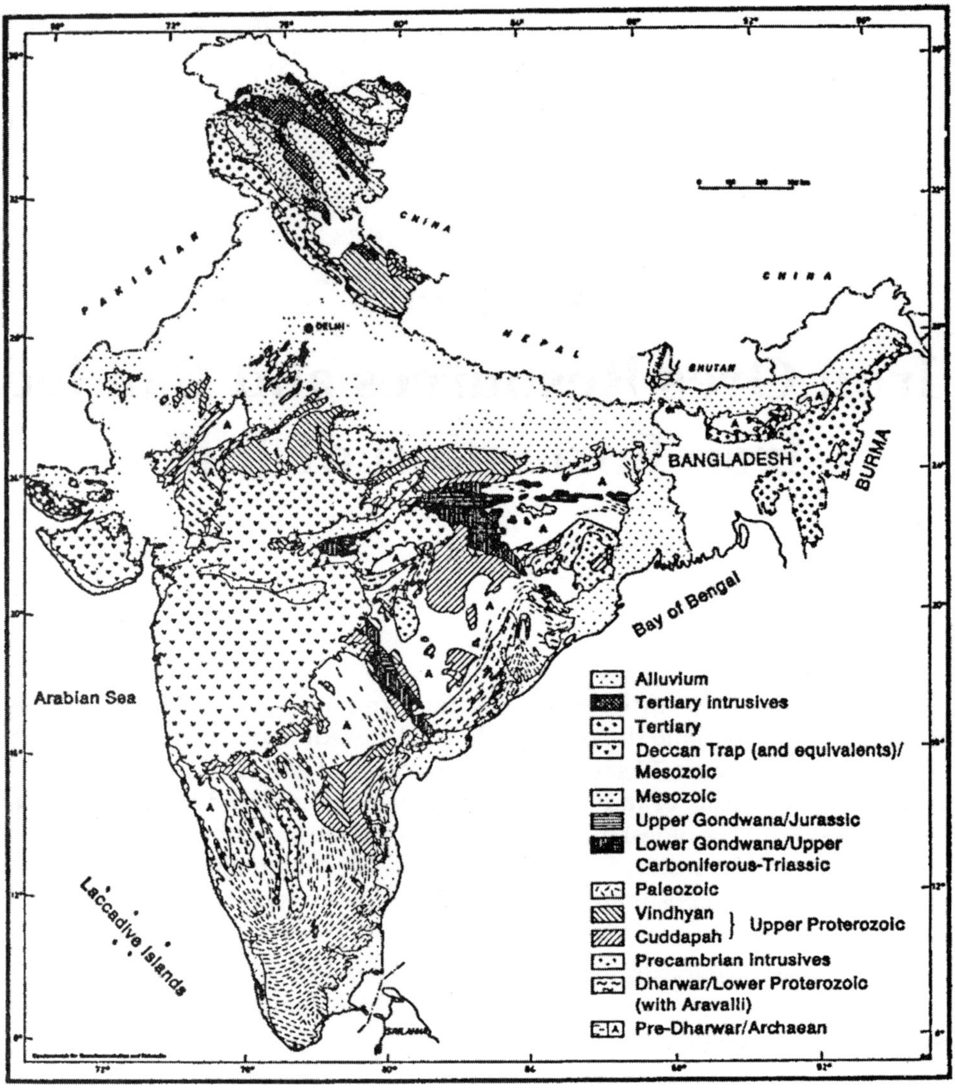


**Figure 3.1: Generalized Geology of India**

In addition while in Tamil Nadu some good deposits of magnetite rich banded quartzite exist other deposits occur in southern India in parts are found in Andhra Pradesh near East Coast, magnetite also occur in Salem district and its adjacent areas.

## Genetic Types

Iron ore deposits of India have been broadly divided into the following six groups on the basis of their modes of occurrence and origin.

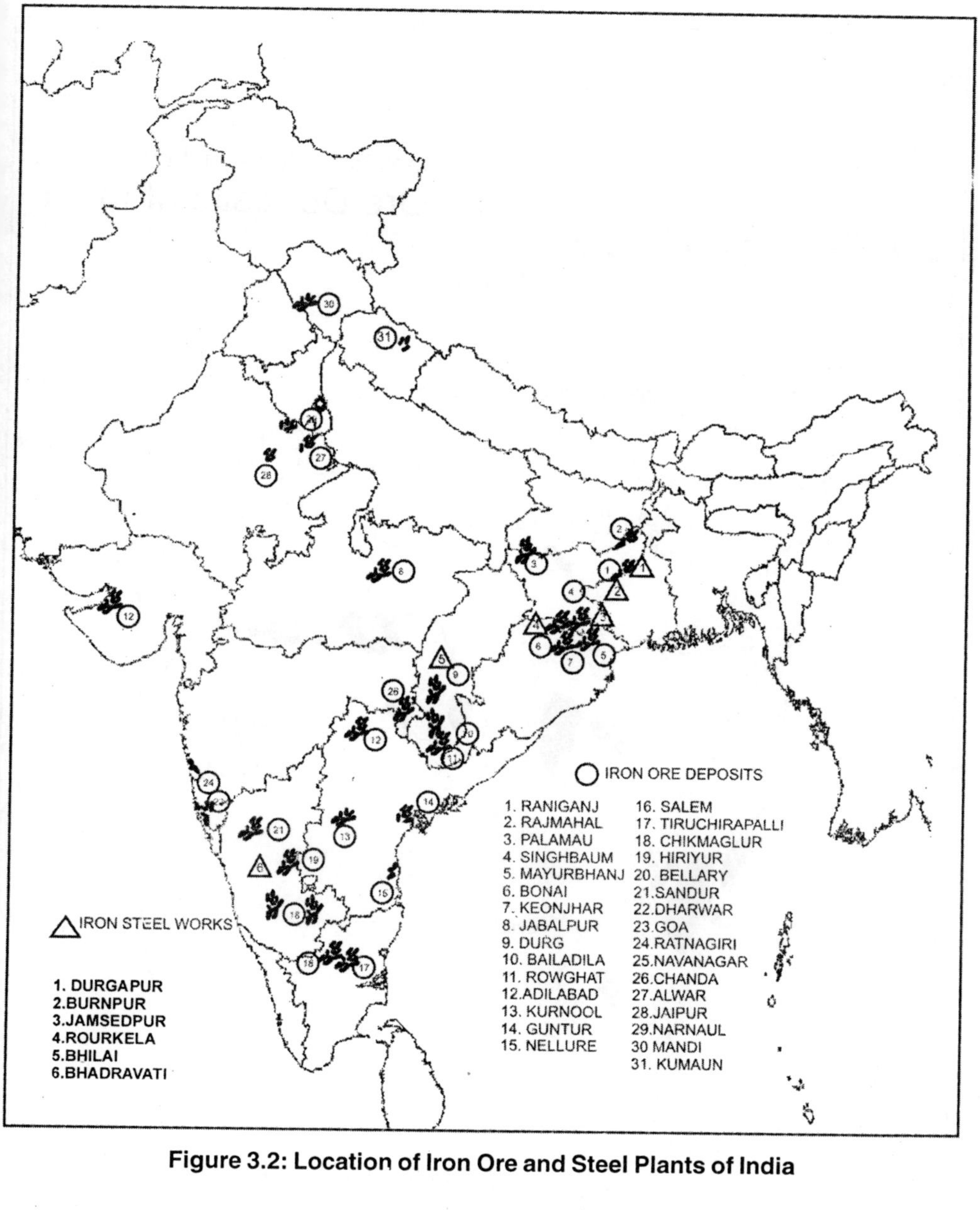


**Figure 3.2: Location of Iron Ore and Steel Plants of India**

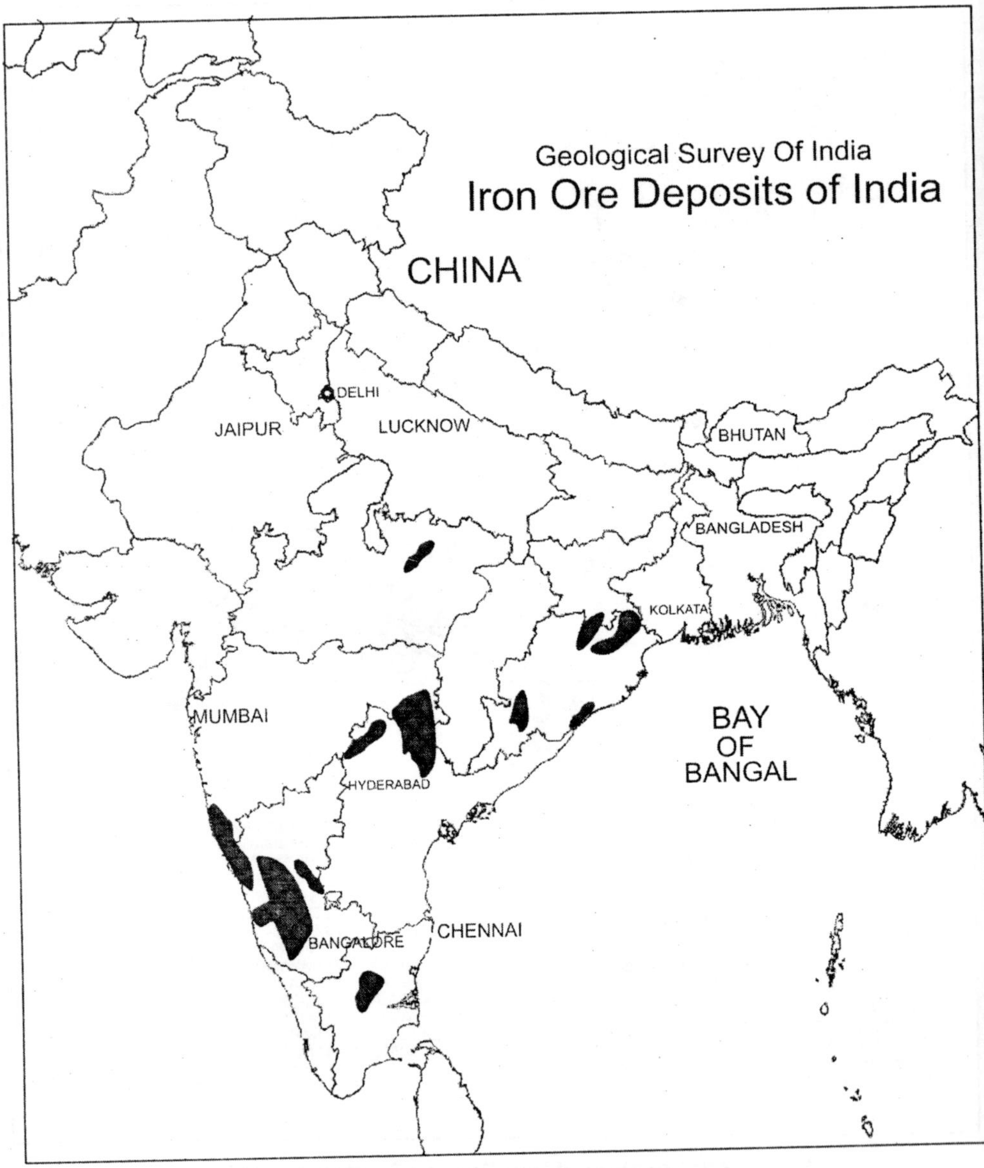


**Figure 3.3: Iron Ore Deposits of India**

## 1. Banded Iron Formations of Precambrian Age (BIF)

The BIF deposits are very well developed in India. Most of the Indian deposits are similar to those of the Lake Superior region of U.S.A., Brazil and Venezuela. Extensive outcrops of BIF are found in the states of Jharkhand, Orissa, Chhattisgarh, Maharashtra, Karnataka, Goa and Tamil Nadu.

The common names used in India to designate BIF are Banded Hematite Quartzite (BHQ), and Banded Magnetite Quartzite (BMQ). In other parts of the world, names used are Taconite (Lake Superior), Itabirite (Brazil), Jaspilite (Western Australia) and Calico Rock (South Africa) have been used to designate BIF. In the recent years BIF has come to be generally acceptable both in field term as well as stratigraphic term to designate iron rich sedimentary rocks.

### Classification of BIF

Gross (1965) distinguished two main types of iron formations from the Precambrian era *viz.* Algoma type and Lake Superior. *The Algoma type* is dominating the Archean age and are characterized by their banding and absence of ooliatic and granular texture. These are generally limited to lateral extent and closely associated with volcanic rocks and grey sediments. Carbon and pyrite rich black slate are common in them.

*The Lake Superior type* on the other hand, has the characteristic of the Protozoic era and is characteristically very extensive and closely associated with clastic sediments like quartzite and pelitic rocks without showing any direct relationship will volcanic associates. The BIF of India generally possess the characteristics of Algoma and Lake Superior types especially in the Archean schist belt.

There is yet another distinct type of iron formation which is seen mostly confined to the granulite terrain. This is generally a weakly-banded magnetite-quartzite forming part of a supra-crustal sequence of quartzite, mica schist marbles, meta-volcanic, and amphibolites, completely engulfed in a voluminous mass of tonalitic gneiss. The formation is highly folded and metamorphosed under granulite facies condition. Typical example are iron - ores, formation of granulite terrain of southern India like, Tamil Nadu, Andhra Pradesh, Karnataka, and Kerala and these are different from those of the Archean Schist Belt.

Therefore, the iron formation in the Indian shield can be divided into two main types: (a) such iron are deposits lying within the high grade region and (b) such iron ore deposit which are confined to Archean Schist belt.

Among these, the first type, namely those occurring within the high grade regions of Archean granulites and gneisses and represent formation of an older age group (>3,000 m.y.) formed in distinct tectonic environment and were later incorporated within high grade mobile belt.

The next type, namely those occurring in the Archean schist belt and the more extensive types, are the ones confined to the schist belts formed during the period between 2,900-2,600 m.y.. These types of deposits are confined to the states of Jharkhand, Orissa, Karnataka, Maharashtra, Chhattisgarh and Goa. They represent an important source of rich iron ore deposits in India.

## Origin of BIF

The origin of the BIF is still not settled, for they have always been debated and as such a final option is not viable at this point of time. There are inputs from several attempts and investigations in India as well as in other parts of the world where similar BIF deposits occur. Yet broad generalizations exist, which suggests that the large and most widespread proportions of deposits are of sedimentary origin. The volcanic nature of the period during which the Archean iron ore formation were deposited have been also recognized (*e.g.* Isua Formation). A controlling factor was possibly the nature of the ocean water during the Archean times. The Eh and pH of ocean water appears to have been significantly different from those of later years.

One view is that iron formation was deposited in shallow inland lakes, fresh water being considered as a more likely way of transport of silica, and iron from earths crust quite similar to the present day laterite crust. Periods of intense deposition was proceeded by a long period of accumulation of dissolved iron and silica in such sedimentary forms.

A different view is that the iron formations are essentially a produce of diageretic replacement of primary carbonates. Although there are evidences of replacement but the process cannot fully satisfy for vast amounts of iron in such BIF formations.

The character of such late Archean – early Protozoic atmosphere is also taken into account to understand deposition of BIFs. The atmosphere at that time, as deciphered, was rich in carbon dioxide, nitrogen and was deficient in oxygen. Enormous quantities of iron thus got accumulated in the oceans and lakes. Subsequently, it is postulated that when life first appeared, photosynthesis took place, which resulted in the release of bulk oxygen. Thus oxygen combined with dissolved iron, precipitated it, which resulted in formation of iron deposits. However, iron formations as old as 3,000 m.y. show that the build of oxygen in hydrosphere took place much earlier.

Thus, the distinctive chemical composition as suggested by iron ores formation (BIFs) restricted mainly to iron and silica, to the exclusion of other metallic compounds and origin of uniform banding can not be explained through inorganic chemical precipitation process alone.

There exists, thus, differing opinions and concepts of various works in explaining the origin of BIFs. The existing knowledge about the BIFs appears not only inadequate to build a good theory of origin, suggesting perhaps that a single mode of origin for all BIFs does not seem to be feasible.

## Characterization of BIF Type of Iron Ores

Let us briefly examine what makes the BIF formation so special? We know that the BIF's have given rise to huge accumulations of iron to produce a commercial interest of both quantity and quality in having a high percentage of Fe in them. In India nearly 90 per cent of the iron ore mined comes from the BIF's. In these the main ore minerals are hematite, and magnetite. Important deposits are located, as mentioned earlier in the southern regions of Jharkhand; Keorjhar; Sundergarh and Bonai districts of Orissa; Bellary district in Karnataka; Baster district in Chhattisgarh; and in Goa.

Magnetite ore deposits are mainly restricted to Chickmaglur district of Karnataka and Salem and north Arcot districts of Tamil Nadu, as well as Prakasam district of Andhra Pradesh.

Therefore, different types of iron ores derived from Banded Hematite rock found within the deposits of the group are (*i*) Massive ore, (*ii*) Laminated ore, (*iii*) blue dust.

In addition, float ore accumulated on the slopes and foothills appear to be a result of disintegration of in-situ ore bodies. The float ores are of different sizes and of different quality in regard to the iron percentage.

## 2. Sedimentary Iron Ore Deposits of Siderite and Limonitic Composition

These types of iron ores are also called bog iron deposits. They are generally consisting of siderite and limonitic ores. They occur often in association with the iron stone shells of Lower Gondwana formations in India, within the coalfields of Jharkhand and West Bengal (namely Jharia and Raniganj coalfields). They occur also with the Tertiary formations of Assam and other small occurrences elsewhere in the Himalaya and appear to be a result of hydration, which converts siderite into limonite stones at the surface. Such deposits are mostly heterogeneous in grade, as well as in their mode of occurrences. Iron minerals are here accumulated as irregular bodies in stream beds, and typically at the bottom levels of bogs and marshes where Lower Gondwana sedimentary beds have deposited along with the organic debris. In upper Assam such deposits occur in Lakhimpur and Sibsagar districts and are mainly of two types (*a*) clay ironstone, and (*b*) impure limonite.

In Raniganj area, the sedimentary iron ores occur in the form of thin beds of iron ores of variable thickness and frequently in Ironstone shale group of the Damuda series in Raniganj coalfield. The ore is mostly grey iron carbonate but near the surface it has been weathered to form into brown hydrated oxide.

Clay ironstones are also known to occur in the Karanpura and Auranga coalfields.

## 3. Laterite Ores Derived from Sub-aerial Alternations

Laterite types of iron ores are derived from the sub aerial alteration of rocks, such as gneisses, schists, mafic lava and so on, in humid and hot climatic conditions in the eastern states of India. By examining the composition of these laterites it is possible to attribute that some of these may be of economic value and could be exploited in the time to come. One limitation of them is a high level of alumina content along with such elements as titanium, nickel, chromium and manganese. Such deposits of laterite ore are mostly concentrated at the top due to alteration process of the iron bearing parent rocks. They could be of variable colours – red, yellow or brownish hematite and goethite being common. The capping is usually thicker over the mafic rocks for obvious reasons, Such occurrence contain high percentage of primary iron, associated with coal, nickel, chromium manganese and titanium. Large stretches of Deccan Basalts flows and, gnises in the Western Ghats and in the Chota Nagpur, (Ranchi, Plateau) in Jharkhand state as well as the schistose rocks of many areas like those of Sandur are covered by such laterite tops.

### 4. Iron Ores Formed by Magnetic Activity

A zone of apatite magnetite rock is found closely associated with the Singhbhum Sheer Zone (the copper belt thrust) occur in minor bodies. It is understood that these have been formed by magmatic activity associated with Precambrian diastrophic cycle when the rocks of the shear zone were thrusted and subsequently intruded by acid to intermediate igneous rock (soda granites and associated suite). The magnetite containing rocks is a mixture of apatite and magnetite with some biotite, chlorite and subordinates quartz. This is mostly found to occur on the hanging well side of the copper lode. Here the apatite magnetite ores are associated with granodiorites.

### 5. Titaniferous – and Vanadiferous Magnetite

The titaniferus vanadiferous magnetite deposits of south eastern Singhbhum, Mayurbhanj, Keonjhar in Jharkhand and Orissa states, and in Hassan district of Karnataka are associated with gabbroid and ultra-mafic rocks. These types of ores of Jharkhand and Orissa occur as thin veins, lenses and pockets in gabbroid and ultra-mafic rocks which are often altered to serpentine, steatite and even to epidiorite. Magnetite and limonite are present in them, and in several occurrences appreciable quantities of hematite ore is also obtained.

In the state of Karnataka, small lenses like bodies of titaniferious magnetites occur in Tumkur district. These are generally associated with ultramafic rocks and they occasionally contain chromite as well. Such deposits contain up to 55 per cent to 61 per cent of iron content. In Hassan district, titaniferous magnetities occur as linear bands with prominent outcrops in a narrow belt of Dharwarian rocks, comprising amphibolites and hornblende-schist. These are surrounded by the Peninsular Gneiss having been intruded by an ultramafic complex suite.

### 6. Fault and Fissure Filling Deposits

Fault and fissure filling deposits of hematite are minor occurrences found in Veldurty and Ranalla, Kota in Kurnool district of Andhra Pradesh. Such ore bodies occur in a fault zone traversing the gneisses and formation of the Cuddapah Group, they extend over a length of several kilometers. The ore lenses form low hillock and ridges, project out well above the ground. Some of these occur as veins and stringers in the fault zone. The ore is generally hematite and often slightly specular in character, at places even jaspary when it is somewhat siliceoes.

## Distributions and Brief Description of the Deposits

It has been mentioned earlier that large deposits of iron ore are mainly confined to the states of Jharkhand, Orissa, Chhattisgarh, Karnataka and Goa. However relatively smaller yet important deposits are found in the states of Maharashtra, Andhra Pradesh, Tamil Nadu, Kerala, Rajasthan and Haryana.

In addition, we find small deposits of iron ores in the states of Assam, Meghalya, Nagaland, West Bengal, Himachal Pradesh, Uttar Pradesh and Jammu and Kashmir. However they are at present of no economic significance.

The iron ore occurrences are given in Table 3.1 whereas details has been given in Table 3.2. It is important to summarize the age-wise (geo-chronological group) of the iron ore deposits of India in a tabular form for the convenience of our readers.

**Table 3.1: Geological Setting of the Iron Ore Occurrence in India**

| *Formation* | *Nature of Ores* | *Occurrence* |
|---|---|---|
| Quaternary | Laterite | Several occurrences, mainly derived from formations such as the basalts of Deccan Traps |
| Tertiary | Ironstone | Southern Indian region – Travancore, Malabar etc. |
| Miocene and Eocene | Ironstone | Assam, NE States, Uttar Pradesh (Kumaon region) |
| Jurassic | Iron stone in Rajmahal inter-troppean beds. | West Bengal (Birbhum) Jharkhand (Rajmahal) |
| Gondwana (Barakar Mahadeva) | Ironstones and siderite Siderite | West Bengal (Birbhum) Jharkhand – Auranga coalfields |
| Triassic Ironstones and shales | Iron stones and siderite Hematite and goethite | West Bengal – Raniganj Coalfield Kashmir region |
| Cuddapah Bijawar Gwalior | Hematite and ferruginous quartzite | Madhya Pradesh, Gwalior, Indore Andhra Pradesh – Cuddapah |
| Precambrian Mafic and Ultra-mefic rocks | Titaniferous and vanadiferous magnetite | Jharkhand – SE Singhbhum; Orissa – Mayurbhanj Karnataka |
| Granodiorite | Apatite-magnetite rocks | Singhbhum |
| Granite | Magnetites (residual) | Assam – Jantia Hills; Karnataka – Kudremukh |
| Banded Iron Formation | Hematite (Massive shaly and powdery) | Orissa – Sundergarh, Keojhar, Mayurbhanj; Karnataka – Simoga, Bellary-Hospet, Dhawar; Jharkhand – Singhbhum west; Maharashtra – Ratnagiri and Chandrapur; Chhattisgarh– Bastar (Bailadila) and Durg; Madhya Pradesh-Jabalpur |
| Banded Iron Formations (Metamorphosed) | Magnetite - quartzite | Tamil Nadu – Salem, Tiruchirapalli; Kerala; Andhra Pradesh – Guntur, Karnataka – Shimoga, Chickmaglur, Himachal Pradesh – Mandi |

## Reserves of Iron Ores in India

Hematite and magnetite are the most important iron ores in India. Amongst them, the main deposits of hematite iron ore are situated in the states of Jharkhand, Orissa, Chhattisgarh, Karnataka and Goa. Magnetite is the other main iron ore and occurs in the form of Oxide either within the igneous or in the metamorphosed banded iron formations. Chief magnetite deposits are situated in Karnataka, Andhra Pradesh and Tamil Nadu

Iron ore reserves are grouped category wise *i.e.* proved, probable and possible corresponding to the measured, indicated and inferred; as well as according to grade (Tables 3.3 and 3.4a&b).

**Table 3.2: State-wise Brief Description of Iron Ore Deposits in India Updated from Indian Minerals Year Book of IBM**

| *Name of State* | *General Description* | *Name of Deposit* | *Ore-Minerals* | *Reserve in MT* | *Remarks* |
|---|---|---|---|---|---|
| Jharkhand | Iron ore, consisting primarily hematite in banded iron formation in Singhbhum region. They occur as low ranges and hills. Titaniferous magnetite and apatite magnetite occur in SE Singhbhum | **Hematite Ore Deposits of**<br>a. Singhbhum- Noamundi, Gua, Kiripura, Neghatuburu, Manoharpur, Chiria<br>b. Ranchi region – Sikorda, Bagdaur, Mahantol<br>c. Small occurrences in Santhal, Parganas, Dhanbad, Hazaribagh, Sahabad districts. | Hematite (BIF) | 3281 MT | |
| | | **Magnetite Deposits**<br>a. Singhbhum region - Ramchandra Paher, Kudado, Pathorgora, Khejurdari, Dublabera, Sindurpur | Apatite Magnetite | 7.547 MT | |
| | | b. Palamau region - Gora village, Sua and Kauria, Biwabathan area. | Ti-magnetite Magnetite | | |
| Orissa | Precambrian Iron Ore group of rocks of Singhbhum-Keoghar-Borai Belt containing high grade hematite ore run through Keoghar Sundargarh districts. In addition to hematite, magnetic (Ti-bearing) are also found in some places. | **Hemetite Ore Deposit**<br>a. Keojhar – Thakurani, Bolani, Jhillung-Langollota, Joda, Gandhanordar, Malangtoli, Bansupani, Guati, Gurubera and minor occurrences from Jiyang, Joribehel, Kateonoti, Bhadrashi, Koisa, Kasia Kurbandh, Dulk, Jolapuri, Baldo.<br>b. Sundargarh – Barsua, Mankarnacha, Balia, Pahar, Khondadhav, Mithurda, Patroposi.<br>c. Jajpur – Tomka, Daitari<br>d. Mayurbhanj, Gurumahisani, Sulaipet, Badampahar<br>e. Naurangpur – Hirapur, Umrakot<br>f. Sambalpur Lohakhand- Naibassa Hill<br>g. Dhenkund – Malaygiri range | Hematite (BIF) | 4177 MT | |

*Contd*

**Table 3.2–Contd...**

| Name of State | General Description | Name of Deposit | Ore-Minerals | Reserve in MT | Remarks |
|---|---|---|---|---|---|
| | | **Magnetite deposit**<br>– Titanium bearing magnetite from Kumardubs - Betjharan | | | |
| Chhattisgarh | Precambrian Iron ore group of rocks consisting of Banded Hematite jaspar and quartzite. These are similar to those of Singhbhum Keonjhar iron ore belt. They occur in several places in Chhattisgarh and M.P. Large high quality deposits occur in Bastar and Durg district. | **Hemetite Deposits**<br>a. Bastar Dist.- Rowghat ore and Chottadongar deposits<br>b. Duntewara dist – Bailadila hill-range comprises 14 deposits.<br>c. Durg dist – Dalli-Rajhara, Kanchar, Jhasandali, Koudekosa and minor occurrences near Khairagarh Bela, Katul, Kassa, Jurle Khev.<br>d. Kankar Dist – Ari, Dongri, smaller deposits at Dulke, Kalwar, Dongar-bar, Lohattar.<br>e. Minor deposits in Jashpur, Bilaspur, Rajgarh districts | Hemetite (BIF) | 2278 MT | Reserves of both Chhattisgarh and M.P. considered together |
| Madhya Pradesh | Precambrian Iron ore group of rocks comprises of banded hematite and quartzite (as in Chhattisgarh state) | **Hemetite Deposits**<br>a. Jabalpur Dist – Kanhwar Plateau, Agaria, Bijori, Ghosalpur, Lora hills, Ghoghra, Sitondi Saroli.<br>b. Chattarpur Dist – Dalipur, Nimkhera, Deora, Chungwah.<br>c. Small occurrence in Betul, Jhabua, Nimar, Rajgarh, Sagar, Satna, Sidhi, Tikamgarh, Gwalior, Mandsaur, Narsimhapur | Hematite BIF | 152 MT | |

*Contd...*

**Table 3.2–Contd...**

| Name of State | General Description | Name of Deposit | Ore-Minerals | Reserve in MT | Remarks |
|---|---|---|---|---|---|
| Karnataka | Iron ore deposits here are divided into 3 groups:<br>1. Banded hematite quartzite of Dharwar group.<br>2. Metamorphosed banded magnetite quartzite.<br>3. Magnetite deposits with titaniferous magnetite in association with ultra-mafic rock | **Hematite Deposits**<br>a. Ballery District – Ballery-Hospet deposits<br>b. Chitradurga District - Sivaganga and Hiriyur, Medikeripura, Kedlegudum Bhimsamundra, Kajra<br>c. Shimoga Dist – Siddarahotti, Channagiri, Joldhal, Ganpur, Bhadigund, Shankar-guddo, Kumsi, Chattanhatti, Agumbe Visaniguda, Kodachadri, Kutebara<br>d. Bijapur Dist – Amirgarh, Bassargi, Bisral, Aipole, Hiremagit Ramthal.<br>e. North Karara Dist – Halkhamba, Shiroli, Kunarg, Katimedi, Hudsa, Anmod, Kuveshi, Diggi, Joidu, Talaginkera, Maringudi, Huntaganis, Yellapur.<br>f. Tumkur District, Karikurikhi, Chikanaya Kanthalli, Janehara, Kuni,<br>g. Small occurrences in Bijapur, Dakshin Kannad, Dhaiwar, Hassan, Mysore district. | Hematite<br>BIF | 1315.60 MT | Most important iron ore deposits are Sandur hills of Bellary Hospet, Bababudan hills Kudremukh-Gangamula range. |
| | | **Magnetite Deposits**<br>a. Chikamagalur District – Bahabaidan Hill, Kudremukh, Gangamula.<br>b. North Kanara Dist – Kodalgadde, Apsarakinda.<br>c. Mandya Dist, Tippur, Husegu, Hullehalli.<br>d. Chivemegdur Dist - Near Massrik<br>e. Bhadavati | Magnetite<br><br>Vanadi-ferous magnetite | 3843.9 MT | |

*Contd...*

**Table 3.2–Contd...**

| *Name of State* | *General Description* | *Name of Deposit* | *Ore-Minerals* | *Reserve in MT* | *Remarks* |
|---|---|---|---|---|---|
| Goa | Several deposits of Iron ores occur. Banded hematite quartzite of Precambrian age is mostly in pink python horizon. Ores are – hematite with minor occurrence of limonite and goethite | **From NW to SE** more than 30 iron ore deposits have been located. These are listed here:<br>1. Advalpale 2. Nanora 3. Bichulem Sirigao,<br>4. Bordem- Sarorna 5. Sanguelim 6. Arvalem<br>7. Gudhem Dignemsurla 8. Velguem - Palo,<br>9. Pissurlem – Sonshi 10. Usgao<br>11. Conquirem 12. Poient-Siudem 13. Sacorda,<br>14. Sond-Deven, 15. Gavarem-Molpura<br>16. Balooruem 17. Bimbol-Siguo 18. Suetioti-Taitoli 19. Codli 20. Samtone-Quirlapole<br>21. Dudal, 22. Kaloy 23. Manlinguem<br>24. Tulem-Motto, 25. Barazan-Villeno,<br>26. Sirigal- Undorna- Argod 27. Rivona-Columbe 28. Lanvovem – Navelim<br>29. Sukorna – Vichurdrem 30. Netrolim<br>31. Camona- Conda 32. Batul. | Probably Hematite (BIF) with small amount of magnetite and limonite. | 79.85 MT | Bicholem-siringaon + Volguem pale are the best deposits. |
| Maharashtra | Iron ore deposits are located in associated with Iron Ore group of the Archean. This group comprises older schist and unclassified rallies. These have been by metamorphosed sedimentary rock such as quartzite, BHQ, Phyllite.<br>Iron ores seem to have been derived from BHQ by process of leaching of silica. | **Hematite Ores**<br>a. Sindhudurg Dist – Redi, Tirvada- Ajgaon – Guldave. Sateli-Starda, Sateti-Talwara, Talesane-ajgaon, Kalre, Podye Degve-Darde, Galel, Galel North and Galel South.<br>b. Chandrapur Dist- Lohara, Pipalgaon, Asola<br>c. Gadchiroli Dist, Surajgarh, Bhamragarh, Dewalgaon, Puser, Damkodwavi, hill-range.<br>d. Bhardawa Dist, Khursipar Konhoti<br>e. Ratnagiri Dist – Molvan, Kunda, Savantvedi<br>f. Small occurrences are located in Kolhapur, Nagpur, Satara (North) Nanded, Yeotmel districts | Hematite (BIF) | 273 MT | Economically viable deposits occur in Chandrapur Sindhdurg and Gadchiroli districts. |

*Contd...*

**Table 3.2–Contd...**

| *Name of State* | *General Description* | *Name of Deposit* | *Ore-Minerals* | *Reserve in MT* | *Remarks* |
|---|---|---|---|---|---|
| Andhra Pradesh | Rest of the iron ore deposits are located in Dharwar sediments of Purana Formations. However, low iron ore also occur in upper Gondwana and laterite cappings on baselts of the Deccan Trops. Magnetite and Hematite both occur in them. | **Hematite Ores**<br>a. Anantpur Dist, Balapuram, Siddapuram, Rayadurg, Talut, Motopanagudi, Velpurnadurg Kambedur, Gollepalle, Oddapalam, Muchakpalle.<br>b. Guddupal Dist – Chabeti, Rajampet, Ponduluri, Venkata Palli, Erregurtakuta, Mantapampelle, Pendhimri, Pagadalapalle.<br>c. Kurnool Dist – Veldwets, Ramallakoto<br>d. Nedove Dist, Rassnapalem, Chundi, Polenava, Chetuva, Swarrnamukhi, river<br>e. Khammam & Waranged districts. Kottaguderian Motala, Timmapur, Nilanehe, Bayyaram Opulapuram. | Hemetite (BIF) | 89 MT | |
| | | **Magnetite Ores**<br>a. Prakasam Dist – Ungole, Pernametta, Konijedu, Sarnanpudi, Bard, Gundel Kamma group, Byrepalle, Errapalle, Timmavasam and Manikeshvaram<br>b. Khamman dist, Utla, Tatraiyapatti, Gopalpur.<br>c. Vishakhapatnam Dist, Sitarampur, Darbanblom, Konda<br>d. East Godavari Dist – Addatigala, Devipuram. In addition small deposits are located in Adilabad, Chittoor, Guntur, Karim Nagar, Krishna, Medak, Nizamabad, Vishakha-patnam, Srikakulam and Warrangal Districts of the state | Magnetite (BIF) | 1309.7 MT | |

*Contd...*

**Table 3.2–Contd...**

| *Name of State* | *General Description* | *Name of Deposit* | *Ore-Minerals* | *Reserve in MT* | *Remarks* |
|---|---|---|---|---|---|
| Tamil Nadu | Iron ores are located in small relative to other major deposits. Several magnetite quartzite bands occur in some areas especially along the northern side of Kaveri River | **Magnetite Ores**<br>a. Salem Dist. – Kanjamalai, Godumdai, Malath angi, Tumbal, Alongadu, Suryagaddi, Paduvalhi Tainandamalai, Kollaimelai, Puchaikalai Aptur.<br>b. Tiruchirapalli Dist– Valasirannani, Urakkari<br>c. Dharampuri Dist – Titlhamalai Alambadi<br>d. South Arcot & North Arcot Dist. north of Talankumar, Budamangalam.<br>e. Nilgiri Dist. – Nilgiri Hills, Tatarrenu, Ar Vankadu, Devla. | | | |
| Kerala | Several bands of magnetite quartzite have been recorded with the Charmodate and gneissic groups of rocks. | **Magnetite Ores**<br>a. Calient- Kozikode Dist. – Cheruppa, Eleyettimala, Nanminda, Naduvallur, East & West Hills, Banda, Alanpura.<br>b. Kottayam Dist. Kitapare, NW of Idikki, Kallipare, South of Panamkutty, Nullaninod, Neriyamangalam, Ernolu, Rendav<br>c. Palghat Dist. – Attapely Valley, Kilur, Mannambatti, Karivallur, Valur, Nadupetti, Elival West.<br>Small occurrences have been reported from Kollam and Trichur districts. | Magnetite (BIF) | 39 MT | |
| Rajasthan | Minor deposits of Iron Ores occur in different areas of the state. In Udaipur and Jaipur districts, hematite ore occur in the Alwar Series of rocks. In Jhurghum and Sikar district are hematite & magnetite occurrences have been located within the Ajabgarh series. | **Hematite Ores**<br>a. Jaipur Dist – Morija, Lalsot, Nimia, Rampura<br>b. Udaipur Dist – Nathara Kapasa. | Hematite | 20 MT | |
| | | **Megnetite Ores**<br>a. Jhurghum Dist- Tanoda, Raipur, Jaintapura, Kali Pahari, Gaonle<br>b. Sikar Dist. – Narda- Nanagwas, Bagoli, Sarai | Magnetite with layer of hematite | 0.15 MT | Magnetite is in lowl amounts |

*Contd...*

**Table 3.2–Contd...**

| *Name of State* | *General Description* | *Name of Deposit* | *Ore-Minerals* | *Reserve in MT* | *Remarks* |
|---|---|---|---|---|---|
| Arunachal Pradesh | Small occurrences of iron ores have been reported in Subansiri & Siang district. Boulders of magnetite hematite ores known to be associated with quartzite and shelly phyllites unit. | a. Subansiri Dist – Lamdak, Godak Village, Western Feamt of Simmi river, Tarai, Kimin Jaihung<br>b. Siang Dist – Tribin, Yomcha. | Hematite and magnetite (BIF) | | These occurrences have no economic significance |
| Assam | Iron ores glow have been located in lower Brahmaputra valley. Banded magnetite-hematite quartzite rocks. They show an association with gneisses and amphibolites of Precambrian age. | a. Goalpara Dist- Chandardinga, Kumri, Lengupura, Dipika, Chatanbari,- Pandoba, Pahar- Bamandanga<br>b. Bongaigar Dist – Malai<br>c. Kokrajhar Dist. – Chakrasila<br>Small occurrences in Jainta Hills, Khasi Hills, Lakhimpur, Sibsagar and Mikir Hills are known | Hematite magnetite (BIF) | | These occurrences have no economic significance |
| Nagaland | Iron ores in form of magnetite with NS, Co, and Cr occur with ophirolite suite of Nagaland. | a. Deposit has been located in Pokphur village in Tuensang dist.<br>Other small bodies have been located with the ophirolite suite in Phek district. | Magnetite | | They have no economic significance |
| Jammu & Kashmir | Hematite containing beds ore located in Batliaz formations of Precambrian age in Poonch district. Hematite chart aoccurs in Udampur district which are within Sirben Limatara Group | **Hematite Ores**<br>a. Poonch district – Khandi Iron ore<br>b. Udhampur district – Matah, Kotala, Sangar | Hematite | | They have no significance |
| Himachal Pradesh | Small occurrences of hematite-magnetite have been located in association with quartzite schist phyllites in various parts of the state. | **Hematite Ores**<br>a. Kullu Dist.- Roshal, Yargi, and Garahan<br>b. Lahul & Spiti Dist. – Thango Formation, Southeast of Muthi.<br>c. Shimla Dist – Rohru tehsil, Narain, Shekal, Pujarli Shil. | | | They are of no economic significance |

*Contd...*

**Table 3.2–Contd...**

| *Name of State* | *General Description* | *Name of Deposit* | *Ore-Minerals* | *Reserve in MT* | *Remarks* |
|---|---|---|---|---|---|
| | | **Megnetite Ores**<br>a. Kangra District – Dharmsala, Bis, Kohad.<br>b. Kinnir district – Mangrala<br>c. Mandi district – Rama Bhet, Sangalwara, Jhungi, Kohar, Khas, Buragoran<br>d. Sirmaur district – Kambari, Nahan, Lana, Chatta. | Magnetite | | No economic significance |
| West Bengal | These are no iron ore deposit of economic significance in the state.<br>Minor occurrences are located in different geological succession *e.g.* iron bearing sands of rivers. Recent age laterite which cap the Rajmahal basalts. In addition titaniferous magnetite ore minor occurrences are found within the Archean rocks of the state. | a. Purulia Dist.- Manbajar, Surpur, Gaurangdih, Jholda, Buroajora, Baud, Panchet Hill, Tamkhur, Aspani<br>b. Bankuna Dist – Biharnaths Hill, Bagjobra, Ambikanagar, Ruparhir Tepra, Kharidungri, Mukhtnanipur, Barcha, Dedua, Salua, Dvargram, Purapani, Kuchaipal, Manla, Pukura<br>c. Midnapur Dist. – Bhankabhanga, Sarisabasa, Jarna, Dublakono<br>d. Durdiwan Dist. Raniganj Coalfield, Barren Meaicef shela<br>e. Birbhum Dist, Namgulia Tamla, Ganpur, Deocha, Korda, Deodina, Sopohadi<br>f. Dayeding Sambalbong<br>g. Jalpaiguri dist- Buxa Bazar, Raimatang-Goapota | Magnetite and Hematite | | No economic significance |
| Haryana | Magnetite rich iron ore occur in minor concentrations and discontinuous band within dolomite and siliceous marbles of Ajabgarh series. | **Hematite Ore**<br>Mahendragarh Dist. – Rajawan Sonk.<br><br>**Magnetite Ore**<br>Mahendragarh Dist. Anti-Biharipur, Dhandta, | Hematite Magnetite | 8.08 MT | Minor economic significance |

*Contd...*

**Table 3.2–Contd...**

| *Name of State* | *General Description* | *Name of Deposit* | *Ore-Minerals* | *Reserve in MT* | *Remarks* |
|---|---|---|---|---|---|
| | Sometimes hematite occurs also within calcareous quartzite as minor accumulations. | Dhancholi. | | | |
| Meghalya | Magnetite occurs as minor accumulation in alluvial sands and ultra-mafic rocks in the Sung valley. | a. Sung Block<br>b. Muscot block | Magnetite | NA | No economics significance |

**Table 3.3: Indian Reserves of Iron Ores (Hematite and Magnetite mainly) in Million Tonnes**

| Grade | Recoverable Reserves as on 1.4.1995 | | | |
|---|---|---|---|---|
| | Proved | Probable | Possible | Total |
| Hematite Total | 5106 | 2360 | 2577 | 10052 |
| Grades Lump – high grade | 410 | 294 | 106 | 810 |
| Lump Medium Grade | 1056 | 751 | 582 | 2389 |
| Lump Low Grade | 488 | 204 | 358 | 1050 |
| Lump Unclassified | 77 | 91 | 470 | 638 |
| Fines High grade | 224 | 95 | 17 | 336 |
| Fines Medium grade | 1600 | 441 | 356 | 2397 |
| Fines Unclassified | 21 | 48 | 296 | 365 |
| Lumps and fines high grade | 44 | - | 7 | 51 |
| Lumps and fine medium grade | 150 | 1 | 7 | 158 |
| Lumps and fines low grade | 23 | 1 | 50 | 74 |
| Lumps and fines unclassified | 18 | - | 28 | 46 |
| Blue dust | 76 | 4 | - | 80 |
| Black Iron ore | 2 | 6 | 4 | 12 |
| Others | 3 | 3 | 4 | 10 |
| Unclassified | - | - | 4 | 4 |
| Not known | 14 | 1 | 13 | 28 |

**Table 3.4a: Iron Ores in India: State-wise Reserves/Resources Iron Ore (Hematite) as on 1-4-2005 (Unit: 000 Tonnes)**

| State | Reserves | Remaining Resources | Total Resources |
|---|---|---|---|
| All India: Total | 7004168 | 7626220 | 14630388 |
| Andhra Pradesh | 39596 | 123443 | 163038 |
| Assam | – | 12600 | 12600 |
| Bihar | – | 55 | 55 |
| Chhattisgarh | 760512 | 1970275 | 2730787 |
| Goa | 458704 | 254244 | 712948 |
| Jharkhand | 2494433 | 1541323 | 4035746 |

*Contd...*

**Table 3.4a–Contd...**

| *State* | *Reserves* | *Remaining Resources* | *Total Resources* |
|---|---|---|---|
| Karnataka | 940430 | 735792 | 1676222 |
| Madhya Pradesh | 33917 | 171021 | 204938 |
| Maharashtra | 13997 | 251359 | 265356 |
| Meghalaya | – | 225 | 225 |
| Orissa | 2251777 | 2508848 | 4760625 |
| Rajasthan | 10813 | 19035 | 29848 |
| Uttar Pradesh | – | 38000 | 38000 |

**Table 3.4b: Magnetite Reserves/Resources**

| *State* | *Reserves* | *Remaining Resources* | *Total Resources* |
|---|---|---|---|
| All India: Total | 58504 | 10560977 | 10619481 |
| Andhra Pradesh | – | 1463541 | 1463541 |
| Assam | – | 15380 | 15380 |
| Bihar | – | 2659 | 2659 |
| Goa | 50112 | 164057 | 214169 |
| Jharkhand | 3391 | 6879 | 10269 |
| Karnataka | – | 7811784 | 7811784 |
| Kerala | – | 83435 | 83435 |
| Maharashtra | 621 | – | 621 |
| Meghalaya | – | 3380 | 3380 |
| Nagaland | – | 5280 | 5280 |
| Orissa | 156 | 54 | 210 |
| Rajasthan | 4225 | 522652 | 526877 |
| Tamil Nadu | – | 481876 | 481876 |

*Source*: Indian Bureau of Mines.

# Production of Iron Ores

## World Scene

During 1980-88 the global iron ore market came down heavily on the verge of imbalance in supply and demand of ore. However, at the end of 1988, the world economy started recovery with clear signals of strong growth of iron ore production. This was clearly demonstrated in the year beginning from 1993, as can be seen in the Tables 3.5a&b and 3.6.

**Table 3.5a: Global Top Five Iron Ore Producing Countries (2003–2009) Million Tonnes**

| *Country* | *2003* | *2004.* | *2005.* | *2006* | *2007* | *2008* | *2009* |
|---|---|---|---|---|---|---|---|
| China | 122.7 | 145.7 | 197.6 | 278.4 | 365.0 | 366.0 | 234.0 |
| Australia | 212.0 | 234.7 | 257.5 | 275.1 | 299.0 | 349.8 | 394.0 |
| Brazil | 245.6 | 276.5 | 292.4 | 318.6 | 336.5 | 346.0 | 300.0 |
| India | 99.1 | 120.6 | 142.7 | 180.9 | 206.9 | 214.0 | 257.0 |
| Russia | 91.8 | 97.0 | 95.1 | 102.5 | 105.0 | 99.9 | 100.0 |
| World Total | 1074.7 | 1184.9 | 1309.0 | 1491.9 | 1664.0 | 1724.6 | 1588.0 |

**Table 3.5b: Iron Ore Resources and Production Between 1980, 1990, 2000 and 2005**

| *Grade* | *Resources as on 1-1-1980* | *Production between 1980-1990* | *Resources as on 1-4-1990* | *Production between 1990-2000* | *Resources as on 1-4-2000** | *Production between 2000-05* | *Resources as on 1-4-2005** |
|---|---|---|---|---|---|---|---|
| Hematite | 11469 | | 12197 (+728) | | 11426 (–771) | | 14630 (+3204) |
| Magnetite | 6095 | | 10590 (4495) | | 10682 (+92) | | 10619 (–63) |
| Total | 17564 | 470 | 22787 (+5223) | 656 | 22108 (–679) | 532 | 25249 (+3141) |

Figures in parenthesis indicate decrease (–)/increase (+) in resources.

*Notes*: 1. These resources do not include around 1000 million tonnes of hematite iron ore recently discovered by DMG, Chhattisgarh in Kabirdham district.

2. Above resources are with cut-off grade +55 per cent Fe and roughly up to 50 meter depth estimated with sparse and far-between drilling.

*Source*: Indian Bureau of Mines, Nagpur

**Table 3.6: World's Largest Iron Ore Producers, early 2010**

| *Company* | *Base* | *Capacity mt/yr* |
|---|---|---|
| Vale Group (CVRD) | Brazil | 417.1 |
| Rio Tinto Group | UK | 273.7 |
| BHP Billiton Group | Australia | 188.5 |
| ArcelorMittal Group | UK | 78.9 |
| Fortescue Metals Group | Australia | 55.0 |
| Evrazholding Group | Russia | 50.4 |
| Metalloinvest Group | Russia | 44.7 |
| AnBen Group | China | 44.7 |
| Metinvest Holding Group | Ukraine | 42.8 |
| Anglo American Group | South Africa | 41.1 |

*Contd...*

**Table 3.5–Contd...**

| *Company* | *Base* | *Capacity mt/yr* |
|---|---|---|
| LKAB Group | Sweden | 38.5 |
| CVG Group | Venezuela | 37.9 |
| Cliffs Natural Resources | USA | 34.6 |
| NMDC Group | India | 32.6 |
| Imidro Group | Iran | 29.8 |
| CSN Group | Brazil | 28.0 |
| Shougang Beijing Group | China | 26.5 |
| US Steel Group | USA | 23.5 |
| ENRC-Eurasian Natural Resources | Kazakhstan | 19.7 |
| Wuhan Iron and Steel Group | China | 18.6 |
| Total capacity | | 2177.3 |

*Source*: Steelonthenet.com.

## Indian Production Scene

Amongst the states of the country, Chhattisgarh (including Madhya Pradesh) is the largest producer of iron ore. Other important states are Goa, Orissa, Jharkhand and Karnataka.

# Chapter 4

# The Banded Iron Formation and Iron Ore Deposits of Eastern India

## Introduction

Rich iron ore deposits of high grade where the iron percentage is more than 60 per cent, eastern India account for more than half of the total current annual production of more than 180 million metric tonnes of iron ore in India. After nearly a century of active mining the estimated remaining iron ore resource of the eastern Indian deposits is in the order of five billion metric tonnes at >60wt per cent Fe (*see* also Chapters 3 and 10). The best grade and largest East Indian deposits are virtually all hosted by Precambrian banded iron formation (BIF) of the Iron Ore Group (IOG) (Jones, 1934; Dunn, 1937; 1940, 1941; Spencer and Percival, 1952; Krishnan, 1982; Banerji, 1977; Sarkar, 2000; 2002; Acharya, 1993, 2002; Sarkar and Gupta, 2005; Beukes *et al.*, 2008). The following description is from Mukhopadhyay *et al.*, (2008). Major strata bound ore deposits occur in the BIFs of the eastern IOG in the Gorumahishani-Badampahar range, western IOG in the Noamundi-Joda-Malangtoli-Bursua-Gua-Chiria ranges, and in the southern IOG in the Daitari-Tamka range. Relatively minor amounts of low-grade ores occur as ancient colluvial detrital conglomeratic ore deposits in the Late Mesoproterozoic Kolhan successions around Chamakapur and Baljori villages (Mukhopadhyay *et al.*, 2007) as well as Quaternary alluvial deposits close to major BIF-hosted deposits.

There are differences in opinion regarding the origin of the BIF-hosted iron ore deposits of eastern India. They are generally believed to have formed through preferential leaching of silica from BIF/BHQ (banded hematite quartzite) in response to *supergene* weathering and tropical lateritization processes (*e.g.*, Dunn 1937; Krishnan, 1982; Banerji, 1977). A syngenetic hypothesis for the origin for the BIF-hosted high-grade iron ores (Spencer and Percival, 1952; Misra, 2006; Acharya, 2002) has also been invoked. An alternative hydrothermal model (*e.g.*, Mukhopadhyay *et al.*, 2002; Beukes *et al.*, 2003; for the Noamundi Deposits), or a combination of supergene and hydrothermal processes (Sarkar and Gupta, 2005 for eastern Indian deposits) have been put forward. In more recent times Beukes *et al.* (2008) and Mukhopadhyay *et al.* (2008) proposed a *supergene-modified hydrothermal model* for the deposits of the Noamundi area based on field relationship, petrographic and geochemical proxies (Gutzmer *et al.*, 2006).

## An Overview of the Iron Ore Group

The iron ores of eastern India are virtually restricted to the BIF-bearing Paleo-Mesoarchean greenstone successions of the Singhbhum craton. The craton is one of the oldest Paleo-Mesoarchean cratonic nuclei of the peninsular India. It is a composite mosaic of Archean greenstone-granitoids and Proterozoic supracrustal successions (Acharya, 1993; Saha, 1994, Mukhopadhyay, 2001). The oldest granitoid is referred to as the Older Metamorphic Tonalite Gneiss (OMTG, 3,400 m.y.) that includes enclaves of metasedimentaries of the Older Metamorphic Group (OMG, 3,500-3,800 m.y.; *see for reviews* Saha, 1994; Sarkar, 2000; Mukhopadhyay, 2001; Misra, 2006). The OMTG is intruded by several granitic plutonnes collectively referred to as the Singhbhum Granitoid with three phases of emplacement between 3300 m.y. and 3100 m.y. (Mukhopadhyay, 2001; Misra, 2006). The Singhbhum Granitoid is the aerially most extensive unit and encloses the BIF-bearing Iron Ore Group (IOG). Younger Neoarchaean to Mesoproterozoic volcanosedimentary successions unconformably overlie the granite-greenstone successions (Dunn, 1940; Iyenger and Alwar, 1965; Acharya, 1993; Saha, 1994; Mazumdar, 1996; Sarkar, 2000; Mukhopadhyay, 2001; Misra, 2006; Mukhopadhyay *et al.*, 2006; 2007).

The IOG low grade metamorphic greenstone belt successions comprise banded iron formation (BIF), mafic-felsic volcanic rocks, chert, shale and minor carbonate (Jones 1934; Acharyya 1993; Saha 1994; Mukhopadhyay 2001; Beukes *et al.*, 2008). The greenstone belts occur as three large detached enclaves within Singhbhum Granitoid. These enclaves are informally referred to as the western (Noamundi-Joda-Koira-Malangtoli-Bursua-Chiria), eastern (Gorumahisani-Badampahar) and southern (Malaygiri-Tamka-Daitari) IOG. Iron ore deposits occur in BIF host units in all three areas of greenstone belts. However, the economically most important deposits are located in the western IOG, in the Noamundi-Joda-Koira-Malangtoli-Bursua-Chiria range. From base to top, it includes thick, massive, or pillowed metabasalt, lower phyllitic shale-tuff (locally with thin carbonate and supergene manganiferous mineralization), BIF, and upper phyllitic shale (Ghosh and Mukhopadhyay, 2007; Beukes *et al.*, 2008). The main regional structure controlling the outcrop belt has been described as a northeasterly plunging synclinorium-the *'horseshoe synclinorium'*, with overturned western limb (Jones, 1934; Dunn, 1940; Sarkar and Saha, 1962). The name comes from the fact that the resistant BIF results in a range of hills with a typical horseshoe-shaped outcrop pattern. The synclinorium has been later cross-folded along an east-west axis (Chatterjee and Mukherjee, 1981; Ghosh and Mukhopadhyay, 2007).

The high-grade iron ores of the Western IOG are mainly composed of hematite. In contrast the smaller deposits of the Eastern IOG are mainly composed of magnetite-rich stratabound bodies in a thick BIF unit (Mukhopadhyay *et al.*, 2008). These deposits are located along the Gorumahishani-Bdamapahar range. The eastern IOG is folded into several steep anticlines and synclines with early steep isoclinal folds trending NNE-SSW and late open folds with axis trending WNW-ESE.

The BIF-bearing metavolacnics succession of the southern IOG is well exposed along the Tomka-Daitari Ranges (Prasad Rao *et al.*, 1964; Chakraborty *et al.*, 1980; Acharya, 2002). The succession consists from the base upwards of massive and pillowed basalts with a few thin grey to green chert interbeds, felsic to intermediate volcanic and volcaniclastic rocks (tuffs), bedded chert and BIF (Mukhopadhyay *et al.*, 2008). The BIF unit here is more than 120 m thick and hosts the Daitari and Tomka hematite-rich iron ore deposits. A podiform chromiferous ultramafic body (Aug´e *et al.*, 2003; Mondal *et al.*, 2006, 2007) that forms the most important chromite resource of India in the Sukinda Valley overlies the BIF with a thrust contact (cf. Banerjee 1997). The ultramafic body and the greenstone succession of the Daitari-Tamka range are unconformably overlain by a thick siliciclastic shelf succession, the Mahagiri Quartzite (Mukhopadhyay *et al.*, 2008) that includes detrital chromite grains in its lower parts.

Until recently there was no direct age for the IOG successions. A minimum age of ~3,200 m.y. was provided for the Iron Ore Group by granitoids intrusive into the three outcrop belts (cf. Paul *et al.*, 1991; Misra, 2006). Mukhopadhyay *et al.* (2008) obtained 3,506±2 Ma U-Pb SHRIMP zircon age from the dacitic lava from the southern IOG around Daitari.

## Iron Ores

Iron ores of the Singhbhum craton (Figures 4.1 and 4.2) occur as stratabound orebodies within the BIF protolith or else in subordinate amount as detrital colluvial ores in ancient geological formations (Mukhopadhyay *et al.*, 2007) or Quaternary to recent alluvial deposits. The detrital ores are seemingly derived from the stratabound mother orebodies. The main stratabound orebodies are essentially hematitic in mineralogy, though magnetite/martite dominated orebodies occur in the Gorumahishani-Badampahar range of the eastern IOG.

The stratabound orebodies are hosted by the prominent BIF-units in each of the IOG outcrop belts. Thickness of the BIF protoliths may range from 120 to 220 m. Besides the major BIF-bearing unit, several thinner (a few metres) BIF units in the lower manganiferous shale of the western IOG are also mineralized and are locally mined.

Megascopically the ores are of two major types, namely, hard massive/laminated ore and soft/friable ore that can grade to completely incoherent blue dust variety. The high-grade hard orebodies have been found to near completely replace the BIF protolith

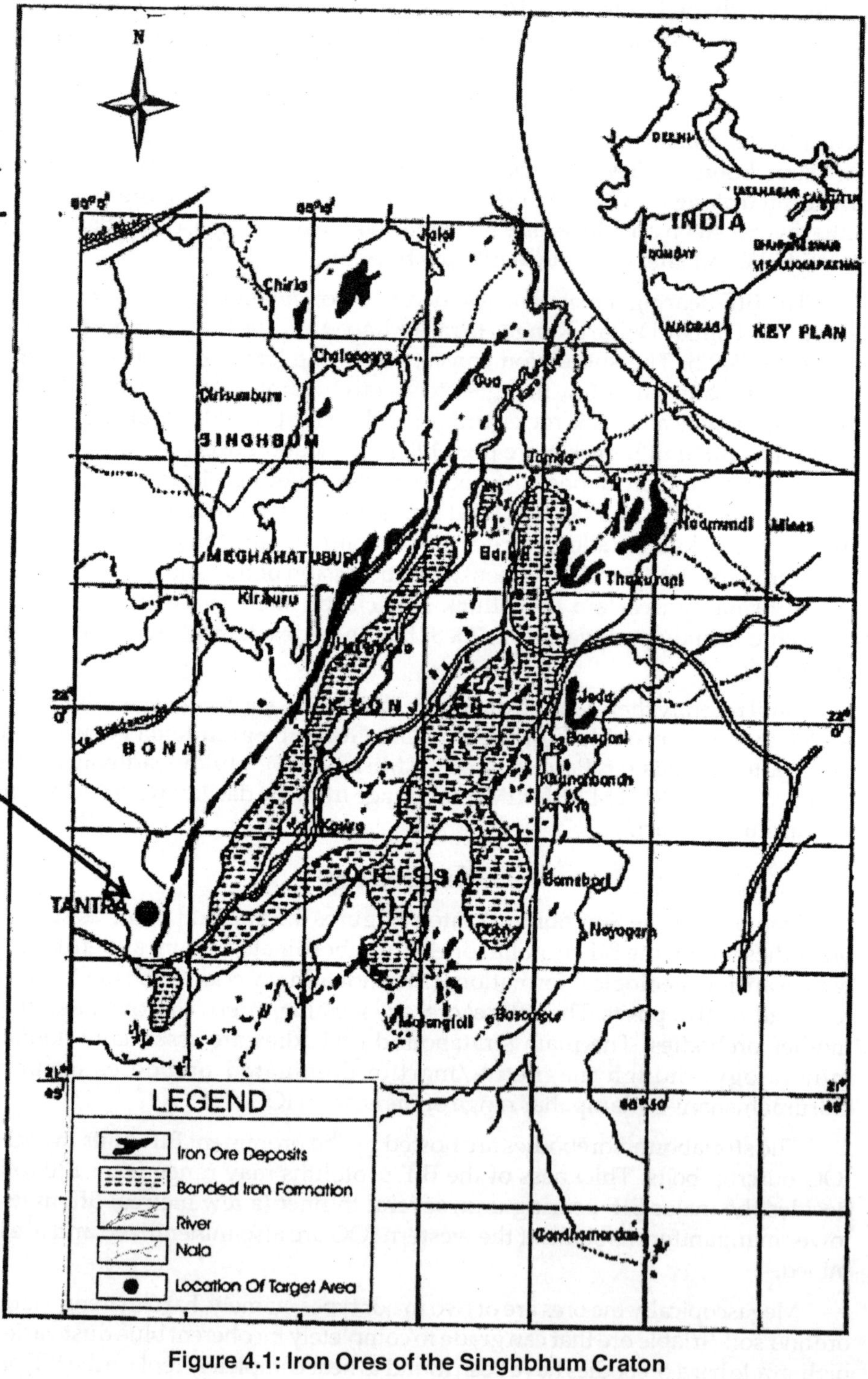


**Figure 4.1: Iron Ores of the Singhbhum Craton**

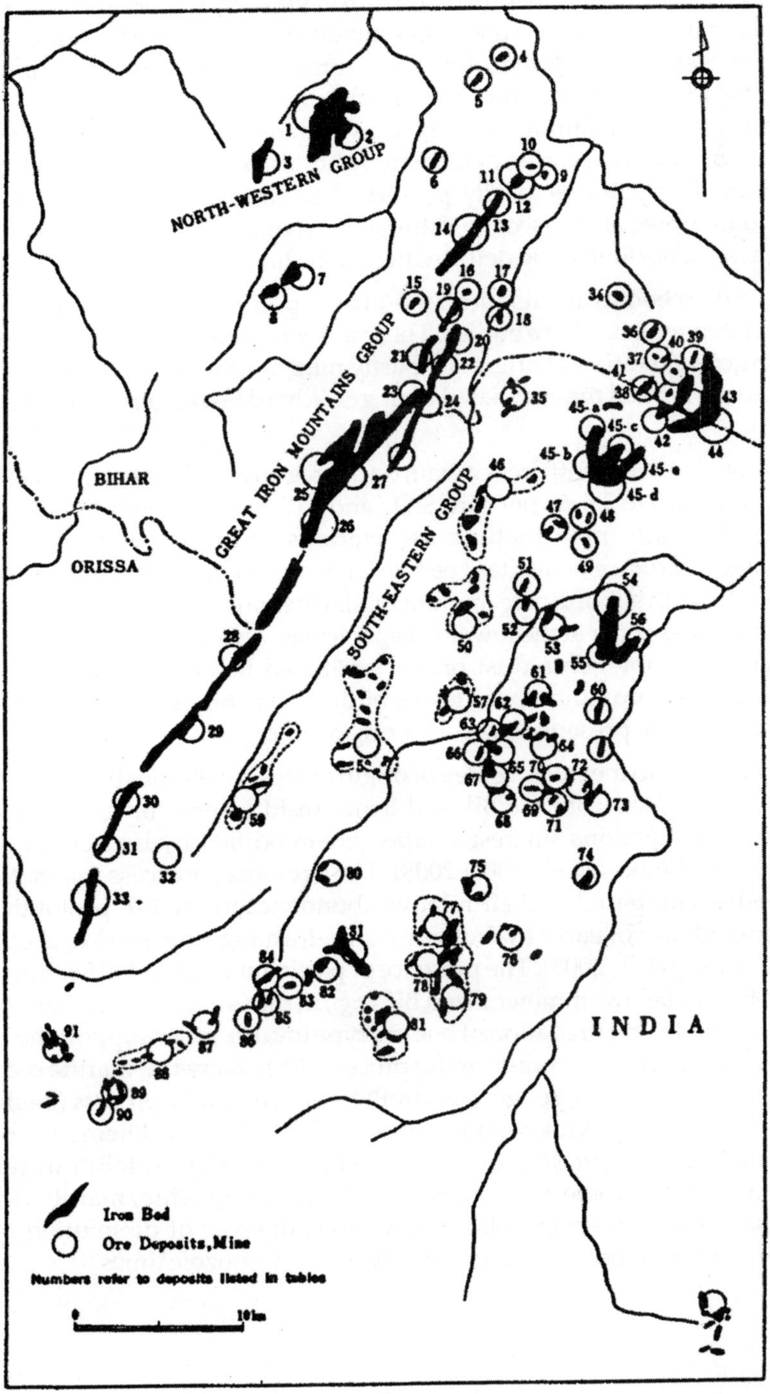


**Figure 4.2: The Iron Ore Deposits in the Singhbhum Area, Singhbhum–Orissa Region (from C. Nishwaki, 1970)**

or might grade to unmineralized BIF through partly mineralized BIF both vertically and laterally. Locally, the orebodies include patches of partly mineralized BIF. The orebodies strictly follow the folded form surfaces of the BIF protolith and consequently the attitude of the orebodies varies with the changing attitudes of the BIF units. Although relative timing of ore genesis with respect to the deformation is yet to be resolved, lack of pervasive deformation fabrics in platy hematite-rich orebodies and intricate fold patterns locally preserved in essentially monomineralic orebodies without appreciable viscosity difference among strata suggest that ore formation might have postdated the deformation of the host BIF.

Soft orebodies are also stratabound to specific units in the BIF host and closely associated with hard ore bodies. These are considered orebodies that resulted from supergene alteration of originally partly mineralized BIF by the same hydrothermal fluids that formed the associated high-grade hard hematitemartite ores (Beukes *et al.*, 2008).

Both hard and soft ores contain on average 64 to 67 wt per cent Fe, 1 to 2.8 wt per cent $Al_2O_3$, 0.5 to 3.6 wt per cent $SiO_2$, and 0.05 to 0.1 wt per cent $P_2O_5$. The hard ore mineralogically may include associations of martite-hematite±magnetite or hematite±martite or hematite±goethite. The soft ores and blue dusts are predominantly hematitic with subordinate amount of martites and goethite. In general the martite-rich hard ores occur at the lower/deeper levels. This type of ore commonly grades to either soft friable/blue dust ore or laminated hematitic ores. The goethitic ores commonly occupy the upper levels of deposits and are distinctly the products of oxidation in the present-day weathering profile.

Contrary to the existing idea of origin of these orebodies by supergene process of leaching of silica from the BIF and hence residual enrichment of Fe-ore minerals, recent investigations suggest a supergene-modified hydrothermal process of ore formation (Beukes *et al.*, 2003; 2008). The presence of excess magnetite/martite in orebodies compared to their relative abundance in the BIF-protolith provides the major evidence of early hydrothermal ore-forming process (Mukhopadhyay *et al.*, 2002; Beukes *et al.*, 2008). The presence of partly mineralized BIF relicts, the existence of orebodies below unmineralized BIF (*e.g.*, in the Gandhamardan ore deposit, OMC, Orissa) and lateral gradation of one ore type into the other support the hydrothermal ore genesis as primary ore-forming process. The magnetite-martite ores are believed to be the products of hypogene hydrothermal ore genetic process (Beukes *et al.*, 2003; Beukes *et al.*, 2008; Mukhopadhyay *et al.*, 2008). The hard hematitic ore have been explained as the product of replacement of the BIF-protolith in relatively low-temperature hydrothermal system peripheral to magnetite/martite-rich ore-bodies. The soft ores have been related to various degrees of dissolution of $Fe^{2+}$ during supergene oxidation in acidic groundwater in Cenozoic times.

# Chapter 5

# Banded Iron Formations, and Iron Ore Deposit of Orissa–Jharkhand Region

## Introduction

In India most of the Proterozoic iron ore deposits are stratiform and hematitic like the rest of the world. The planar features of the ore bodies are parallel to bedding of BIF. Clastics are mostly absent and fine-grained shales exist above and below BIF. In the field the ore bandings thin or thicken (from mm to even 0.3 m.) and are parallel to bedding of BIF to start with and hence produce sediment- type- stratiform deposit.

Since times of the Jones (1934) the Iron ore deposits of Orissa and Jharkhand have received great attention due of their being high grade and large size. Here mining is done by simple quarrying. If the present day production of a very high scale these ore deposits continues at this rate, then they would be exhausted in the near future. This may make imperative to mine out lower cut-off grade and also go for ore beneficiation (*see* also Chapters 9 and 10).

These deposits are mostly associated with sedimentary BIFs of Achaean to Proterozoic age; the grade of deposits increases with time. Each deposit is continuous, uniform and homogeneous, based on their chemical sedimentary characters and includes the gangue minerals which downgrade quality of the deposits. Hence primary and secondary processes upgrade deposits by enriching the grade due to beneficiation is now being adopted by several mining companies operating in the region.

## Regional Geological Pattern

Geology of the Singhbhum-Orissa region has been one of the best geologically studied regions of the country because of Noamundi and Gua iron ore deposits (extension of Orissan iron ore district) and Gorumahisani, Sulaipat and Badampahar iron ore deposits (in Mayurbhanj dist. Orissa) as well as for the copper and atomic mineral deposits of Singhbhum shear zone that discontinuously extend upto Dakura, 16 kms south of Baripada in Mayurbhanj district. The Iron Ore Supergroup-bearing northern Orissa is separated from Talchir Gondwana rocks and Eastern Ghat Supergroup by Sukinda Thrust zone (northern fault of Gondwana basin). The iron ore district of Orissa-Jharkhand is, thus, confined to the Singhbhum-Sukinda thrust belts in the north and south (Acharya, 2001) (Figure 5.1).

The Iron Ore Super Group (IOSG) has three stratigraphically horizons of BIFs in space and time, which are structurally, stratigraphically, mineralogically, petrologically, metamorphically and ore-deposit-wise different from each other (Acharya, 2000, 2005). The following description is from Acharya (2008).

BIF-1 is narrow, Banded Magnetite-quartite (BMQ)-type, thin banded and extensive from Pallahara to Gorumahisani with Amphibolite facies metamorphism (grunerite) and often higher and exhibits at least 6 periods of deformation but with no big ore deposits so far known. BIF-2 forms Daitari-Tomka basin that dies out at Harichandanpur. It has three periods of deformation and suffers higher phase of green schist facies of metamorphism. BIF-3, the 'Horse-shoe' basin (Joda-Koira Basin as JKB) is the youngest with Dhanjori Sandstone and younger volcanics at its base. It has the best grade and extensive ore bodies each of more than one km in length at times. With not much of complicated folding, the basin forms independently with youngest BIF (BIF-3) in the entire region and the thickness of bands of hematite/chert exceeds 30 cms at times.

GHSV Prasada Rao (1964), had recorded more than one BIF horizon in this entire region and significantly the opinion on Kansa quartzite, south of Daitari deposit to be of Dhanjori age and not of Kolhan as recorded by him earlier is very important in recasting the regional stratigraphy. A two-tier system was suggested by Banerjee (1974) whereas Acharya (2005) conceived of a three-tier system. This has been found to be valid by repeated field checking when the second one has been observed to be intermediate to BIF-1 and BIF-3. An unconformity runs between the rocks of Daitari basin and Dhanjori sandstone, which, at different places, has acted as an angular unconformity, disconformity and nonconformity. BIF-3, as mentioned earlier, is post Dhanjori sandstone and volcanics in the intra-cratonic basin between Singhbhum-Granite Complex (SGC) and Bonai granite.

Large deposits associated with BIF-1 are not yet known. But the BIF is magnetite-rich and structurally complex. They, with the associated rocks show upto sillimanite and kyanite grade of metamorphism. The thickness of the BIF is less in comparison to its length. The ore minerals are essentially magnetite and secondary ones. Jasper and chert almost do not exist since they are recrystallised.

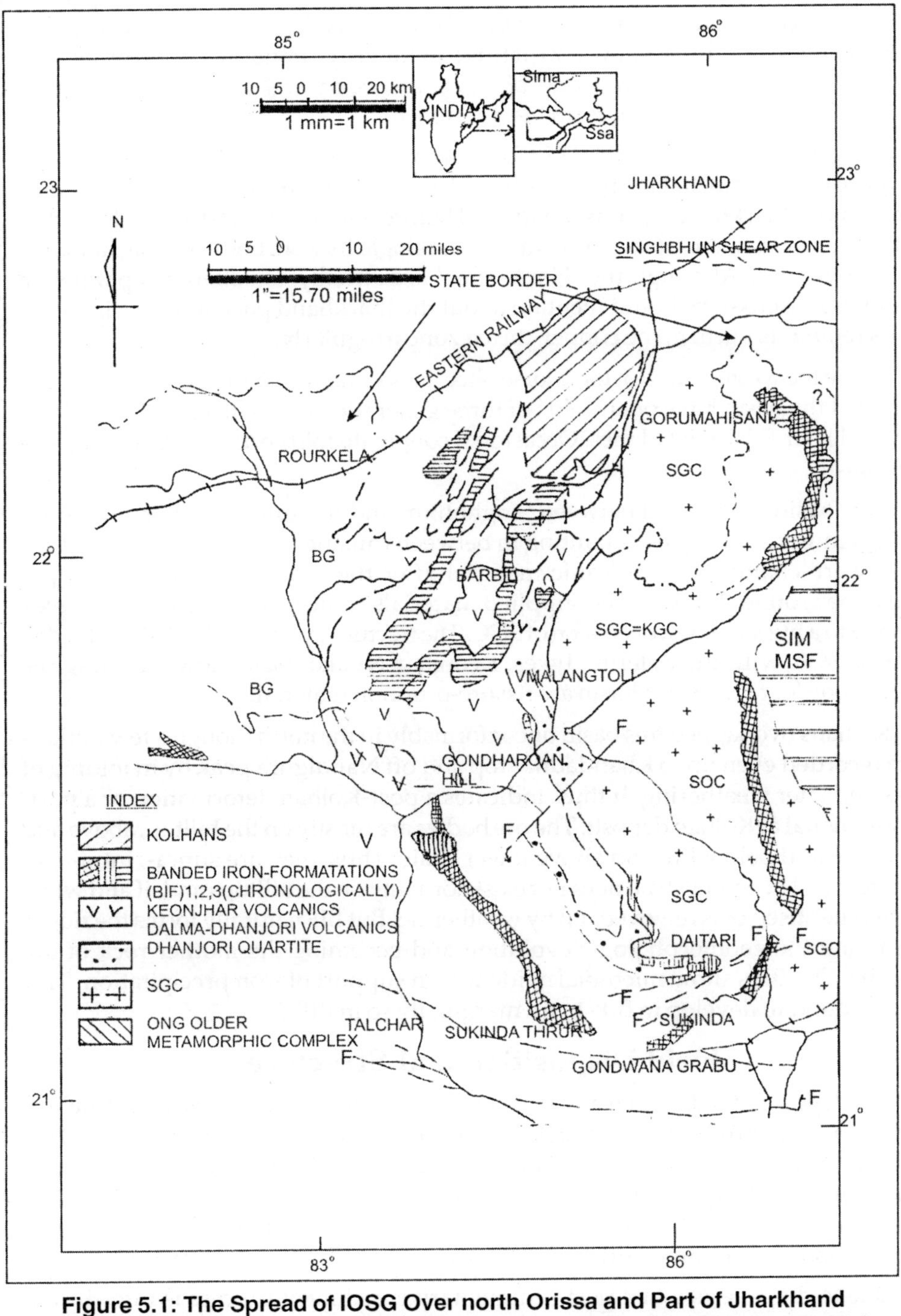


**Figure 5.1: The Spread of IOSG Over north Orissa and Part of Jharkhand (BIF-1 in Jharkhand is not shown). Basic volcanics surrounded BIF-3 (J-K basin) on three sides barring north. The basin forms between KGC/SGC and Bonai granite (BG) intracratonically. Daitari- Tomka basin (BIF-2) is older to DQ and younger to BIF-1 basin, which (BIF-1) forms a regional closure at Sukinda area (from Acharya, 2008).**

BIF-2 forms Daitari-Tomka basin but is often considered as the same as BIF-1. Detailed field mapping shows structural inequality, mineralogical difference, stratigraphic dissimilarity, metamorphism presence of large and small ore bodies associated with BIF-2 to bring forth the difference.

BIF-3, the Joda-Koira Basin (JKB) forms a small, shallow but highly rich iron and manganese ore basin that forms a 'U'-shaped exposure of BIF, northern part of which comes under Jharkhand State as mentioned before. Its western limb extends further north to turn westward upto Chiria (the largest single Iron ore body of Asia) and then runs southward. Although the 'Horse-shoe' is normally considered separately a basin-wise discussion should mention about the Jharkhand part of the basin. BIF-1 has its remnants north of the copper-thrust zone irregularly.

While the western limb of the 'Horse-shoe' is isoclinally folded with dip westward the rest of the basin have open-folds of three generations *i.e.* with early E-W, NNE-SSW and later E-W axial planes. Occasional conjugate folds occur at different parts of the basin.

This basin, developed between Singhbhum and its equivalent Bonai granites (B.G.) is caused by a series of faulting in between causing the basin to form and the faults were channels for volcanic material after the sedimentation of Dhanjori sandstone around the SGC. The supplied materials come from the granite complex pointing to a huge amount of erosion of SGC. The fracture-system in the basin extended towards SGC with the dolerite dykes. Keonjhar-Nuakot basic flows forming the western border of the BIF-3 basin are fissure-eruption material.

Kolhans overlapped this basin unconformably in the north though a few outliers were recorded even up to Khandadhar top and off Nandigura peak by in folding of rocks and later weathering. It thus, indicates a post-Kolhan deformation or a post-deformational at Kolhan deposit. The ore bodies are mostly on the hilltop, above and inside BIF and below BIF and above lower shale. Thus, they are supra-, intra- and infra- to BIF. The upper shale does not exist normally on the hilltops and, if and when so, gets lateritised or is removed out by weathering. But BIF naturally forms the ridges controlling the geomorphologic evolution and becoming the mother-rock of ore deposits. The BIFs show microbial evidences in support of iron precipitation. This has not found to develop in BIF-1 and marginally so in BIF-2.

## Field Disposition and Structure

Ore deposits of sedimentary association, like that of iron ore, one finds parallelism of extension of ore bodies and BIF when the former is syn-sedimentary. This relationship broadly exists even if later enrichment makes it wider and thicker. In Gandhamardan, Jajang, Malangtoli, Thakurani, Kurbandh and many such localities broad infra- or supra-BIF deposits exist in such fashion. Even depending on chemical precipitation such a framework remains as one sees at Tomka (Acharya, 1964).

Due to diagenesis when post-sedimentary enrichment process is introduced, banded chert gets enriched with hematite or replaced by iron-oxide/silica, subsequently metamorphism brings in recrystallisation of new ore minerals are formed while the gangues partly get removed.

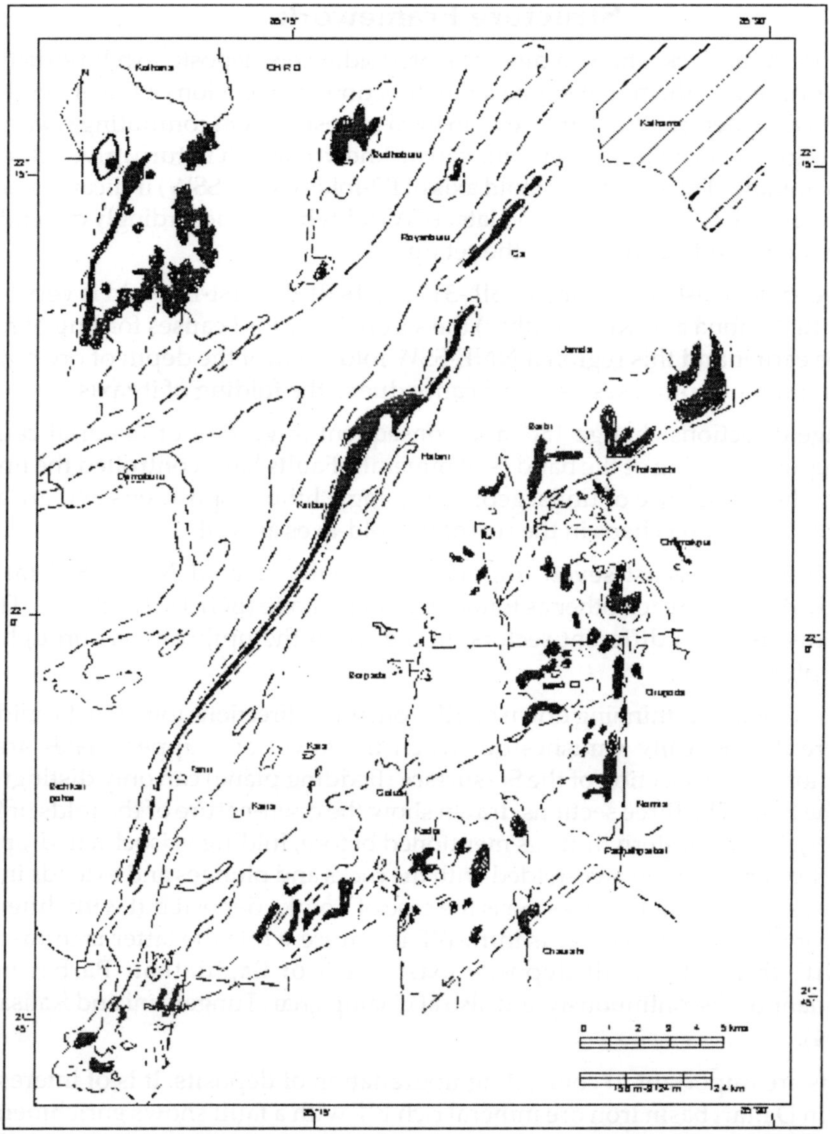

**Figure 5.2: The 'Horse-shoe' of Jones (1934) with Iron Ore Bodies (Black) Associated with BIF-3. Adjacent dashed-lines west of Kiriburu are outer limbs of BIF. Modification includes the presence of faults (F1-F7) and completion of the closure in the south. The western limb is over folded eastward with high westerly dip. The eastern limb dips west but at a much lesser amount and forms open folds. The southern limit is apparently up-faulted and its displacement is due to F-5 fault. The faults are somewhat parallel to each other and the dolerite dykes in SGC maintain the same trend; these faults, with different throws, make the bottom of the basin irregular and are gateway for Mn- solution for later enrichment. The basin is intracratonic. Inset shows Kolhans extend upto 6 (Khandadhar hill top) indicating a large size of the older Kolhan basin. Loc. 1. Chiria east, 2.Ghat kuri, 3. Gua, 4. East of it, 5. Nandugira, 6. Khandadhar. (from Acharya, 2008)**

## Structure Framework

Iron ore group rocks show folding. The pre-folding ore deposits exhibit structural elements printed on them that suggest the direction of extension of the ore body in addition to their deformation and trend in local exposures. On computing several of them the regional structural behaviour can be known, which in turn, gives clues to successful mining. Thus, folding of fold axis of B2-folds (NNE-SSW) indicates south/northward plunge/s of ore bodies and later (EW) folds behave accordingly depending on culminations and depression of the set up.

Of the three phases of folding in BIF-3 basin (JKB), the first-EW fold is very local in the south, (Dubna and Khandadhar) the second E-W fold causes folding of fold-axis of the earlier and this regional NNE-SSW fold; control the depth of ore bodies and stratigraphic depth loses its significance due to the folding of its axis.

Plunge directions change 180° and consequent migration of material causes thickening and thinning of the band/s of minerals. Faults have controlled the linear extension, disappearance of units, geomorphology, litho-dispositions and are also responsible in creating chaos in the run of the fold-axes as well.

The JKB has at least seven important mutually related NNE-SSW faults, statistically parallel to each other as found in Bonai granite (BG), JKB and SGC. Their roles are discussed in different sectors. In the south the upthrow has brought in northerly plunge.

The basin exhibits thinning down of BIF from three directions towards the middle part where it practically vanishes out when the lower and upper shales are in juxtaposition. The projection of the So-surface (Bedding plane) can only distinguish them in the field. The three sections drawn show the open-nature of the folds of JKB (Figure 5.3). In the western limb, as mentioned before, folding is isoclinal, dipping west. The Daitari ore body is co-folded with the rocks and plunges and extends in the same way as the associated rocks. So is the case of Tomka deposit but with different direction or plunge. The former is infra-BIF in nature while the latter is intra- and supra- BIF. Intra-BIF small deposits exist north of Baghiathali Parbat upto Harichandanpur discontinuously and also at Champajhar, Tungaisuni and Kalisagar (Figure 5.4).

Faults are important in controlling upgradation of deposits. It is of interest to note that in Daitari basin iron ore mineral rich BIF with a fault shows enrichment of fault zone with iron material. With no ore mineral bands- there is no secondary enrichment of faults. BIF, in Daitari basin, even shows no or very little ore mineral bands for kilometers and the analysis showed only 2-3 per cent of iron in the BIF. This may bring in the question of it being considered as BIF. But along the strike this change of mineral facies does exist (Figure 5.5).

Faults are of immense importance than hitherto realised. They complicate folded rock exposed differently. Older and younger shales (without BIF in between) become difficult for identification. Folding of the fold-axes, folding of fault planes, right side up position of rocks etc. are made difficult for interpretation if continuous mapping is not done in the basin. Thus, it may look strange to observe that shales at Dalki, Fagua,

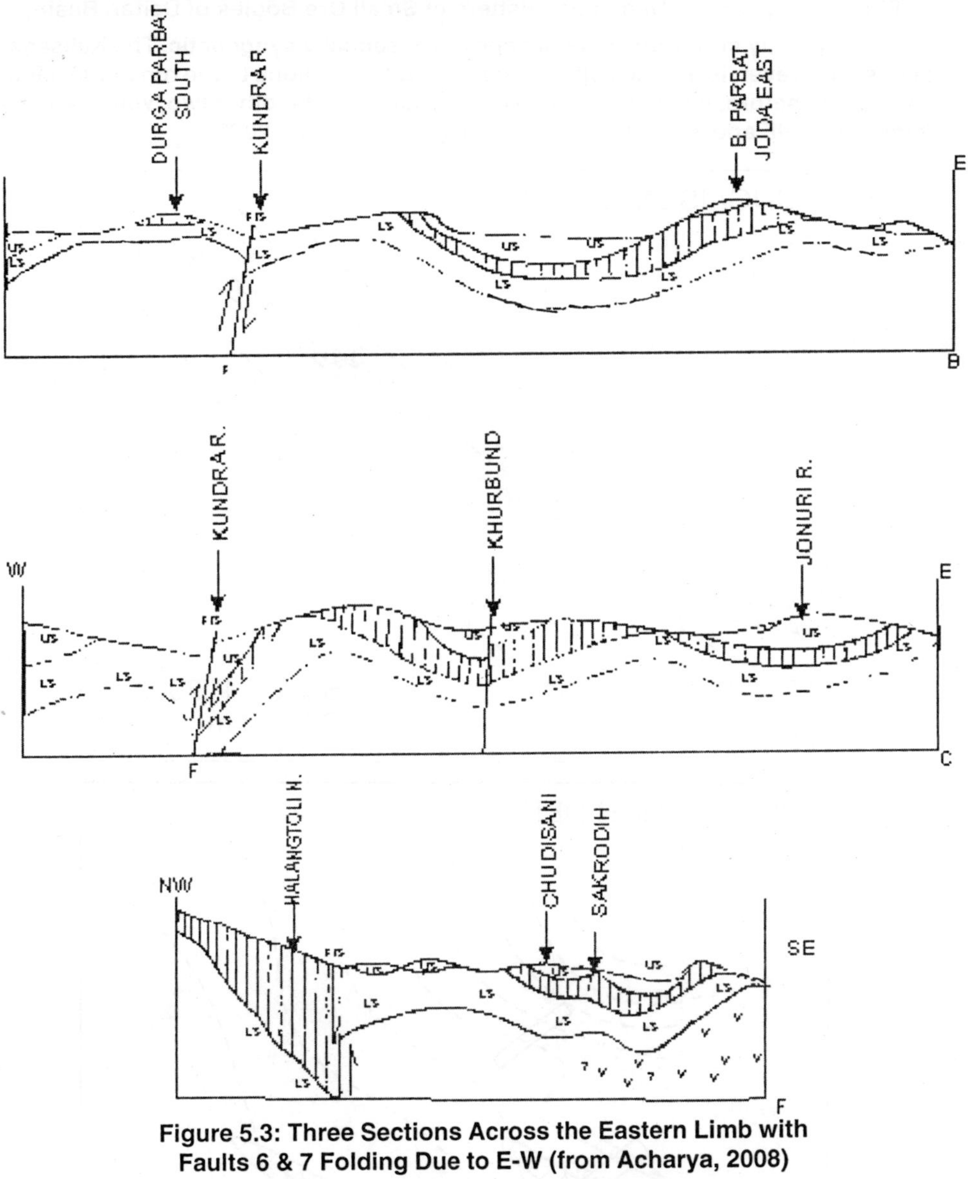


**Figure 5.3: Three Sections Across the Eastern Limb with Faults 6 & 7 Folding Due to E-W (from Acharya, 2008)**

Joda-west, Inganjharan (Joda-east), Dubna-Gonua sector, Rajabasa, Mahulsuka, Patmunda and Koira etc show older shale with Mn-ore bodies (Acharya, 2005). Faults even show opposite sides thrown differently causing problems of mapping and interpretations. These faults are found to horse-tail with branches going in different directions.

After checking the roles of structure and stratigraphy in shaping the 3-D configuration of the ore bodies as noted above, planning for exploration should be done.

**Figure 5.4a,b and c: Deposition Pattern of Small Ore Bodies of Daitari Basin**

**They are mostly stratiform in nature and are essentially syngenetic. The Kalisagar deposit, however, is due to fault zone mineralisation oblique to the run of BIF. More limonitic in nature, it is naturally of lesser grade than the other two, which are co-folded with BIF and are intra-BIF in nature (from Acharya, 2008).**

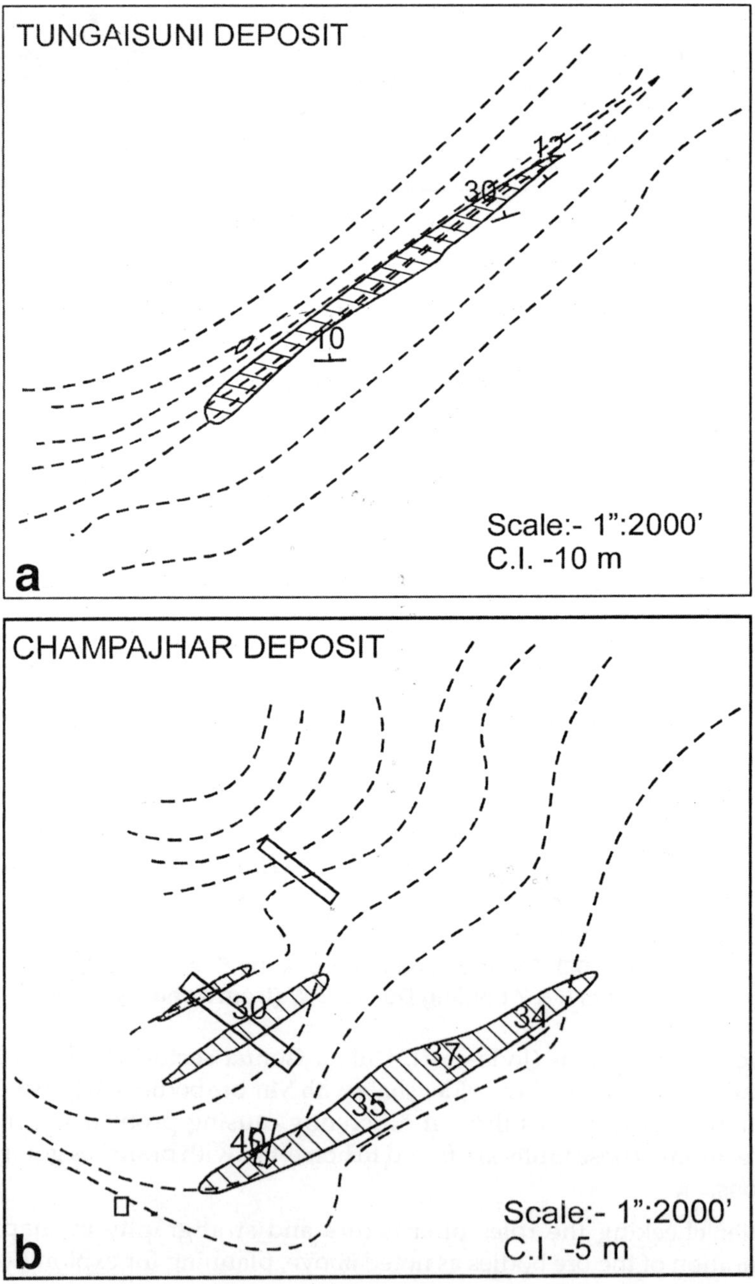


*Contd...*

**Figure 5.4–Contd...**

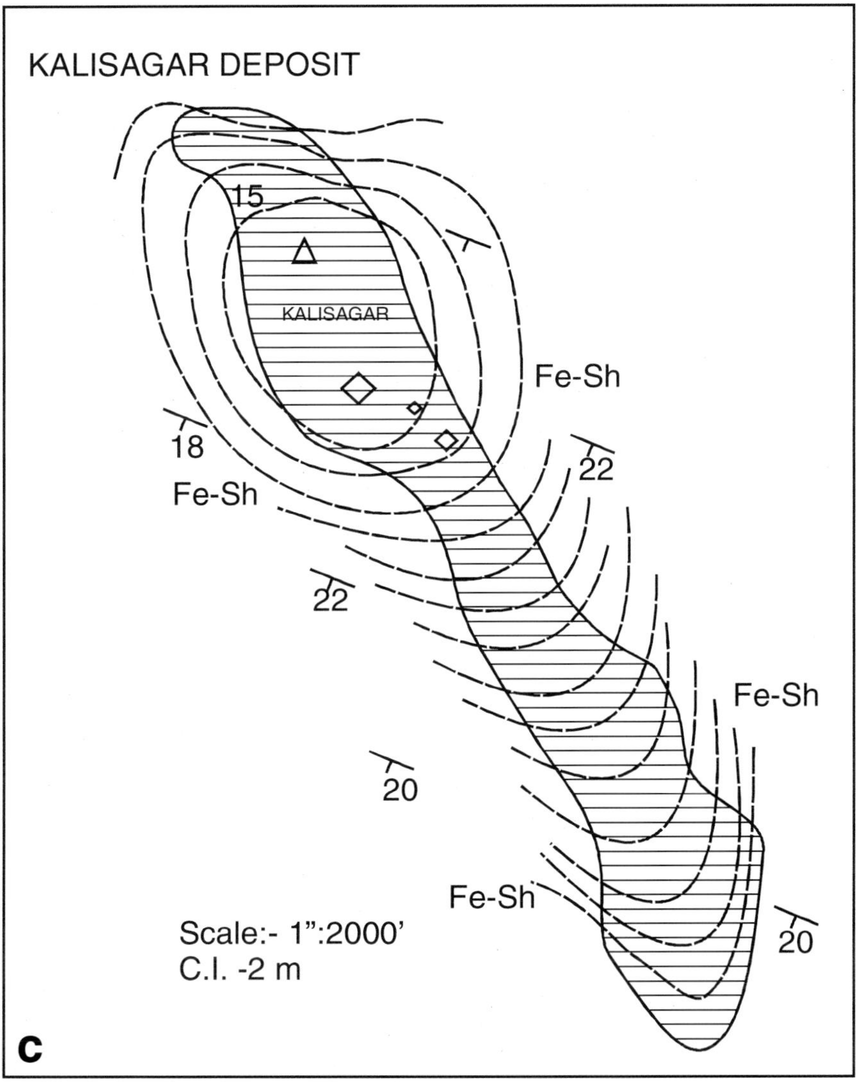


A good part of the shales exposed inside the basin is older shale, which shows certain disturbances uncommon to the upper litho-horizons; this partially explains the complicacies in sequence stratigraphy. The main faults have brought forth sudden depths of the basal floor in the intra-cratonic grabenised basin inside which manganese bearing sediments were filled and later remobilized along the reactivated faults to cause the formation of manganese ore deposits of excellent grade below BIF. (The case of Kachha is one of the good examples). Except a few, towards the middle part of the basin, almost all Mn-ore deposits are fault-controlled. Horse tailing of faults result in cobalt and nickel mineralisation in them as well (Acharya, 1983).

Field occurrence of the BIF deposits in different mines in the region is shown in Figures 5.6a–g.

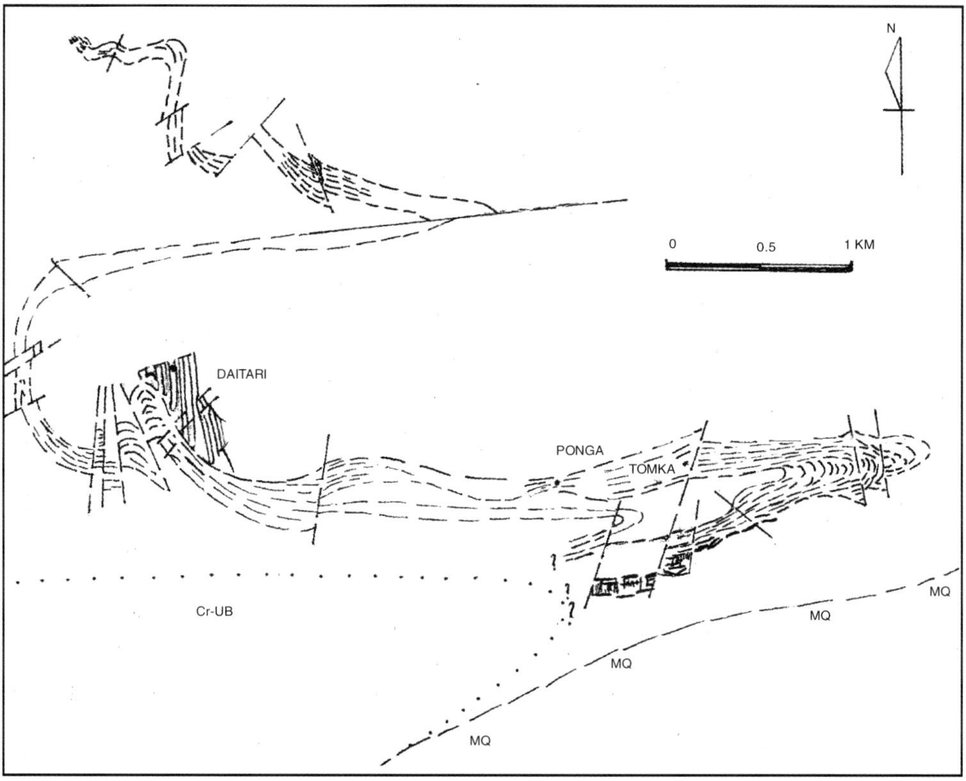


**Figure 5.5: A Very Much-Generalised Geological Map of Part of Daitari-Tomka Basin Showing Only the Spread of BIF. Dashed part contains hematite varying roughly from 25- 60 per cent with deposits where these zones are traversed by faults. The clear zone shows minimal iron-oxide (2 to 5-7 per cent ) when faulted, silica comes along the fault; this suggest that deposits are mostly supplied by the ore materials from depth along the faults (from Acharya, 2008).**

## Stratigraphy

**Table 5.1: The Stratigraphy of the Region (after Acharya, 2000)**

| | | *Kolhan Basin* | *Kolhan Deposits* <br> ——— *Unconformity* ——— |
|---|---|---|---|
| IRON | Joda-Koira Basin (BIF-3 basin) | Upper pelites | Volcanics, Ultrabasic dykes, (Clastics and mixed shales) Fe-shales, and banded shales with all its variations. |
| | | BIF-3 | Banded hematite chert/Jasper/and iron ore bodies and their variations |
| ORE | | | |
| | | Lower | Stromatolitic dolostone/limestone, fe-shale (irregular) Banded shale |
| | | Pelites | Banded manganese formations(B Mn F) banded Mn-ore minerals and shale ores within this |

*Contd...*

**Table–Contd...**

| | | *Kolhan Basin* | *Kolhan Deposits*<br>——— *Unconformity* ——— |
|---|---|---|---|
| SUPER | | | Variegated shales Tuffs & Tuffaceous shale/phyllite. |
| | | | ——— Unconformity (and Disconformity) ——— |
| GROUP | Dhanjori Group | | Keonjhar-Nuakot lavas (with intratrappeans), sills & dykes (Palasponga), in Dhanjori S.G.C. (= Newer dolerite) B2 folding (of Daitari basin) Dhanjori (= Kansa quartzite), fe-phyllites Conglomerate (bouldery locally) Ca 2,300-2,400 m.y. |
| | | | Unconformity, Disconformity and angular unconformity with BIF-2 and non-conformity with SG Daitari-Tomka Basin (BIF-2 basin) |
| | | | Unconformity (and nonconformity) Malayagiri-Gorumahisani basin (BIF-1 basin) |
| | | | ——— Non-conformity ——— |
| | | | Singhbhum Granite ≅ Keonjhar granite, ≅ Bonai granite) + some more Granites in S.W. area (Phase-I and II) |
| PRE-IOSG PRE- | | | (Older to BIF-I) C 3,300 m.y. Tonalite gneiss (OMTG) C 3,400–3,500 m.y. |
| CAMBRIAN | | | Mica schist, fuchsite quartzite, Para-amphibolite, |
| | | | Hornblende-schist etc. C 4,000 m.y. |

Most of the shales show a percentage of tuff in them suggesting volcanic activity throughout the period of sedimentation; that even outlasts the younger shale. Volcanism, thus, is pre, syn- and post-basinisation and later evolution. This brings in the possibility of the role of exhalations during the sedimentation history of the basin. Mn- ore- mineralogy supports the idea as well. Quantification of the ore - deposits –volume, when done, may show if the provenace could have supplied the total amount. An exhalation theory is otherwise, and also normally, should, therefore, be accepted. The presence of todorokite in Mn-ore supports this view. Like BIF, that shows alternations of chemical bands of iron oxides and silica in the lower shales of Dubna and Churisahi quarries, banded manganese formation does exist. It is partly chemical, though mostly mechanically formed layers of fine shale due to repetition of incoming Mn-mineral from the medium with fluctuations of Eh and pH indicating formations of Mn-protore was completed prior to the precipitation of the overlying BIF, the former being shaly, is not physiographically prominent and can be traced only in freshly quarried mines while BIF, in contrast, forms regional hill ranges.

## Condition of Migration and Deposition of BIF and Iron Ore

Most of the ore deposits of iron are stratiform and run grossly parallel to BIF while Mn-ore bodies appear along fault planes as well in addition to being syn-sedimentary. At Cheliatoka peak a sizable piece of current bedding feature was found

**Figure 5.6a-g: The Field Occurrence of BIF in the Region**
**a: Bedding plane, folded, bedding style of BIF in mines from the region.**

c

d

Thakurani Mine - Orissa

(Acharya, 2000) and at two other places BIF showed features simulating current bedding in the basin although plenty of penecontemporaneous deformation feature are available. These agree with the regional pattern of the basin. The BIFs, therefore, suggest a stage of provenancial peneplanation to account for chemical sedimentation. Volcanics and tuffs support an exhalative hypothesis that takes deeper root because of mineralogy and existence of volcanism in the entire time-span (pre- to post-sedimentation).

Shale patches inside BIF formations are considered regular because clearing of suspended material (like-shale particles) cannot be guaranteed and a flutter in them often may result in shale deposits as intra-BIF occurrence. In normal stratigraphy banded hematite shale is rather commonplace before and after BIF precipitation acting almost as end members with BIF in the center as beginning and end of chemical sedimentation of BIF as a unit.

The provenance of this basin means granite and basalt with older metamorphic complex. While the role of granite may not be that important, the role of volcanics is very valuable. The Keonjhar-Nuakot volcanics shows ≈ 2 per cent Mn-Oxide while Sandur volcanics (southern India) gives ≈ 7 per cent Mn that shows its reappearance as Mn-deposit in the lower sediments (Mishra, 1978). Add to it the exhalative materials, the answer is then found. In the case of iron, things are somewhat different. A huge hydrous fluid system has to be brought about to account for transport and migration of metal content to the basin with suitable Eh and pH conditions (a changed P-T milieu) for deposition of oxide of iron sufficiently to form an ore body. Later influx of material enriches the ore- body- grade and also volume. The capsule is not only fittingly suitable to this basin but also offers an excellent concept to account for the origin and exponential enlargement of size of the ore deposits. Leep and Goldrich (1964) have shown the metal supplying capacity of even granites. The volcanics, capable of a volume-wise better supply, can certainly be counted for more iron for BIFs and ore bodies.

Under normal conditions chert and iron oxide components in BIF are chemically formed and are considered original (Maynard, 1983) because their distribution is not controlled by extraneous factors like: metamorphism, deformation, depth of burial, proximity to intrusion, (the basin has only one ultrabasic and a few dykes of late state intrusion).

This is, therefore, superbly suitable for study to conceptualise ideas on formation, evolution and genesis of rocks as well as associated ore deposits. The sedimentary (chemically controlled) and penecontemporaneous deformation feature like current bedding at lower ore body of Gandhamardan and just below Cheliatoka peak and a somewhat larger feature on the last turn of the stream before the Khandadhar fall of Sundergarh district, 'flowery features' and 'flame structures' at Mankarnacha and many other places, 'cut and fill' feature in BIF at Kuradih nala, west of the ridge and a host of many diagenetic feature almost everywhere suggest ideas on formations, development and genesis of the ore deposits (Acharya *et al.*, 1982, 2000). One observes that the oxide facies is most important; the carbonate and sulfide facies are less so. While a change over from siderite to hematite is normally traceable along the hill-cut road to Khandadhar Township (Figures 5.7–5.8), many other locations indicate that the carbonate facies extended much more than hitherto realized. In Daitari basin this is found at a few places like Ponga. Thus, BIF shows a range of mineralogical variation inside the iron-oxide bands. In Daitari range banded chert-quartzite shows preferential replacement of saccharoidal quartzite by iron oxide (Acharya, 2004). In banded hematite shale, often the hematite is partly later as traced on the slopes north of Tomka peak and further east. Thus, the banding in BIF may also be considered to be partly non-sedimentary and is of replacement type; this however, cannot be fully quantified. It is possibly partly true but certainly does not occur as a regionally effective process but nevertheless, has its own importance in places below and above BIF.

With a smaller range of variation of Eh/pH and with a good potential of iron oxide in solution, a 30 m thick ore body has been found below Gandhamardan and elsewhere below BIF; this has slowly allowed coming in of silica that forms bands (≈ 1 cm) of Jasper/chert in contrast to very thick hematite bands. If presumably they have been deposited in sub-basins (with almost fixed chemical parameters), shown by NNE and E-W faults, on the floor of the basin, continuously formed chemical deposits will be physically discontinuous during their reactivation although they will be in the same strike and have similar attitudinal parameters. Field evidences

**Figure 5.7: Showing Stages in Evolution of Iron Ores (from Acharya, 2008)**

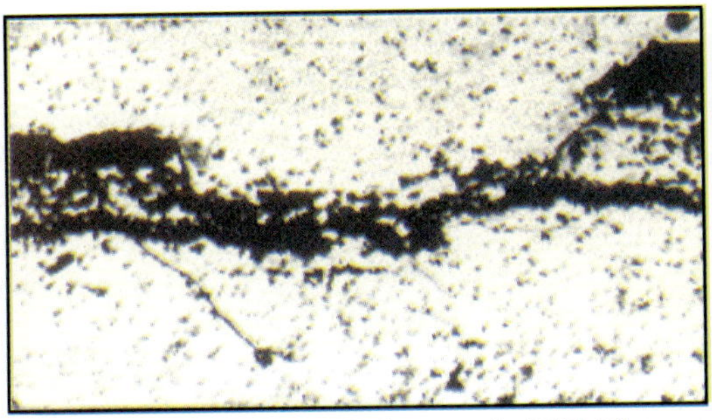

a: Primary cut and fill feature in BIF. The jasper band (black) is cut (bottom retained) a younger band of siderite replaced by hematite (bright white). This obviously suggests a 'right side top' position and assists in establishing stratigraphy. Loc. Kuradih Nala (x20, RL).

b: Hematite band (thick) with dots of silica (black) is filled from top (vug filling) by chert and siderite changed to hematite.Both these two indicate westerly top (at the outer side) and inner top at the eastern side of western limb because of isoclinal nature of folding of the limb. c. Micro oolitewith/without iron nuclei. They often coalesce to become larger. Hematite and goethite are associated. Loc. Roida (x50 RL).

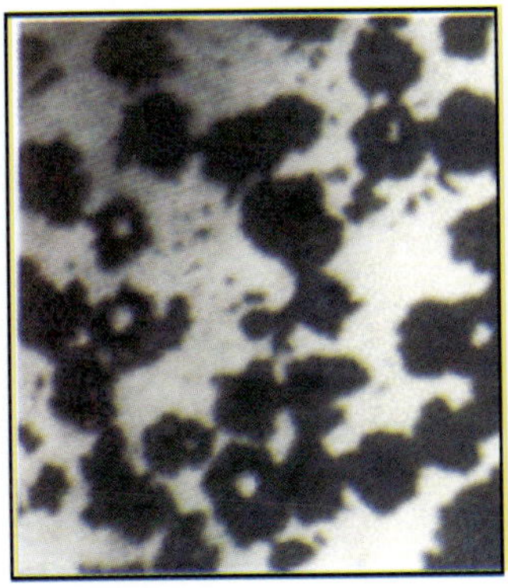

c: Algal structure (?) in ferruginous shale each grain is either peripherally iron-rich or, mixed with silica, in uniform distribution inside. Irregular shape, needlelike extensions is the rule in aggregation. Loc. Roida north. (x30 RL).

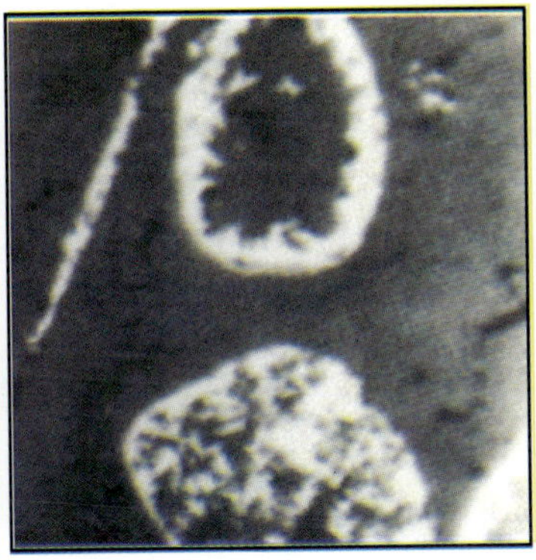

d: Banded chert alternating with granular replaceable (bg iron so!) quartz. The fracture-filling iron solution selects one band-type to replace it. Can this mean BIF may be partly hydrothermal (?) and be named also as 'Pseudo-BIF), (PBIF). Loc. west of Ponga-Daitari Hills.

e: Bedding plane stylolite containing BHJ with cross cutting vertical silica veins. Stylolite bands thin down with iron bands thickening. Bedding planes of BIF are stylolites. Iron from other bands migrates causing its depletion in the latter. The veinlets cut the entire band. Loc. Khandadhar (x20PL).

*Contd...*

**Figure 5.7–Contd...**

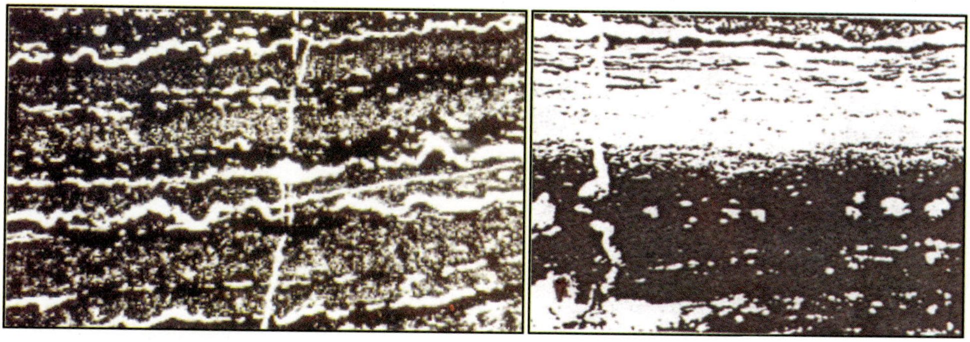

**f: The early diagenetic silica veinlets (vertical) confined to two iron oxide bands is deformed by superincumbent load and later cut by horizontal- diagenetic iron oxide. Loc. Khandadhar east (x20 PL).**

indicate infra-BIF ore body gradually gives place to formations of BIF with thicker iron-oxide bands, which upward, give place to thicker silica bands. This interplay has resulted in sedimentary boudins of BIF (horses) in ore and vice-versa. This finds beautiful expression of itself at Tomka, Champajhar Tungaisani, Kalisagar. In the eastern limb of the BIF-3 basin, iron ore, thus, has excellent grade, which are used for sponge iron due of its compactness because of direct sedimentation with least disturbance by syn -or post structural complications. Massive ore body with 69.2 per cent of iron has been found in Khondband (infra-) and also elsewhere.

It looks that the ore-body type that is an outcome possibly of a syn-sedimentary deformation with associated recementation and enrichment. This ore body type is of excellent grade, sufficiently compact for any tough use (not much powder) although the sizes of ore boulders are not unduly large. Occurring usually at a few present- day hilltops, they are found below certain ore zones as well. As the exposures change down to other ore-types. The differently sized flattish fragments maintain a somewhat parallel nature of existence. They are regarded to be formed by basinal oscillation prior to their consolidation. The groundmass has a differently generated ore mineral and, thus, forms another younger stage of neo- mineralization (Acharya, 2000).

It is known that metamorphism causes recrystallisation that is achieved by regrouping of elements in a different order befitting to the new chemical environment. The Daitari-Tomka Range deposits although underwent metamorphism (of higher grade of green schist/ facies but rarely touching amphibolite-facies at depth. Acharya (1964) do not show significant change.

One observes that oxide facies in BIF sedimentation is most flourishing and most of the siderite material is hematitised. The sulfide facies, developed naturally at depth, is of little consequence in ore formation. So is the case with the silicate facies that shows banded grunerite-quartzite in BIF-1 basin extensively, but less so in Daitari basin. It is frequently observed in BIF-I at Gorumahisani and Badampahar west Mayurbhanj district and around Malyagiri.

**Figure 5.8: Showing Stages of Iron Enrichment**

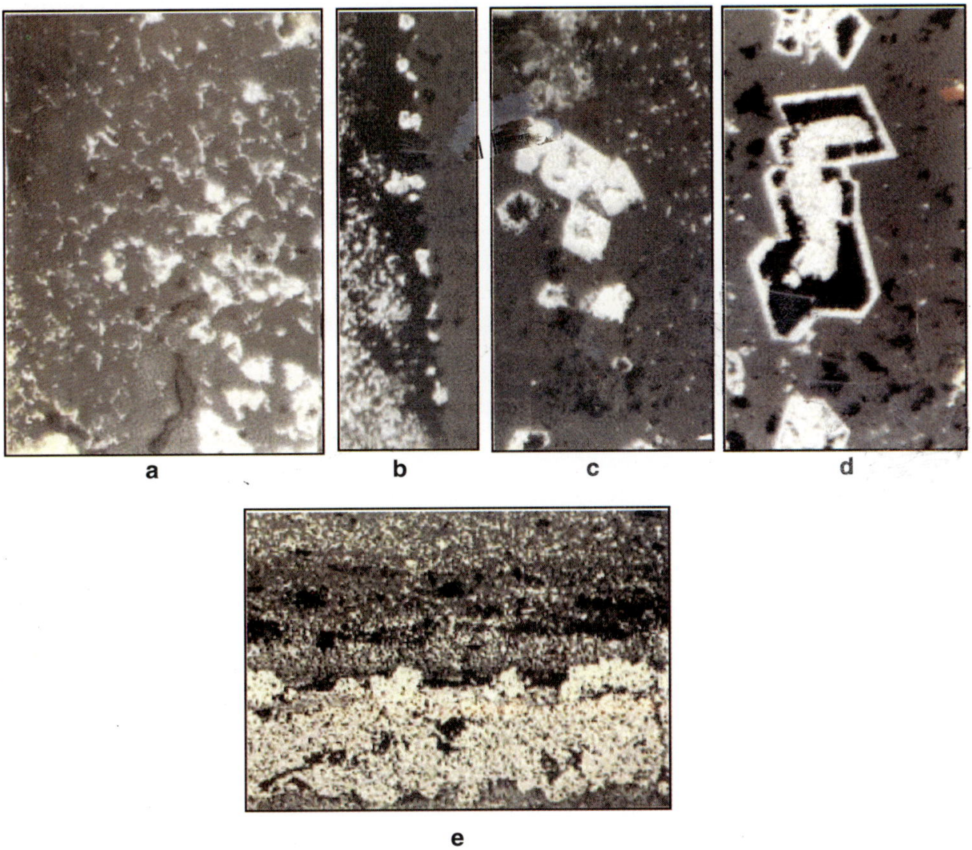

**a: Poor BIF showing chert/quartz/jasper grains bordered by hematite (both diagenetically recrystallised). Hematite shows a tendency for forming bigger crystals when silica grains coalesce. Loc. East of Khandadhar (x20RL).**

**b: A thin part of a BIF that shows pepper and salt texture of silica and iron oxide (much finer grain size) exists; thus the exact beginning texture of diagenesis is yet to be quantified). Grains of hematite along the stylolite (bedding plane). To its right is quartz vein (grey later) and to the left is dark black chert with no hematite in an otherwise 'pepper and salt' milieu- indicating migration to form larger grains. Loc. East of Khndadhar (x20RL).**

**c: Hematitisation of siderite in BIF. The role of siderite in BIF formation is much more than realised and mostly the hematite bands and altered product of siderite. Loc. Road cutting before reaching hill top camp-Khandadhar (x20 RL).**

**d: An excellent band of siderite showing two stages of siderite formation and two stages of its hematitization. Black patches are siderite below the polished level of chert. Loc. East of Khndadhar (x20RL).**

**e: A diagenetically recrystallised and enriched ore-band (hematite) alternating with chert/jasper band showing diagenetically somewhat reoriented pepper and salt texture. This is an indication of a stage of iron increment by pulsation of diagenetic evolution (from Acharya, 2008).**

Pockets of blue dust in BIF and ore bodies indicates *in-situ* leaching of flux-materials and consequential concentration of iron materials. Between Thakurani and Bolani hills sits Barbil on such a deposit, huge in nature but only at depth and partly mined. The degree of *in-situ* leaching is prominent.

## Minerography Studies

Studies have shown the role of diagenesis in ore-fluid migrations and readjustment to upgrade ore quality. Diagenesis has enriched the metal content and at times, the impurities as well (silica mostly) complicating the simple nature of primary ore mineralogy. Generations of minerals are introduced into the litho-system upgrading/downgrading the ore deposits and ore minerals in BIF as are the cases location- wise.

Any approach on genesis of ore deposits has to take care of source, transport medium (essentially hydrous), metal migration, deposition and later sequence of enrichment. PT conditions make the deposits mono- or multi-mineralic based on elemental distribution. In case of iron ore, weathering and lateritization are also big parameters controlling ore body formation and evolution. In the diagrams (Figures 5.9 and 5.10) from the beginning of banding in BIF up to the formation of ore deposits have been shown with microscopic details. These show how at different solution of ore flux into BIF/ore bodies and upgrade the ore both in quality and quantity and the role of diagenesis as a natural mineraling process at different parts of time specially when continuity of volcanism is evidenced in space and time up to the end of sedimentation. Thus, it is clear that provenance of volcanism play the most important role/s in supplying the ore-material and sedimentation, followed by diagenesis, compaction, dehydroxidation, weathering and supergene enrichment (where weathering has been possible) have played dominant roles to bring in the deposits. Removal of silica and consequent loosening of ore –bands causes the biscuity ore to form and the dissolved iron oxide migrate bottomward to upgrade the protore bodies or is wasted. It fixes the iron-oxide into the lower horizon, thus, reducing the volume and upgrading the iron oxide percentage, causing a double benefit. Certain degree of solution (by weathering) is continuously in progress at the top level to reduce the bulk there and to atleast partly refix the ore materials at depth. The textural evolution of the associated minerals is quite evident. Although partly qualitative, this process of enriching ore deposits should be valid if in space and time these processes do not change and there is no evidence in its favour.

To add to it remanent magnetic studies of ores vis-a vis BIF go a long way to prove both syngenetic /epigenetic nature of the deposits with reference to the host rock (Acharya, 1967). While the Daitari deposit is considered to be both syngenetic and epigenetic (poly-genetic), the ore bodies of JKB are genetically found to be similar but with mutually different time frames and more (in number of times) polygenetic than the former.

With better understanding of genesis in spite of not much of borehole data (bore holes hardly go beyond the bottom of ore bodies) a sequence stratigraphy has been attempted on a rather wide canvas that needs further fine- tuning continuously (Acharya, 2005).

Ore microscopic combined with petrologic studies reveal growth pattern of iron-ore minerals as shown in Table 5.2.

From all these different approaches certain ideas on genesis could be developed which may be drawn up as follows.

**Figure 5.9: Polished Section of Iron Ore Showing**

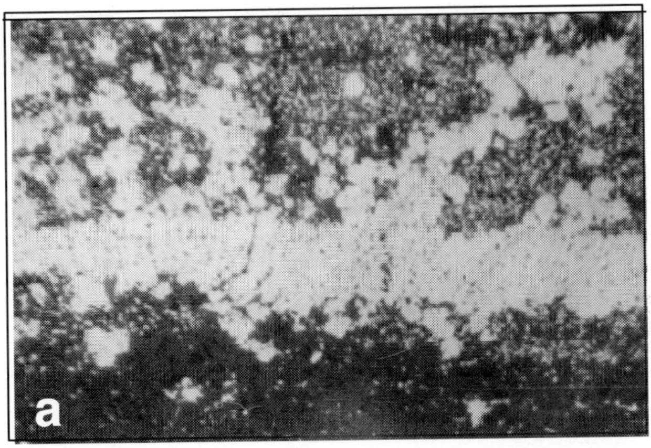

**(a) "Flame structure" above a band (white) of hematite indicating top direction. This is a common feature around Makarnachha in BIF that suggests normal stratigraphy. The chert band (black) shows purity of silica indicating migration (?) of iron oxide particles band ward during diagenesis. Siderite band is indicated from its shape and changeover to hematite with/without magnetite is possible. This is completely a picture of diagenetic stage. Loc. Mankarnachha (x20 RL).**

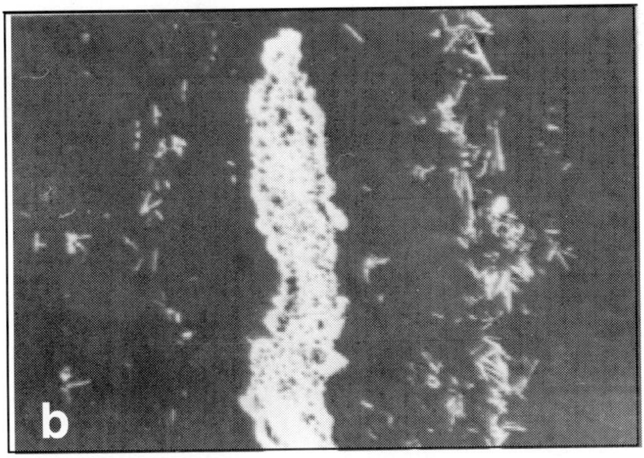

**(b) During stylolites (black dotted line) in hematite band. Note complete absence of hematite grains in chert band on both sides indicating migration into the band and gradual thickening of the hematite. Loc. West Kumritanr. (X20 RL).**

*Contd...*

**Figure 5.9–Contd...**

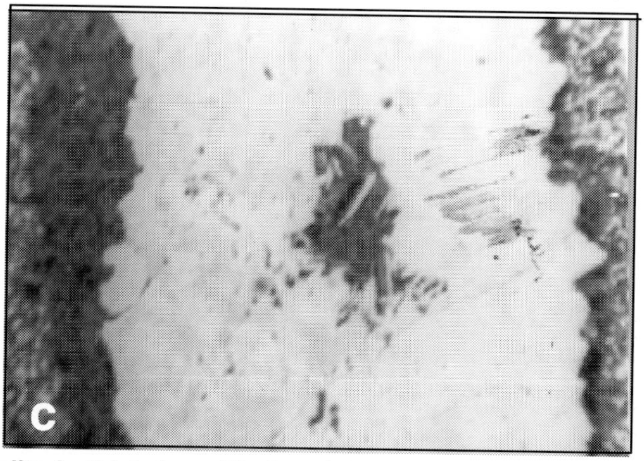


**(c) During stylolite in thick hematite band, hematite starts forming along and after stylolite widening the thickness. (X20 RL).**

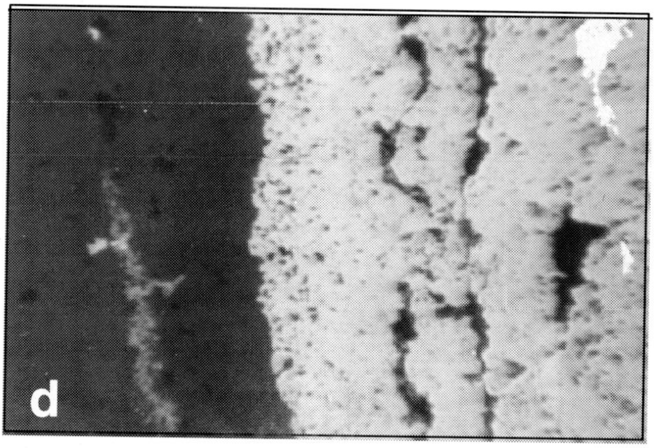


**(d) A very thick band of hematite with borders conforming the obtuse angle of siderite faces. The grey part is magnetite after siderite and the rest is hematite after magnetite.Most of the thick bands of hematite are formed during diagenesis; its primary banding might/might not have been due to thin hematite. Note the absence of iron oxide on both sides where silica remains in pure form. This is considered to be due to migration Loc. North of Kumritanr. (x20RL).**

Banded Hematite Jaspar (BHJ)

Banded Hematite Quatrate (BHQ)

Banded Hematite Shale (BHS) as sedimentary iron ore deposits. The ore bodies BIF in general holds BHJ, BHQ, Banded hematite Shale, as the sedimentary iron ore deposits. The ore bodies are stratiform and are infra-, intra- and supra- BIF in occurrence. Sedimentary boudinisation of ore body is to be kept in mind during mining; one can think of a chemical basin manifested this way physically. The second

**Table 5.2: Paragenetic Sequence of Mineral Formation**

| *Minerals and Events (G)* | *Depositional* | *Diagenetic* | | |
|---|---|---|---|---|
| | | *Very-Early* | *Early* | *Late* |
| Silica 1 | — | | | |
| Hematite 1 | — | | | |
| Siderite 1 | — | | | |
| Magnetite? 1 | — | | | |
| Sedimentary structures Retained through diagenetic stage | | | | |
| Silica 2 | | — | | |
| Hematite 2 | | — | | |
| Siderite 2 | | — | | |
| Synerisis – first stage of compaction | | | | |
| Silica 3 | | | — | |
| Compaction and bending of silica veinlets due to load of sediments | | | | |
| Stylolites formation and silica veins | | | | |
| Silica 4 | | | | |
| Recr. Hematite 3 | | | — | |
| Recr. Siderite 3 | | | — | |
| Recr. Chert 5 | | | — | |
| Penecontemporaneous deformations, brecciation, slumps, slips and folding | | | | |
| Conversion of siderite to magnetite 2 and later hematite 4 (martite) and a few wider veins of silica 6 Recryst. He. (thick bands) 5 | | | | — |
| Recr. Siderite 4 | | | | — |
| Recr. He. 5 cross cuts wider silica veinlets and slow death of stylolite | | | | |
| Recr. He. 6 | | | | |
| Recr. Silica (Pure) 7 | | | | — |
| Giant siderite 5 | | | | — |
| Replacing He. 7 | | | | — |

fold system in JKB is most important in controlling the extension of ore bodies in space. The third one causes thickening and thinning and brings in a variable depth factor to search ore. The infra-BIF ores are low in silica and alumina while the supra-BIF ores outsource $Al_2O_3$ from upper shale. Crystalline manganese ore bodies are usually remobilized along fault planes and other weaker zones. Manganese ore below lower shales does not occur. Wad (manganese-shale as mine waste) has 7 to 32 per cent Mn (Acharya, 1983) and wad is an aggregation of different Mn-rich shale types whose petrochemistry suggests presence of certain important uncommon elements. Both iron and manganese have been outsourced into the Jamda-Koira basin from the provenance and also through exhalation. The ore bodies are strongly stratiform and structurally controlled and these two features broadly control the shape and size of

**Figure 5.10: Polished Sections of Iron Ores**

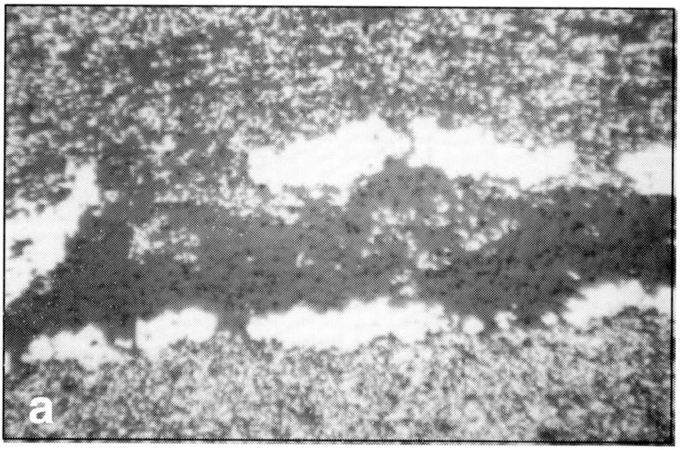


**(a) Banded hematite jasper, thick jasper bands but with rich hematite dust inside (pepper and salt) and thinner bands of diagenetic hematite prior to mid-silica band. Note a tendency for development of schistosity (black thin lines of silica in jasper band). This is almost the first stage of diagenetic silica band often with stylolite that slowly dies out. Loc. Rontha east (x20 RL).**

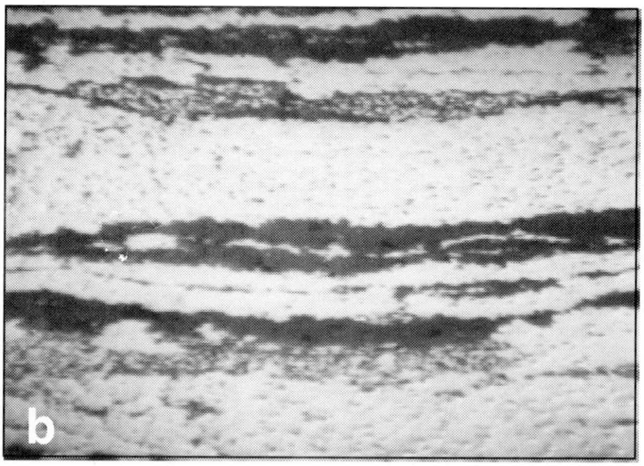


**(b) High grade (iron) BIF. A banded hematite chert/jasper with more than an average of 55 per cent of hematite. While the two thin hematite bands still show the role of stylolite in the thicker ones; they are almost non existent. In silica bands they are "sub-microscopically" visible with diagenetic recrystallisation. Loc. Kurmitar (x20 RL).**

*Contd...*

**Figure 5.10–Contd...**

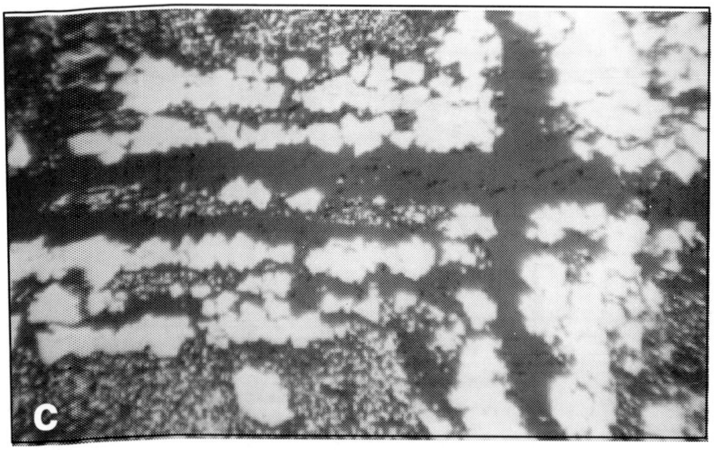


**(c) With good inflow of iron-rich solution the stylolites (both beding plane and vertical) and other features show extensive diagenetic recrystallisation with little space for pepper and salt texture which also supplies iron to the new crystals and remain as silica only. Loc. West Kurmitar area. (x20 RL).**

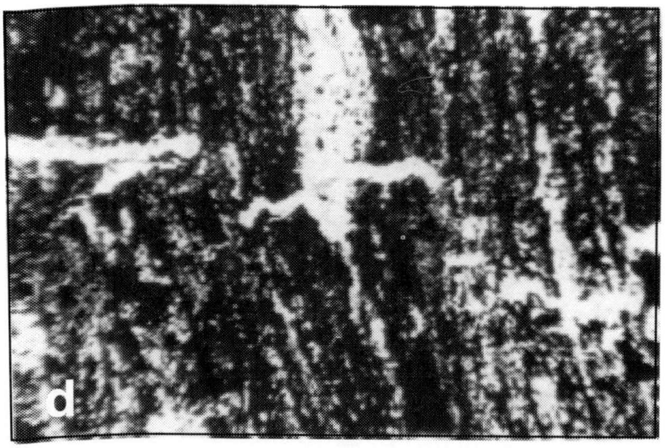


**(d) A mid-grade BIF. Silica and iron oxide laminae are thin and alternating and differently recrystallised in the diagenetic stage at times forming small thin layers of iron oxide and quartz lenses varying dimensions. Note a vertical thin quartz vein cross cutting the entire sequence. But is 'micro-faulted' essentially in one direction along the bedding plane that indicates post-diagenetic bedding plane slip. The slip has been rather commonplace in most of BIF-rocks. Loc. East of Rantha- west of Kurmitar. (x 20 RL).**

the deposits. Both biochemical and abiochemical processes have played their roles to precipitate the iron and also manganese minerals are due to processes of mechanical re-concentration at a much later stage. Many such reworked deposits were mined as 'floats' since iron ore mining started. The iron and manganese deposits are essentially sedimentary but increase in size and grade with stages of diagenetic enrichment in time; this is further aided by re-concentration due to weathering as shown in Figure 5.11..

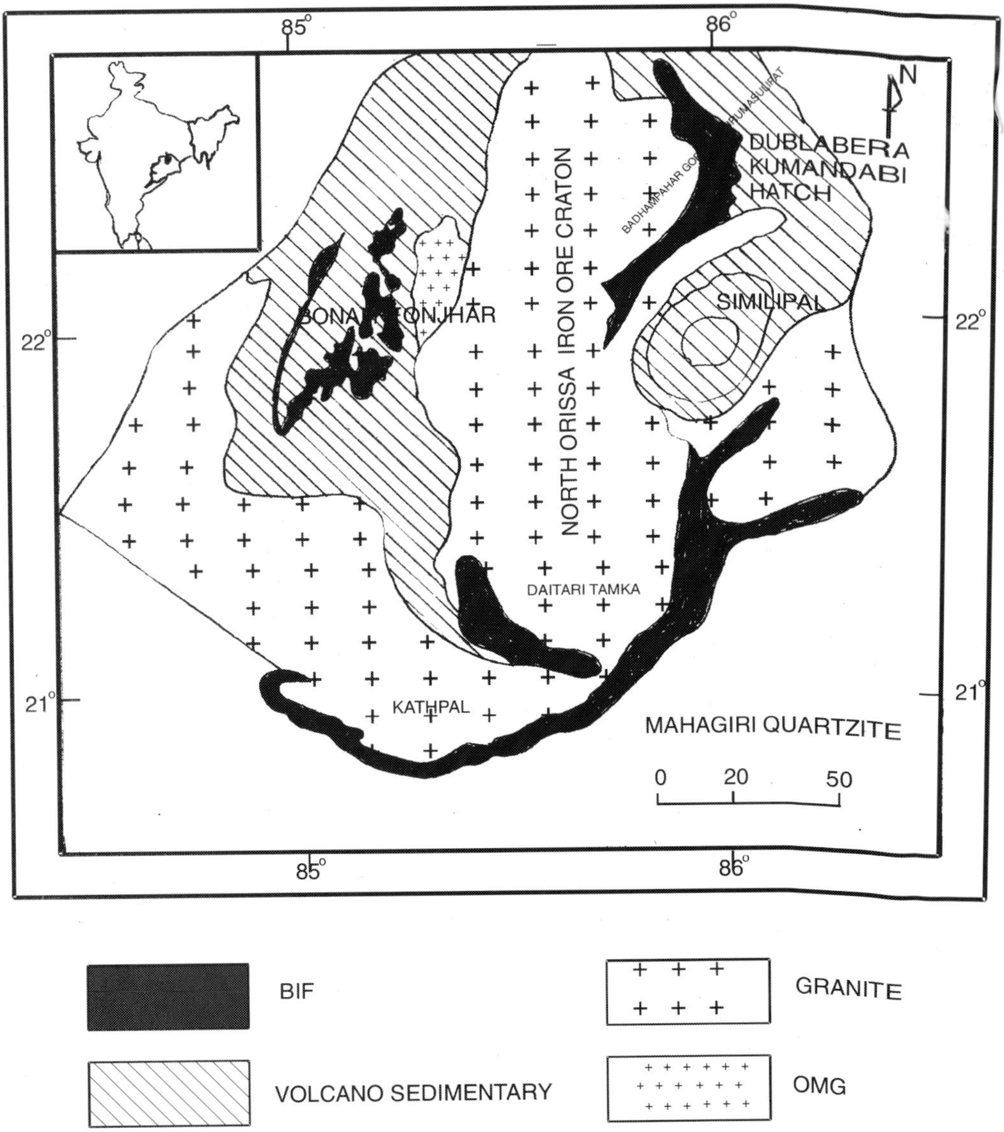


**Figure 6.1: Generalised Geological Map Showing BIF-I, BIF-II and BIF-III Surrounding the NOIOC (from Beura and Singh 2008)**

magnetite, hematite, martite, goethite, specularite and grunerite, and silica minerals (Beura, 2002; Das *et al.*, 2002). The iron mineral in the basin is predominately oxide facies (James, 1954). The mineral assemblages reveal sedimentary signature and subsequently modified by diagenesis and metamorphism (Acharya, 1986; Beura and Singh, 2005a).

The iron-formation and ore deposit are developed in a fault bounded basinal structure (Beura and Singh, 2005b). The spatial disposition of iron deposits in this basin is influenced by the tectono-structural events. The iron formation reveals characteristic features of Archean schist belt and has given rise to commercially exploitable deposit (Beura *et al.*, 2007).

## Geological Framework

BGS belt is located in the northeastern flank of the North Orissa Iron Ore Craton (NOIOC). It is underlain by metamorphosed mafic volcanics and clastic sedimentary rocks. The supracrustal assemblages of the belt comprises Banded Magnetite Quartzite. Banded Magnetite Grunerite Quartzite, Banded Cherty Quartzite is assigned as Archaean schist belt (Beura, 2002; Beura and Singh, 2005a) belonging to the oldest Iron Ore Group under Iron Ore Supergroup of north Orissa (Iyengar and Murthy, 1982; Acharya, 1984, 2000). The iron-formation of the belt constitutes Banded Magnetite Quartzite as the predominant rock type characterized by alternate bands of iron oxide mineral and silica (Chakraborty and Majumder, 1986; Beura, 2002).

The iron-formation consists of iron oxide minerals such as magnetite, martite, specularite, hematite and silica in form of chert. It is characterised by well developed bands, small-scale folds, faults and certain non-diastrophic structures such as pinch and swell and scour and fill indicate primary sedimentary nature (Beura, 2002). The general trend of the area is NE-SW, however towards the northern part it deviates truncating towards N-NNW. The rocks are complexly folded and faulted and have been intruded by ultrabasic and mafic dyke (Beura, 2002; Beura and Singh, 2006). In fact the proportion of grunerite increases towards the contact of basic intrusive.

The depositional basin of BGS belt has probably been originated due to progressive tectonic activities. During the initial stage the cratonic massif witnessed spreading and extension along its margin. In subsequent period, thinning of the cratonic margin was resulted, which led to rifting on further extension. The post rifting grabenisation could develop the BGS basin. This intracratonic basin has been considered as depository of iron formation and iron ore (Beura and Singh, 2005a; 2006).

In many instances supracrustal rocks including BIF were laid down in Early Proterozoic rift basins (James, 1983; Radhakrishna *et al.*, 1986). Stretching of the sialic crust gave rise to thinning and fracturing near the margins of the ancient continental block; this led to subsidence troughs and on further spreading led to volcanism accompanied by deposition of chemical precipitates (Mukhopadhyay, 1989). Archaean continental crust experienced tectonic- magmatic reactivation in disruption and fragmentation in early Proterozoic time (Gaal, 1989). The Iron ore basins of Karnataka have been developed as "intra-cratonic" fringed by volcanics that erupt along fracture zones. Ultimately it led to block-rifting causing zone of depression and subsequent deposition of sediments (Radhakrishna, 1983). The sedimentary setting of Proterozoic iron formation of Canadian Shield (Goodwin, 1973; Dimroth, 1986), Hamersley Group (Morris and Horwitz, 1983) and Transvaal Super Group (Beukes, 1973, 1984) has also undergone tectonic system of basin development. Sawkin (1990) while discussing the spectrum of rift-related metal deposits stated that the iron deposits along with volcaniclastic were formed in the rift –related environments.

The basin so formed in the process of tectonic activities might have become the receptacle to receive chemical precipitates and volcano-clastic materials. These materials have been derived from diversified sources through different processes, which in turn operated by the basin architect and external dynamic events. The basin structure of present study area is an intra- cratonic one that received sediments from terrestrial source through continental denudation, sea water through transgression and regression, deep circulation of marine or meteoric water and from volcanic exhalation product inside the basin.

The ancient cratonic massif, probably of late Archaean, started providing denuded material to the basin of low relief in form of solution instead of clastic inputs because of prolonged period of crustal stability (Mookherjee, 1998). In the course of continued spreading of crustal block, the basin initiated volcanism accompanied by the deposition of chemical precipitates. Low relief basin in the cratonic margin was able to arrest the mineralizing water during the transgressive and regressive stages.

The extensional tectonic regimes along the cratonic margin during time of basin formation generated continuous permeable zones where pressure of mineralizing solution was nearly equal to the hydrostatic pressure that facilitated the deep circulation of marine and meteoric mineralisers (Mookherjee, 1998, 2000).

The BIF was precipitated as chemical sediment in the studied basin from the hydrous Fe $(OH)_3$ solution collected through above different processes (Huber, 1958). Tectonically frame of basin assisted on availing iron and silica minerals, principally, from diversified sources, in interacting in stratified ocean water in association with the Precambrian environment. The stratified ocean water had maintained two major zones; one below chemocline as anoxic water zone and the other above the chemocline as oxic zone. By the process of upwelling the dissolved iron and silica in anoxic water come up to the oxic zone probably in form of hydroxide and precipitated as oxides in shallow water (Klein and Beukes, 1989). The basin environment maintained a restricted environment with a chemical equilibrium condition in scanty oxygen level, alkaline medium, low pressure and temperature, and positive Eh that started precipitating magnetite (Krumbein and Garrels, 1952; La Berge, 1964). In certain conditions, with scanty supply of iron minerals, silica minerals deposited cyclic nature of deposition. Increase in grain size and blurring of bands is the result of recrystallization during diagenesis and low-grade metamorphism (French, 1973; Acharya, 1986; Chakraborty and Majumder, 1986; Beura, 2002).

In the event the basin underwent slow rate of supply of oxygen hydrous $Fe_3O_4$ rather than hydrous $Fe_2O_3$ could be obtained by oxidation of ferrous hydroxide in an alkaline (low Eh). However, with a large supply of oxygen (high Eh) the rate of oxidation was so high that little or no $Fe_3O_4$ is formed (Weiser, as cited by Huber, 1958), where in hematite was the stable mineral of iron. Hematite precipitated as a thermodynamically unstable phase in a gradually increasing oxidizing condition in preference to magnetite, where magnetite was the stable phase (Krauskopf and Bird, 1995). As the chemical system approaches the equilibrium, magnetite would form at the expense of hematite, when equilibrium not attained completion, some hematite would remain though unstable. This would permit that at the apparent range of condition both hematite and magnetite occur together (Krumbein and Garrels, 1952; Huber, 1958). Magnetite and hematite pairs of iron minerals are stable together under specific pH and Eh. (Beura, 2002) as shown in Figure 6.2.

The BGS belt, due to the above cited tectono- sedimentary system, carry a domain of iron ore deposits dominated by magnetite with patchy occurrences of hematite. The sheets/beds of synsedimentary origin rich in iron minerals in the area refer a syngenetic mode of origin (Beura, *et al.*, 2007).

Regional faults have been traced along the periphery of the basin as evidenced by differential altitude and displacement between the adjoining litho-units exhibiting escarpment and vein quartz. The major faults extend in NE-SW direction lying parallel to the regional structural disposition of the BGS belt. Besides, a number of E-W faults have also been noted across the regional trend (Beura and Singh, 2006). There are number of faults along the periphery as well as inside the belt. The basin structure is affected mainly by continuous transverse faults and thrusts followed by numerous concordant to sub-concordant boundary faults.

Polyphase deformation as well as folding episodes of vectorial contrasting nature generated intense cleavages in beds, which led to an increase in permeability of the rocks. This had enhanced the percolation of water into BIF that results in iron ore deposits of supergene type confined to cleavage cracks (Beura, 2002; Beura and Singh, 2005a).

Structural setting in the basin has relationship with ore bodies having being controlled over by the solution channels. The downward movement of water responsible for leaching and subsequent oxidation of ore bodies has been controlled by structure.

The iron deposits are discontinuous and appear lenticular in outcrop pattern; this can be attributed to the folding and faulting rather than to an irregular pattern of iron deposition. Archaean BIF and chert are significant source of iron ore suggesting syngenetic character (Dimroth, 1986; Acharya, 2002). Mineralisation is controlled by structural style; cross faults, closely spaced fractures and folds influence the localisation of the ore deposits (Morris, 1986).

The diastrophisms under iron ore orogeny also have witnessed faults of various dimensions and directions. The iron formation has been cut by a group of major faults striking along the general trend of the area *i.e.* NE and a good number of minor faults in the peripheral zones of the basin. The faulting framework has become the pathways for dykes and ultrabasics. In due course the contact zones have undergone thermal metamorphism to produce grunerite (French, 1973). Elsewhere the pressure zones give rise to specularite (Mücke and Annor, 1993; Beura, 2002).

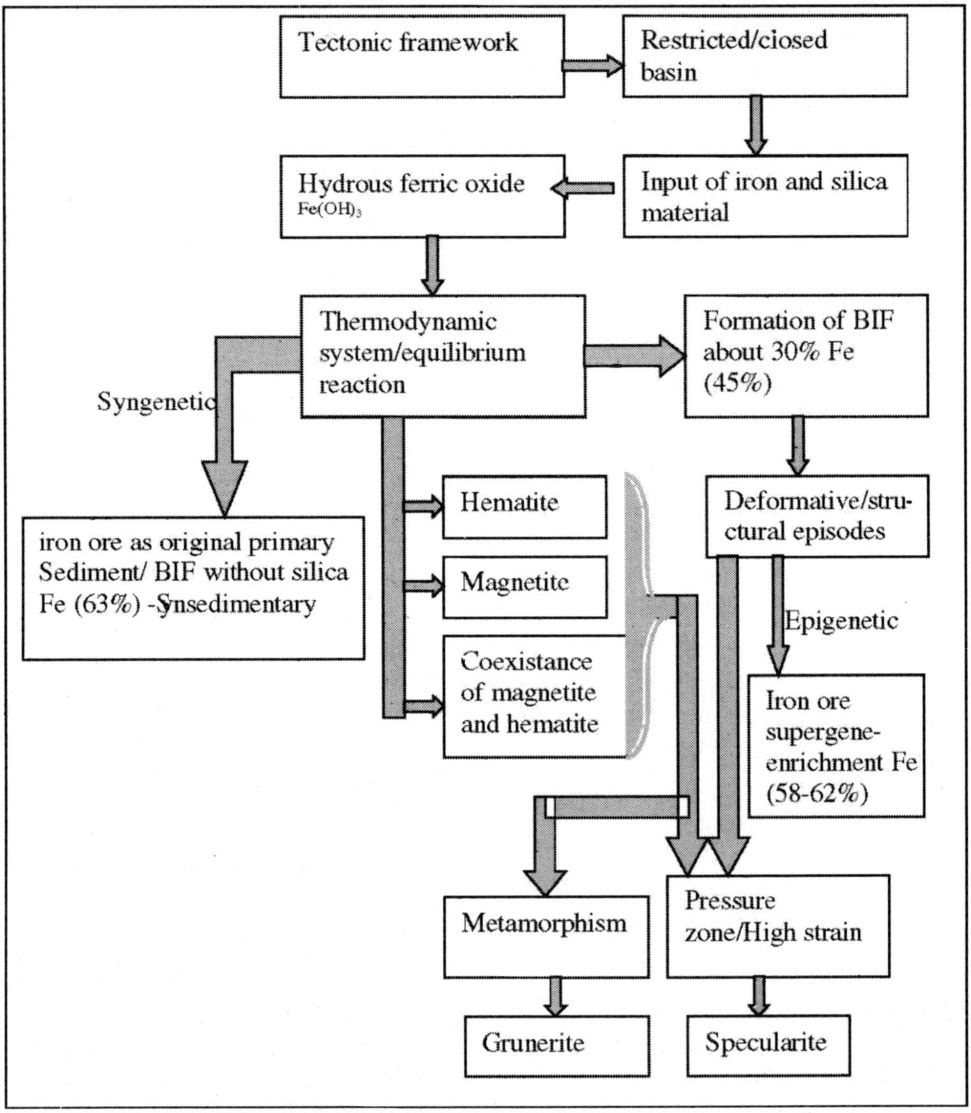


**Figure 6.2: Evolution of Iron Minerals and Ore in the Tectono-metamorphic Milieu (from Beura and Singh, 2008**

The BGS depository basin was intra-cratonic formed by the rifting and grabenization of the craton along the boundary. The present starched out basin shape is due to the effect of deformations. The fault bounded closed basin activated the formation of BIF and ore in thermodynamic regime through chemical equilibrium system.

The BGS belt is experienced with polyphase deformational episodes as well as folding episodes of vectorial contrasting nature generated intense cleavages in beds, which leads to an increase in percolation feasibility of the rocks. This resulted in cleavage cracks filled up with ores. Fault zones act as avenues for migrating large scale meteoric water to form ore bodies by supergene- enrichment process.

Oxidation is facilitated along fault zone, the result of which is the concentration of martitised magnetite. The shear zones are marked by specularite indicate the control of pressure on mineralisation. Presence of grunerite demands its origin in specific P-T environment during deposits metamorphism, which might have been derived from ultrabasic intrusions controlled by tectonostructural events. Iron ore deposits, though discontinuous in nature, have their trend parallel to the regional strike of the belt indicate the structural influence on ore. Presence of volcaniclastic rocks and tuffs in the BGS belt indicate the basin to have undergone active tectonic process. Younger ultrabasics and dolerite dykes that invaded the meta-sediments may be responsible for isochemical change in BIF, endothermic reaction in magnetite, rise in P-T condition and thermal metamorphism.

# Chapter 7
# Iron Formations of Karnataka Region

## Introduction

The iron formations of Karnataka occur in different tectonic environments namely, low grade metamorphic belts, high grade metamorphic belts and cratonic basins. The iron formations which occur in high grade metamorphic belts have often attracted the attention of earlier workers, because of their intimate association with charnockites. Some earlier investigators (Smeeth, 1916; Jayaram, 1912, 1917; Sampath Iyengar, 1920) considered a genetic relationship between the iron formations and charnockites. They were thought of as gravitative differentiates of a charnockitic magma and as interesting additions to the charnockite series. However, later investigators (Devaraju and Sadasivaiah, 1966; Naganna and Mahabaleswar, 1976; Mahabaleswar, 1986) have shown that the iron formations are formed by the metamorphism of iron-rich sediments and have no genetic relationship whatsoever, to the associated charnockites.

## Field Disposition

The Karnataka craton is the oldest part of the Indian shield (Radhakrishna and Naqvi, 1986), with rocks in the age range of 3,800 to 2,500 m.y.. A generalised geological map of the Karnataka craton is appended (Figure 7.1).

The supracrustal rocks which are older than 3,000 m.y. are called Sargur supracrustals (older schist belts or high grade metamorphic belts) and supracrustal rocks younger than 3,000 m.y. Dharwar supracrustals (younger schist belts or low grade metamorphic belts). The Sargur supracrustal rocks are mostly exposed in the southern parts of the craton and are metamorphosed to upper amphibolite to granulite

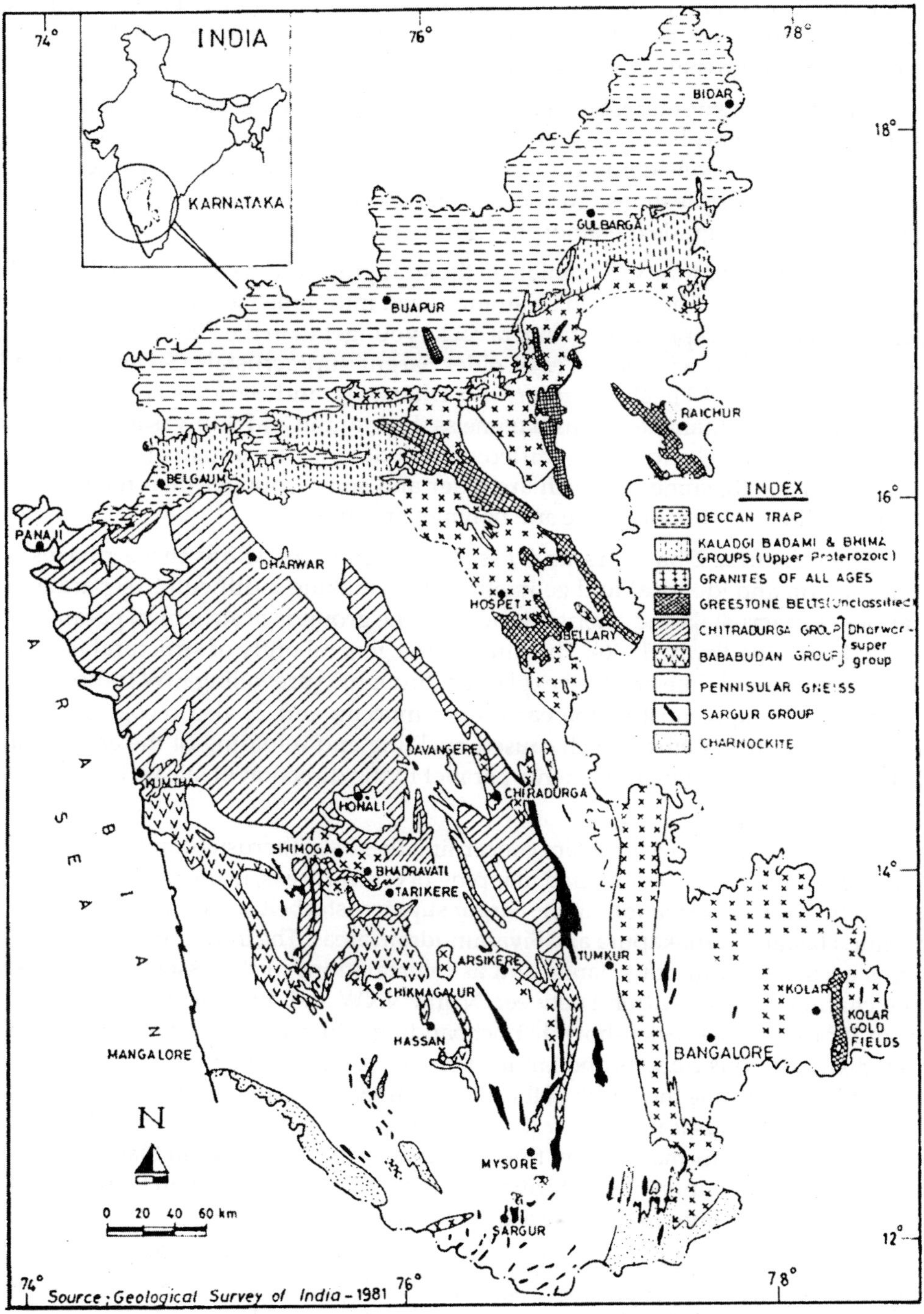


**Figure 7.1: Geological Map of Karnataka Craton Showing the Distribution of the Schist Belts**

grade. They are found as enclaves in the tonalite-trondhjernitic gneisses which are called Peninsular gneisses. Clastic siliceous sediments are absent from these belts and they have high mafic/sedimentary rock proportions.

The Dharwar supracrustal rocks which are exposed in the northern parts of the craton are metamorphosed to greenschist facies, have very low mafic/sediments ratio, and contain considerable amounts of clastic siliceous sediments exhibiting primary sedimentary features. An unconformable relationship between the Peninsular gneiss and the low grade metamorphic belts is envisaged.

There is no unanimity of opinion on the stratigraphy and structure of these two metamorphic belts. These could be summarized into three views: 1) The Dharwar supracrustal rocks represent a group of rocks younger than the Peninsular gneisses and these gneisses carry enclaves of older Sargur supracrustals (Swaminath and Ramakrishnan, 1981); 2) Together, the Dharwars and Sargurs represent one supergroup older than the Peninsular gneiss (Pichmuthu and Srinivasan, 1984); and 3) they represent belts formed at different periods covering a span of at least 1,000 m.y. (3,500-2,500), some of which are older and some younger than the gneisses which are themselves polyphase and polymetamorphic.

The Sargurs, Dharwars and associated gneisses show three phases of deformation and identical fold geometries thus, making it difficult to separate the various supracrustals and gneissic groups on the grounds of structural parameters alone (Mukhopadhyay, 1986). The cause of the general unity of structural features through space and time has been explained through: 1) prevailing E-W compressive directions through most of the early Precambrian; and 2) also recognising late Archaean shear systems, which caused buckling and refolding of the earlier fold belts making all the linear elements parallel to the direction of shear (Drury *et al.*, 1984).

However, the above problem concerning these supracrustals and gneisses can only be resolved by more detailed mapping of critical areas, in the field disposition, ore finds. The iron formations in the Sargur supracrustal belt are found extensively in Satnur, Halagur, Kanakapura and Sivasamudram areas. The iron formations in these areas occur as continuous bands and as intercalations in the associated gneisses and charnockites. They trend between N and NNW and dip east at angles varying from 35° to 60°. The rocks show distinct banding which is due to the occurrence of thin discontinuous ribbons and laminae of quartz alternating with laminae rich in dark minerals. While the width of the intercalations is less than 10 metres, the width of continuous bands is more than 30 metres and their strike length ranges from 0.25 to 4 km. The iron formations are fine to coarse-grained rocks with black to brown colour. The distribution of iron formations in these areas is shown in Figure 7.2 and various iron ore mines in the state are given in Figures 7.3 to 7.7.

The texture of the iron formations varies from schistose to xenoblastic. There is rapid variation in the proportion, distribution and grain size of the minerals. All the minerals are anhedral and contain abundant inclusions. The essential minerals in the iron formations are magnetite, orthopyroxenes, clinopyroxenes, amphiboles, garnet, pyroxferroite. lamellar pyroxenes, and quartz.

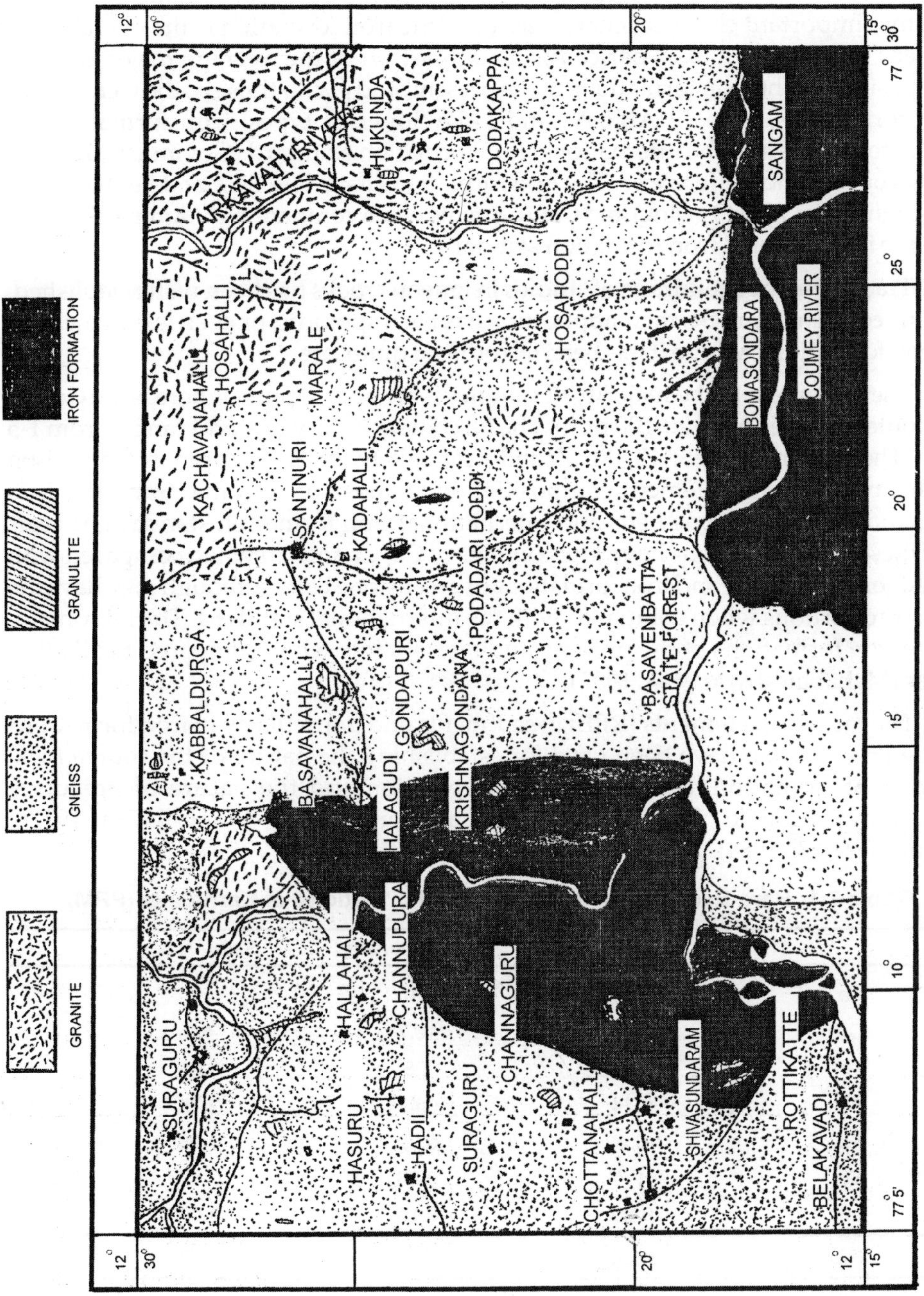


**Figure 7.2: The Distribution of Iron Formations in High Grade Region (Sivasundaram & Sanrur - Halagarh Areas)**

## Chemical Characterization

The iron formations have variable $SiO_2$ contents ranging from 40.61 per cent. The total Fe ($FeO+Fe_2O_3$) ranges from 28-51 per cent. FeO predominates over $Fe_2O_3$ Another important chemical characteristic of the iron formation is the overall high content of MnO (avg. 3.17 per cent). A comparison of the average major element composition of the iron formations of the present study with those of the well known iron formations, namely Algoma and Lake Superior types, iron formations of greenstone belts and the international iron formation standard (Govindaraju, 1980), brings out distinct differences. The iron formations have low $SiO_2$ and FeO contents and higher MgO, $Al_2O_3$, MnO and CaO contents when compared to Algoma, Superior and the international iron formation standard.

Trace element usefulness of studies in igneous rocks has been well established, but in sedimentary rocks their application has been sporadic, or even less in the field of iron formations, where it has been introduced quite late.

The Ba content in the majority of samples is around 10 ppm, whereas the Co, Cr, Cu content ranges from 20-100 ppm. The Ni content is very low and ranges from 1-5 ppm. The proportions of Sr, Zn, Rb, Zr and V range between 20-100 ppm. A comparison of the average trace element composition with those of Algoma, Superior, iron formations of greenstone belts and international iron formation standard, reveals that these iron formations have low contents of Co, Cr and Cu when compared with the Algoma, Superior and iron formations of greenstone belts, although they have the same proportions when compared with the international standard. The Ni content, of the iron formations of the present study is very low when compared to all other types (Mahabaleshwar *et al.*, 1987).

The rare earth elements (REE) in sediments and particularly in iron formations of the Precambrian have been used for establishing the nature of the source rock, process of formation, environment of deposition and the nature of precursor mineralogy (Laajoki, 1975; Laajoki and Lavikainen, 1977; Fryer, 1977a, 1977b; Majumder *et al.*, 1984).

**Table 7.1: Rare-Earth Elements of the Iron Formations of Karnataka (PPM)**

| | *Satnu-Halgu* | *Sivasamudam* | *Satnu-Halgu* |
|---|---|---|---|
| La | 7.7 | 9 | 1.9 |
| Ce | 18.7 | 15.7 | 4.9 |
| Sm | 3.4 | 1.5 | 0.63 |
| Eu | 0.74 | 0.47 | 2.75 |
| Tb | 0.4 | 0.22 | 0.08 |
| Yb | 1.7 | 0.88 | 0.47 |
| Lu | 0.29 | 0.15 | 0.07 |
| L REE | 32.93 | 27.92 | 10.8 |

**Figure 7.3a: View of Vyasanakere Iron Ore Mines**

**Figure 7.3b: Close View of Iron Ore–Banded Hematite**

**Figure 7.4a-b: Close View of Hard BHQ**

**Figure 7.5a: Silicious Iron Ore**

**Figure 7.5b: Folded BHQ in Karnataka Mines**

**Figure 7.6a-b: Marine Beds of BIF in Asundi Mines showing Banded Hematite (b)**

**Figure 7.7a-b: Bedding Joints in Hematite in Asundi Mine (a) and Cross Bedded BHQ in Nagvi Tanda Mine (b)**

The total REE contents of the iron formations vary from 10.8 to 32.93. The REE concentration of the iron formations of high grade terrain of Karnataka is consistent with the REE concentration of Archaean iron formations elsewhere (Appel, 1983; Fryer, 1983).

The behaviour of Ce is also considered to be time dependent. Definite anamolous behaviour of Ce is observed in Proterozoic iron formations when compared with iron formations of the Archaean age (Fryer, 1983). Flat to slightly depleted Ce pattern can be observed in the iron formations of the present study.

Some workers (Fryer, 1977a, 1977b; Laajoki, 1975) suggest that an Eu anomaly can be used as an indicator for oxidising versus reducing environments in the Precambrian atmosphere. Fryer (1983) showed that the behaviour of Eu appears to be time dependent, as the Archaean iron formation was consistently enriched in Eu whereas early Proterozoic iron formations exhibit slightly positive to slightly negative Eu a~amolies. However, the REE patterns of the iron formations of the present study show enriched to slightly depleted Eu anamoly. Based on the behaviour of Eu, it seems rather difficult to say anything about the oxidisation state of the environment during the Archaean period in southern Karnataka. The behaviour of Eu anamoly in the iron formations of southern Karnataka is similar to the observation made by Appel (1983) on the Isua iron formation of Greenland.

Therefore, it can be summarised that the iron formations of the high grade region are associated with pelitic and carbonate sediments and are found as enclaves within the gneisses. Based on petrography, two distinct types are recognised, namely, oxide and silicate facies. A peculiar feature of these iron formations is the occurrence of a variety of silicate minerals, such as orthopyroxenes, clinopyroxenes, amphiboles, garnet. pyroxferroite, lamellar pyroxenes and biotite. Chemical investigation of these minerals indicate that the pyroxenes are represented by ferrohypersthene and ferroaugitc whereas the garnet belongs to pyralspite series. The lamellar pyroxenes are Ca-poor and Ca-rich pyroxenes containing Ca-rich and Ca-poor lamellae respectively. Major element chemistry has revealed that these iron formations are in general comparable with the international iron formation standard with one major difference, that is, that the iron formations of the present study have a very high MnO content (3.97 per cent). Regarding trace elements, the Ba and Ni content of the iron formations of the present study is relatively lower compared with that of iron formations elsewhere. Rare earth elements' concentration is consistent with the REE concentration of Archaean iron formations elsewhere.

It is possible to this postulate that the iron formations of this region mainly consist of silicate and oxide facies. The presence of a variety of silicate minerals in these iron formations is controlled by a combination of parameters, namely, bulk composition, oxygen fugacity and pressure/temperature conditions of metamorphism. The pressure/temperature conditions of metamorphism making use of well known geothermobarometric models have yielded an average PIT estimate of 7.5-8 kb and 650°C. These values suggest that the iron formations have undergone upper amphibolite to granulite facies conditions of metamorphism.

The major, trace and REE geochemistry indicate that these are chemical sediments and silica and iron might have come from volcanic exhalations. Although large amounts of basic volcanic rocks are absent, there are, however, considerable amounts of basic granulites and amphibolites associated with these iron formations which have a tholeiitic precursor. Further, though it is difficult to apply any new model for the origin of the iron formations, with the aid of geochemistry, it does seem probable that these might have evolved under shelf conditions, since the associated sediments namely, pelites, and carbonates have characteristics typical of shallow water marginal facies depositional environments. The high MnO content in these iron formations suggest that there was little separation of Fe and Mn during deposition. This may be accounted for by assuming a narrow range of Eh. Regarding the nature of the original material, nothing can be deduced definitely since precursor mineralogy is completely obliterated because of high grade metamorphism.

# Chapter 8
# The Goan Iron Ore Deposits

## Introduction

Goa is situated on the west coast of India between the Arabian Sea and the Western Ghats. The state has a geographical area of 3610 sq. kms, less than the area of a district of many states. Goa is essentially a highly hilly and rugged track with narrow valleys and linear sandy planes along the coast. The Western Ghats, which are clad by evergreen forest, have a general altitude ranging from 600m to 1000m. In the western margin of the territory along the Arabian Sea there are long and narrow strips of sandy plains and low flat topped laterite hills ranging in altitude from 50m to 100m. Between the Western Ghats on the east and the coastal plains on the west, the territory is undulating with alternate chain of hills and long narrow valleys. The hills range in altitude from 250m to 400m. The Vageri hills near Valpoi however have an anomalous position as these are shifted much to the west of the Western Ghat chain of hills. But yet there is a narrow link between hills and the Western ghats of Surla ghat.

The geology and mineral resources of Goa had not received much attention when the State of Goa was under the Portuguese occupation. There were, however, sporadic attempts made by some geologists and mining engineers of private firms, to study the geology and mineral deposits, after the commencement of iron and manganese ore mining in Goa, in 1947.

The Goan iron ores have been explored extensively by core drilling in 50mx 50m grid interval due to complex folding of ore body. At some places drilling at 25m x 25m grid interval also has been carried out for pre production and quality control purpose.

The deposition of iron ore in Goa is over an area of 90 km$^2$ strike a length of 25 km. The iron ore range from Pale in South to Advalpale in North for the North Goan

Iron ore deposit. Almost the entire North Goan iron ore deposits are of Haematitic in nature except minor occurrence of magnetite.

## Field Disposition

The northern boundary of Goa runs along the Terekhol River (the mouth of the river lies in Goa) on the eastern side, the boundary is demarcated by the Sahyadris, on the west by the Arabian Sea. Southern section is closed off by an elevation about 111 m high near Colem.

The principal geological feature of the land is the extensive lateritization. It is mainly due to Goa's position in the tropical moist climate subject to vast seasonal changes. Lateritic capping is associated with iron and manganese ore deposits.

The iron ore area of Goa belongs to Dharwar (Archaean) System and associated with Banded Hematite Quartzite and Ferruginous Phyllites. Iron ore deposits occur predominantly towards north-north west.

The mode of occurrence of iron ore deposit is of lensoid and blanket type of varying dimensions in the pink phyllite horizon. Superficially, they occupy the crest and slopes of hill ranges, low lying hills and mounds, and are considered to be formed due to the enrichment of the banded ferruginous quartzite and phyllites. The regional distributions of the iron ore follow a general northwest-southeast trend and varying thickness. These rocks are primarily of sedimentary origin and later intruded by igneous intrusions, which resulted in formation of folds and faults.

The iron ore formations of Goa indicate two sets of sequence and transitional epochs and environments of deposition. Iron ore formations of North Goa, are of banded nature formed in geosynclinals basins while those of South Goa are of simple undulating surface forming several indiscrimination indicative of a platform or a carbonic environment. Available literature on structure, mineralisation and mineralogical maturity of deposit indicate possibility of a zone where a clear-cut separation could be made out. Example of such zone is seen in the region between Sancordem and Mollem.

Practically the entire territory of Goa is covered by rocks of the Dharwar Super Group of the Archaean Proterozoic age except for a narrow strip in the northeastern corner of the territory which is covered by Deccan trap of the Upper Cretaceous-Lower Eocene age. The Dharwar rocks which extend in a general north west-south east trend are represented by metamorphosed basic and acid volcanic rocks and sediments at the base overlain by greywacke suite of rocks, which in turn, if followed by pyroclasts and tuffs with the associated chaemogenic precipitates of lime, manganese and iron and ultimately again overlain by greywacks suite of rocks. These rocks have essentially suffered greenschist facies of metamorphism and have been intruded by granitic rocks followed by basic dykes.

## Nature of Iron Deposits

The North Goan iron ore has been divided into three blocks based on field observations and geological setup.

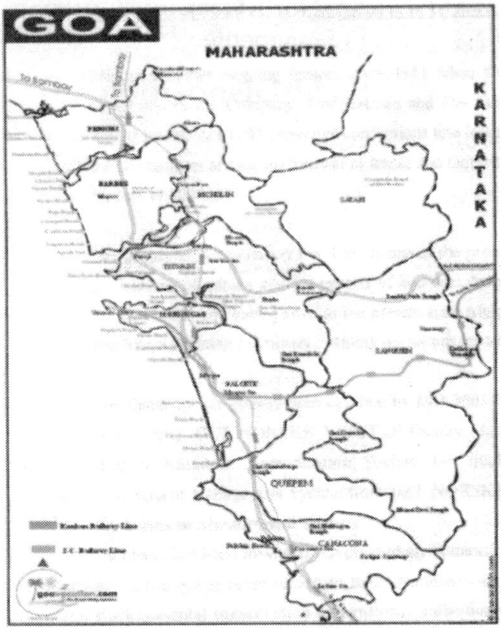


**Figure 8.1: Iron Ore Deposits of Goa**

### Bicholim Block

The iron ore bearing rocks of Bicholim form a part of the entire length of the western limb of the synclinal fold, trending NW-SE direction. This area is characterized by a prominent NW-SE trending dip slip fault which passes along the axial plane of the Bicholim – Sirigao and form iron ore body small local faults have also been observed in the mine working. The strike of the ore body as well as of the associated formations is about N50°W – S50°E with overall dip varying from 45 to 60 degree due NE. These rocks are affected by small folding and a few block faults. The powdery ore bands around 20 – 45m thick occur below low grade lumpy ore underlying lateritic capping. The ore body at places is affected by basic intrusive. Weathering of phyllites has given rise to laterites and this has protected the soft iron ore bodies down below. The iron ore deposits are strata bound; wherein the concentration of iron ore is mainly because of weathering and peneplanation. The iron ore deposits are enclosed within pink phyllite of manganiferous clay lenses. The footwall is generally phyllitic clay and the hang wall is manganiferous clay. The succession comprises:

Laterite/Lateritic Ore–15–20 meters

Iron Ore Lumpy–20-45 meters

### Velguem-Surla Block

This is the biggest block having about 27 mines. The entire area was originally covered with thick capping of laterite below which iron ore is present. Lower portions of the eastern slope are covered with clay formed from weathering of phyllites and

**Figure 8.2a-b: (a) View of Working Mine–Codli Group of Mines, Sesa Goa Ltd.; (b) View of Working Mine–Sonshi, Sesa Goa Ltd.**

**Figure 8.3a-b: Iron Ore Mine (a) Exhaused Mine Pits Converted into Rain Water Harvesting Pits at Codli Mine, Sesa Goa Ltd. (b) Narrain Mines of Sesa Goa Ltd.**

laterite. However, following is the normal succession of litho units observed from bench excavations and inferred from geological mapping and exploration data and showin in Figure 8.4.

**Geological Sequence Average thickness in metres**

1. Soil Cover 0 to 01
2. Laterite/Lateritic Clay 8 to 10
3. Ferruginous laterite / lumpy ore 5 to 10
4. Limonitic / Phyllitic / Mn Clay 5 to 30
5. Low grade Powdery Ore 2 to 10
6. High Grade Powdery Ore 2 to 20
7. BHQ Siliceous 2 to 10
8. Siliceous Clay / Mn Clay mix with silica Foot wall

The ore body occurs in two ridges *i.e.* Dignem and Sonshi ridge. At present working are concentrated in both the ridges.

It is revealed from the geological map and exposed rock formation in the area that the ore body and the associated rocks are folded. The ore formations are associated with the ferruginous phyllitic and limonitic clays on the hanging wall side and

**Figure 8.4: Geological Sequence of Velguem-Surla Block of Goa**

manganiferous clays and schists form towards footwall side. Structurally ore body represents a symmetrically folded, doubly plunging anticline. Pitch of the fold roughly follows the topography of the area. The ore horizon generally consists of parallel ore laminate intercalated with bands of hard ore, limonitic clays. The general strike NNW – SSE with local variation of 10° on either side. Dip of the ore body is 45 – 60° NE. Mineralogically, the ore body consists of mixture or haematite, / Limonite ore upto 62 per cent Fe in case of haematite, martite combination.

The northern part of this block consists of three ore bodies locally named as Bombay, Calcutta and Delhi. These are one below the other. They are 50m, 15m and 20m thick respectively. Calcutta ore is of high grade followed by Delhi and Bombay.

The ore bearing horizons are separated by thick manganiferous clays. Bombay forms the youngest and Delhi forms the oldest ore body. Physico-chemically, they exhibit distinct characters. The Bombay ore body has 5 – 10m thick manganiferous ore, which is transitional zone between Bombay ore body proper and manganiferous clay. They are separated by 50m thick manganiferous clay horizon. The Dehli ore body has phyllitic foot wall. In between Delhi proper ore body and phyllitic basement there is 10m to 40m thick limonitic ore body of 55 per cent Fe grade. In southern portions weathered dolerite intrusions are observed.

### Gavanem Block

The ore deposit of Gavanem Mine occupies the northern part of Gavanem-Malpona iron ore deposit of central Goa. Ore body extends over a strike length of 100 m striking NW – SE and dipping 20 – 40° towards west into the hill. In the Central part of the area the ore body is flatter. The ore body is intruded by dykes at certain places overlying formations below laterite are pinkish brown phyllitic clays. Manganiferous clays form the underlying formation. Lumpy and friable ore columns are followed by powdery ores. The thickness of ore body is varying from 15m to 20m. The beds show minor undulation in the form of gentle anticline and syncline. The deposit has a limb of syncline dipping north-east phyllite, forms both the hanging wall and foot wall side.

## Nature of Ore Goan in Iron Ores

### (*a*) Lateritic Ores

Weathering under tropical conditions has resulted in formation of laterites. The pieces of iron ore are seen embedded within the lateritic mass in this type of ore. This type of ore occurs on the surface. The ore is partly pisolitic and cavernous with some nodules, lenses and bands of haematite and limonitic ore. The recovery of iron ore from this type is lumpy and is low varying from 10 to 20 per cent. The grade of the lumps is low varying from 55 to 58 per cent Fe.

### (*b*) Hard Lumpy Ore

It is dark brown in colour, compact and shows some lateritic patches in upper horizon, followed by distinct lamination at lower horizons containing mostly haematite. This ore zone occurs below laterite and above friable zone. This zone is encountered when the iron ore body comes near the surface due to folding, mainly plunging. The lumpy ore is hard and its grade varying from 55 to 60 per cent Fe. This ore type is found in some of the mines, and friable ore directly occurs below the laterite. The recovery of lumps from this zone varies between 40 – 50 per cent.

**(c) Friable Ore**

This ore when extracted from the mine face crumbles into powdery ore and generally is a mixture of lumpy and fine ore. This ore is commercially known as biscuity ore. It is very porous with thin lamina and poly-ground cracks apparently derived by intensive leaching. The Fe content varies from 55 to 60 per cent in friable ore with lumps recovery of 10 to 20 per cent.

**(d) Powdery Ore**

This type of ore occurs predominantly in all the deposits of Goa. This ore is formed below the zone of friable ore at lower depths and indicates dark greyish brown to brownish grey colour, containing fine haematite crystals. This powdery ore is intercalated with that of yellowish to pink phyllites. This is the main ore zone. It is fine-grained greyish blue to brownish earthy in colour. The Fe content varies from 58 to 65 per cent in powdery ore.

**(e) Siliceous Ore**

The ore is soft and high in silica and low in Fe. The ore is found in some of the mines in Velguem-Surla block. The average grade of this ore is + 40 per cent Fe and $SiO_2$ ranging from 18 – 25 per cent. This is being stacked separately and is consumed on demand directly.

All the three *i.e.* topographical, lithological and structural controls of mineralisation have been observed in iron ore mines of the study area.. It is observed that hills with steep slopes are favourable locales for iron ore concentrations in the form of bands, having distinct lithological control. The iron ore mineralisation is confined only to the ferruginous phyllites or altered siliceous formation *i.e.* B.H.Q. The peculiarity of Goa deposits are that the ore is present in the synclinal trough, fairly deep seated and which are wider and more open.

The origin of iron ore deposits of Goa, is due to enrichment of pre-existing rocks *i.e.* B.H.Q. The corrugation banding so typical of BHQ clearly indicates that silica bands are leached by rain water, resulting in enrichment of iron ore formation. The replacement of quartzite bands in the BHJ by secondary ferric hydroxide has resulted into secondary hematite on hydration is demonstrated by presence of fine banding in the hard massive ore. The descending meteoric water becomes poorer in secondary ferric hydroxide and is thus capable only of leaching silica bands from BHQ but do not deposit any of iron hydroxide. Because of the fineness of grain size and banding, a slightly acidic descending meteoric water, is capable of disabling inter-granular ferric iron within the hematite bands, thus loosening the hematite grains which crumble into fine powder known as blue dust. This is evident from the high percentage of water molecules in form of moisture, which is due to the fact that the water molecule occupies the voids left over by the leaching of quartzite band.

The theory of replacement in ferruginous phyllite also holds good where pH and eH conditions are similar. From the field study the corrugation bands of BHQ indicates that silica bands are removed by rain water with the more resistant haematite bands protruding out. The replacement of quartzite bands in the BHQ by secondary ferric hydroxide which as dehydration has given rise to secondary haematite is amply demonstrated by the preservation of very fine banding in the hard massive ore.

## Resource Outlook

As referred above the iron ore deposits of the region are of complex nature. Structurally, the deposits are cross-folded. The deposits are occurring in low lying and in synclinal basins and are spread more in horizontal planes. The ideal way of exploring such type of deposits is by means of drilling in grid pattern. Delineation of ore body by field mapping becomes very difficult. This necessitated detailed exploration of the deposits at closure grid intervals by drilling at 50mx50m and at places at 25mx25m depending on the complexity.

The exploration carried out in the area is systematic. In most of the mines core drilling has been carried out in a closed grid regular interval in mineralized area. However the area used for dumping within the ML areas are proved barren by drilling few bore holes. The core logs are prepared and analysis & records are properly maintained. Slopes are not stable in some mines of Bicholim & Velguem-Surla block as wall rocks are not strong.

Goa under Portugese rules had granted Title concessions to a maximum of 100ha each which have been subsequently converted to mining leases from 1987. The moderately steep dipping orebodies and the narrow lease areas restrict the depth of mining and the ultimate pit limit. Therefore exploration at deeper depth has not been carried out. Though mineral occurrence continues at depth it cannot be mined. Therefore common boundary working is a routine feature in Goa. The footwall and hanging wall being weak exposure of large area are not permitted from safety angle and sometimes backfilling is carried out to maintain the safety of the pits. This restricts deeper exploration.

The North Goa Iron ore deposits are classified under stratiform, strata bound and tabular ore deposits of regular habit with particular change in trend with sharp to moderate physical contact with bounded surfaces and moderately steep dip. The requirement of exploration as per the field guidelines prescribed under UNFC to categorise reserves under different code applicable for Goan Iron ore deposits

Petrography & Mineralogical studies including gangue and its liberation characteristics have been carried out in all the major working mines like Bicholim, Velguem-Surla and Cudnem etc.

The threshold value of the Goa Iron ores is at present 55 per cent Fe. However, for siliceous ore, the threshold value has been fixed as +40 per cent Fe. The Fe content for the powdery ore exported is +60 per cent Fe with $Al_2O_3 < 2.8$ per cent & silica <3 per cent and lumps is in the range of 59 - 60 per cent Fe with $Al_2O_3$: 2.5 per cent. The ROM grade generally contains on an average 58 per cent Fe which in turn is beneficiated to obtain marketable grade. The low grade ore with 55 per cent Fe is usually blended with high grade to get feed grade of 58 per cent ROM which is fed to beneficiation plants. Thus, it is seen that the quantity of sub-grade generated is almost meagre and all the ore above threshold value +55 per cent Fe is utilised fully.

The Iron ore reserves and remaining resources as on 01.04.2005 as per UNFC for North Goa and South Goa districts of Goa are as presented in Table 8.1a-b.

**Table 8.1(a) Iron Ore Reservces in Goa (in million tonnes) and (b) Grade-wise Reserves**

**(a)**

| *Mineral* | *District* | *Reserves* | *Remaining Resources* | *Total Resources* |
|---|---|---|---|---|
| Haematite | North Goa | 236.43 | 111.74 | 347.87 |
| Magnetite | North Ga | 7.83 | 0 | 7.83 |
| Haematite | South Goa | 222.26 | 142.79 | 365.05 |
| Magnetite | South Goa | 42.24 | 164.06 | 206.30 |

**(b)**

| | *Name of the Block* | *Mineral* | *Grade Category of Reserves* | | | *Total* |
|---|---|---|---|---|---|---|
| | | | *Proved* | *Probable* | *Possible* | |
| Bicholim | Haematite | + 55 per cent Fe | 58 | 13 | 22.0 | 93.0 |
| Velguem-Surla | Haematite | + 55 per cent Fe | 117 | 25 | 10.0 | 152.0 |
| Gavenem | Haematite | + 55 per cent Fe | 5 | NIL | 0.2 | 5.2 |
| | | Total | 180 | 38 | 32.2 | 250.2 |

From the above table it is seen that the total reserves of haematite in three iron ore blocks of North Goa amounts to 250 million tonnes. Out of total 250 million tonnes more than 60 per cent reserves are in Velguem-Surla block. However the demonstrated reserves (both proved and probable together) constitute 245 million tonnes (more than 98 per cent of total geological reserves) in both Bicholim and Velguem-Surla Clusters together.

Further blockage of reserves 1.5 million tonnes of haematite was observed in Bicholim block due to the passage of high tension line and PWD Road through the lease area. Similarly in leases with common boundary, also a considerable quantity is blocked in Velguem-Surla block. These three blocks contribute more than 50 per cent of the total Goan haematitic proved Iron Ore Reserves.

Exploration in the form of core drilling in 50m X 50m grid interval is completed in the aquired areas of all the major mines. However in some mines/leases where the ore body is intricately folded 25m. x 25m grid interval is taken up. The unaquired area which is about 30 per cent of the total lease area may be taken up for exploration after aquiring them. The total 5,505 bore holes with cumulative meterage of 2.73 lakh m in iron ore mines carried out in the area, reveals that the exploration has been carried out in the three blocks *viz.* Bicholim, Velguem-Surla and Gavanem. The reserves

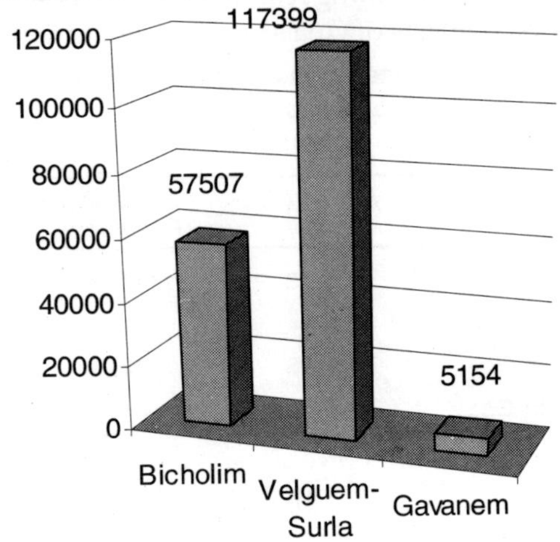


**Figure 8.5: Iron Ore Reserves in Bicholim, Velguem-Surla and Gavanem Blocks of Goa**

of iron ore estimated in all mines of these three blocks were about 250 million tonnes of all categories out of which 180 million tonnes of ore of proved category of haematite have been estimated (Figure 8.5).

The Goan iron ore are fast depleting. As against a total proved reserves of 458 million tonnes of iron ore the state has been producing at rate of about 33 million tonnes, therefore the reserves shall not last long unless very low grade ore is marketed.

# Chapter 9

# Iron Ore-Economics: Facts and Fallacy

## Introduction

The prospect of the iron ore availability with the projected growth of steel capacity in India is a matter which needs attention. There are two divergent views (a) one group led by the mines owners, public and private; and SMEs, advocating for abundance availability of high grade iron ore resources in the country (b) while the user groups are voicing their concern on the non-availability of desired quality and quantity of iron ore on a sustained basis until further systematic exploration is undertaken to augment "Resources" under "Proved Reserve Base".

The mining group advocate that India is endowed with huge resource base of 25.22 billion tonnes of iron ore, hematite and magnetite combined together; 'Reserves (UNFC basis 111, 121, 122)' being at 7.06 billion ton and 'Remaining resources (UNFC basis 211, 222, 331, 332, 333 and 334)' at 18.16 billion tonnes. Of the total reserve base of 7.06 billion tonnes, hematite accounts for 7.0 billion tonnes and magnetite at 0.60 billion tonnes. For a number of reasons, all the reserves may not be accessible to the mining companies and/or SMEs, particularly to those deposits which are occurring in reserve forests, national parks, sanctuaries and ecologically fragile areas like Western Ghat, Kudremukh. This synthesis is based on Ghosh, 2006a,b, 2008 and Ghosh *et al.*, 1996, 2000.

## Indian Production and Comparison

There has been a remarkable change in global steel scenario between 2003 and 2007, when the crude steel production reached one billion ton level in 2004 and maintained the same level of production from 2005 onwards. China is the main driver for such phenomenal growth, registering a significant CAGR at a level of 27.5 per cent between 2003 and 2007. The crude steel production in China was at a level of 184 million ton in 2003 which reached a level of 487 million ton in 2007 (as shown in Figure 9.1).

In India, the crude steel production also demonstrated a robust growth, Cumulative Annual Growth Rate (CAGR) being at a level of 9.50 per cent, next to China but, higher than global average growth at 9.30 per cent between 2003 and 2007. In 2003, the crude production was at 33.6 million ton, which reached to a level 53 million ton in 2007.

The Indian steel industry for the last two decades of control regulation registered a very poor growth. However, the deregulation of the Indian steel industry was initiated in 1992. The 10th and 11th Five year plans have shown a significant growth of the steel industry with Cumulative Annual Growth Rate (CAGR) at 9.5 per cent. The performance of the steel industry during 1992-93 to 2006-07 covering three 5 year plans, namely 8th, 9th and 10th have been shown in Figure 9.2.

It will be observed from the Figure 9.2 that immediately after the deregulation, remarkable growth has been achieved at CAGR of 9.7 percent during 8th Five Year Plan. In 9th Five year plan, the slow down to 6.20 per cent, which was subsequently, picked up a high of 9.5 per cent in 10th and 11th Five Year Plan.

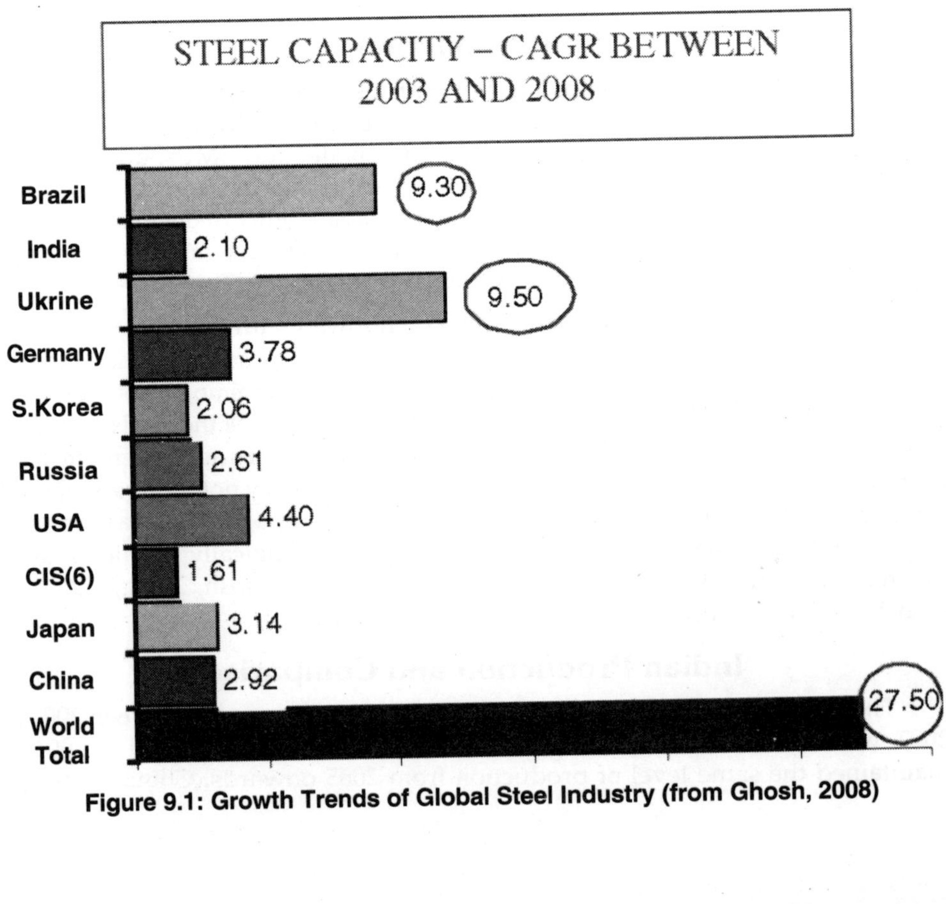


**Figure 9.1: Growth Trends of Global Steel Industry (from Ghosh, 2008)**

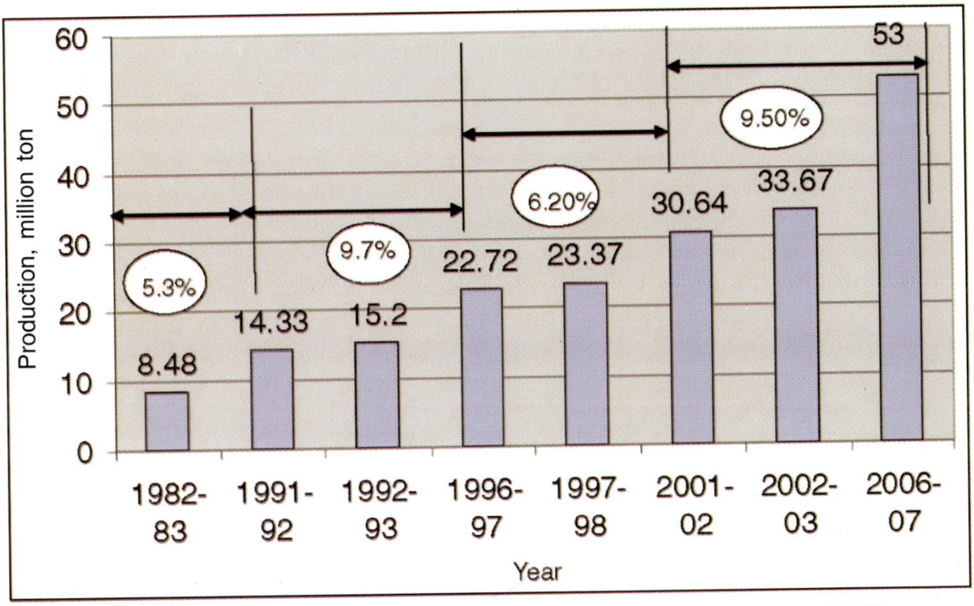


**Figure 9.2: Growth Trends of Indian Steel Industry (from Ghosh, 2008)**

The future projection of steel capacity as reported in the working paper 207 of Indian Council for Research on International Economic Relation (ICRER), 2008 has been presented in Figure 9.3.

Selection of the oxide feed mostly depends on the physical and chemical characteristics of the ore. Depending on the process technology, the oxide feed utilized either as sized ore, agglomerates or fines. However, all the processes aim at achieving

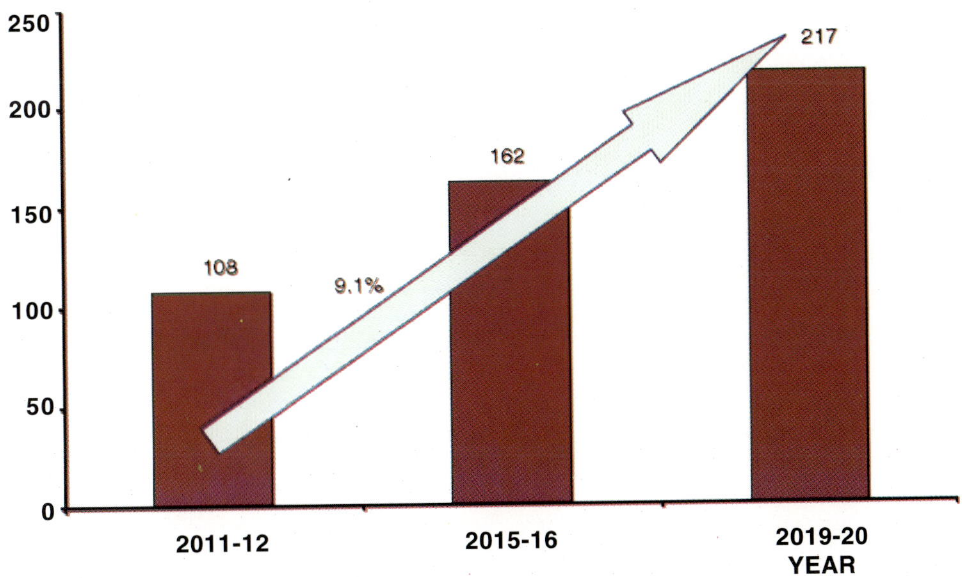


**Figure 9.3: Steel Growth Projection (from ICRER)**

an oxide feed with high Fe content, minimum gangue materials and low impurities like sulphur and phosphorous. The other important factor that governs raw material quality is a consistency in chemical composition, granulometry and physical properties.

For iron making through blast furnace route sized iron ore preferably between 10 mm and 40 mm is charged directly and iron ore fines and concentrates after agglomeration as sinter/pellet. The sized ore should be of high grade, Fe content preferably above 62 per cent with good reducibility and low decrepitation. The ore fines should preferably have 60 percent Fe minimum with low alumina, to yield about 2 per cent alumina in sinter. The lower the alumina content, the better will be RDI of the sinter.

Experience at Tata Steel has shown that reduction of Alumina from 3.1 to 2.1 percent in sinter improves RDI in sinter by about 6 points, which in turn reduces the consumption of BF coke by about 20-24 kg/thm and increases the blast furnace productivity by about 0.1 ton/m$^3$/day. The use of pellets is not practiced in India for economic reason.

## Commercial Classification of Iron Ore

The Indian iron ore can broadly be classified as hard massive ore, hard laminated ore (HLO), soft laminated (Shown in Figure 9.4).

ore (SLO) and blue dust (BD). The typical ore type and their corresponding chemical analyses are presented below:

| Fe | $SiO_2$ | $Al_2O_3$ | $Na_2O$ | $K_2O$ | P | S |
|---|---|---|---|---|---|---|
| % | % | % | % | % | % | % |
| 61.00 - | 0.50 - | 0.60 | 0.010 - | 0.013 - | 0.008 - | 0.031 - |
| 68.00 | 5.00 | 5.00 | 0.01 | 0.02 | 0.02 | 0.01 |

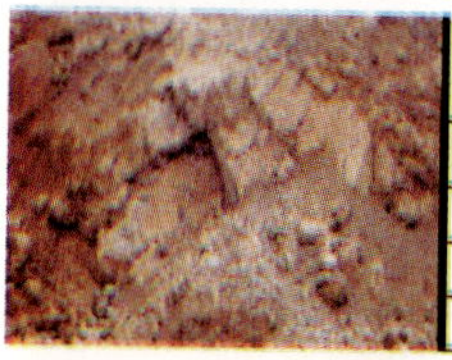

| Fe | $SiO_2$ | $Al_2O_3$ | $Na_2O$ | $K_2O$ | P | S |
|---|---|---|---|---|---|---|
| % | % | % | % | % | % | % |
| 59.00 - | 1.0 - | 1.0 - | 0.005 - | 0.013 - | tr - | 0.005 - |
| 66.00 | 9.0 | 9.0 | 0.008 | 0.018 | 0.063 | 0.008 |

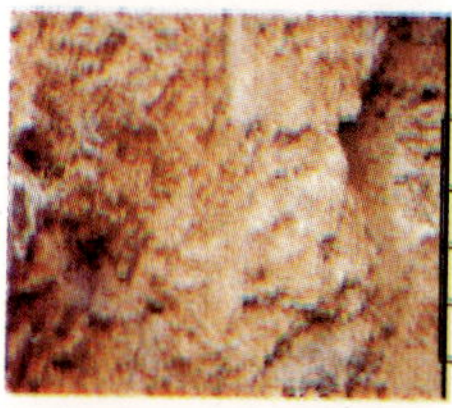

| Fe | $SiO_2$ | $Al_2O_3$ | $Na_2O$ | $K_2O$ | P | S |
|---|---|---|---|---|---|---|
| % | % | % | % | % | % | % |
| 61.00 - | 0.50 - | 0.60 - | 0.010 - | 0.013 - | 0.008 | 0.003 - |
| 67.00 | 5.0 | 5.0 | 0.013 | 0.018 | 0.016 | 0.007 |

| Fe | $SiO_2$ | $Al_2O_3$ | $Na_2O$ | $K_2O$ | P | S |
|---|---|---|---|---|---|---|
| % | % | % | % | % | % | % |
| 64.00 - | 0.20 - | 0.50 - | 0.010 - | 0.003 - | 0.008 | 0.003 - |
| 69.00 | 2.0 | 2.50 | 0.017 | 0.009 | 0.016 | 0.007 |

**Figure 9.4: Commerrical Classification of Indian Iron Ores**

## Iron Ore Fines

It is widely recognized that agglomerates like sinter/pellets would be better feed in blast furnace provided the sinter chemistry and physical properties are maintained at a satisfactory level. However, sinter chemistry will largely depend on the chemical compositions of the iron ore fines together with the thermal conditions of sinter blend which will play an important role in determining the primary melt, formed during sintering, and consequently the sinter structure and quality. The limited incidences of the high grade lump ore in our deposits, ranging between 25 to 35 per cent and the fast depletion of high grade lump ore left no options to the steel plants other than to use iron ore fines through sinter route. The typical analysis of iron ore sinter feed is presented below in Table 9.1:

**Table 9.1: Iron Ore Sinter Feed**

| *Iron Ore Fines (Sinter Feed)* | *Fe, %* | *$SiO_2$, %* | *$Al_2O_3$, %* |
|---|---|---|---|
| CVRD-Standard sinter fines (SSF) | 64.20 | 5.10 | 1.0 |
| Carajas Fines (CJF) | 67.20 | 0.60 | 0.94 |
| Mt. Goldsworthy - HG Fines | 62.90 | 6.64 | 1.29 |
| MBR- HG Fines | 64.00 | 1.50 | 1.50 |
| Bhillai Steel Plant (BSP) - Dalli-Rajhara | 63.76 | 2.38 | 2.48 |
| Bokaro Steel Ltd (BSL) - Kiriburu -Meghahatuburu | 62.9 | 3.14 | 2.54 |
| Durgapur Steel Plant (DSP) - Bolani | 61.8 | 2.3 | 2.8 |
| Rourkela Steel Plant (RSP) - Barsua -Kalta | 62.3 | 2.8 | 3.1 |
| Tata Steel - Noamundi - Joda | 65.67 | 0.9 | 2.6 |
| VSP - Bailadila | 64.83 | 2.07 | 1.81 |

It will be observed from the above table, alumina content in the sinter fines traded in the international market varies between 0.94 and 1.5 per cent. It is observed that $Al_2O_3$ content in sinter is linearly related with sinter productivity (ton/m$^2$/day).

## Reserves and Resources

The reserves and resources estimated by Indian Bureau of Mines (IBM) in different period have been presented in Table 9.2.

It will be observed from the Table 9.2 that total resource estimated at 17.56 billion tonnes on 01.01.1980 was increased to 25.22 billion tonnes in 2005. The Reserves and Resources between 1980 and 2005 have been presented in Figure 9.5.

It is interesting to observe that the total resources of hematite between 1980 and 2005 are steadily increasing while that of magnetite remains more or less steady.

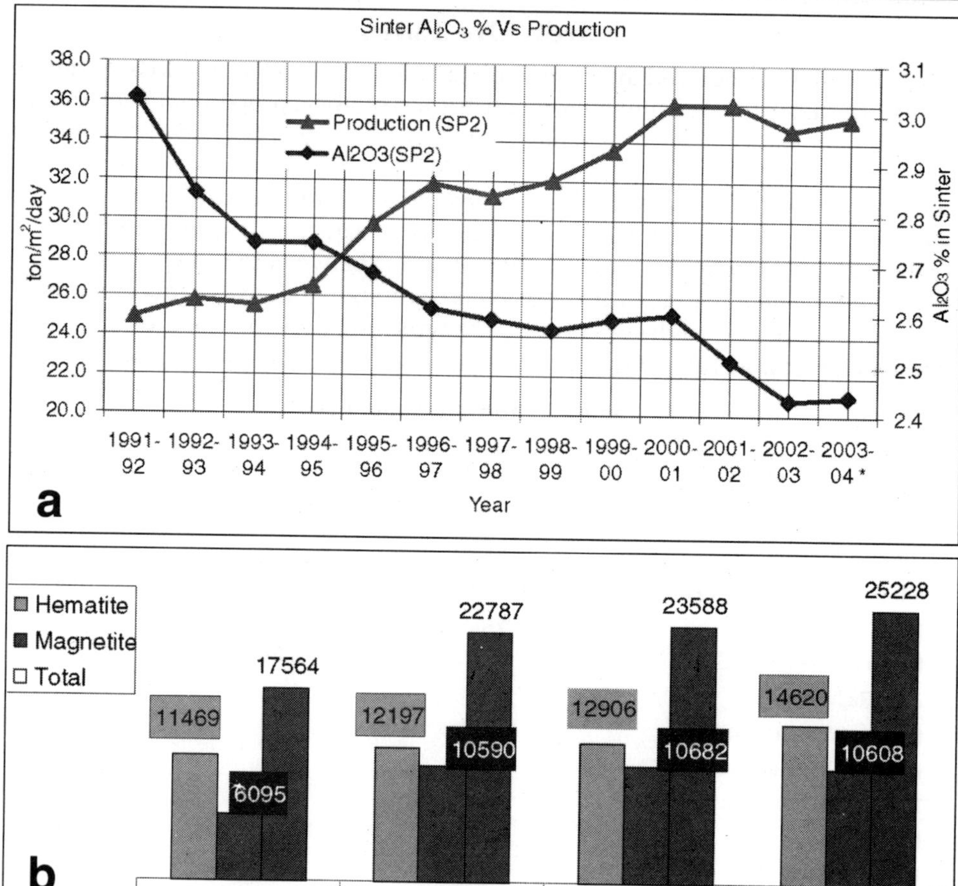


| | 1980 | 1990 | 2000 | 2005 |
|---|---|---|---|---|
| Hematite | 11469 | 12197 | 12906 | 14620 |
| Magnetite | 6095 | 10590 | 10682 | 10608 |
| Total | 17564 | 22787 | 23588 | 25228 |

**Figure 9.5a-b: Sinter $Al_2O_3$ % vs Production**

***Source*: Tata Steel**

Also from Table 9.2, it will be observed that proved reserves remains more or less steady between 2004 and 2005 while the probable reserves (121,122) increased by 28 per cent and remaining reserves by 14 per cent which contributed jointly in increasing the total resources from a level of 22.0 billion tonnes to 25.0 billion tonnes.

In this context, it is pertinent to point out that no systematic detailed explorations have been carried out after 1990 by the major exploration agencies like GSI. Of late, GSI have initiated some exploration.

**Table 9.2: Reserves and Resources of Iron Ore**

| *Grade* | *Reserves and Resources of iron ore (Mill ton)* | | | | |
|---|---|---|---|---|---|
| | *Resources as on 1980* | *Resources as on 1900* | *Resources as on 2000* | *Resources as on 2004* | *Resources as on 2005* |
| Hematite | 11,469 | 12,197 | (a) Reserves: 6025 | (a) Reserves: 6000 | (a) Reserves: 7,000 |
| | | | | Proved (111): 4421 | Proved (111): 4945 |
| | | | | Probable (121): 828 | Probable (121): 995 |
| | | | | Possible (122): 774 | Possible (122): 1063 |
| | | | (b) Remaining Resources: 6881 | (b) Remaining Resources: 5400 | (b) Remaining Resources: 7,620 |
| | | | Total: 12,906 | Total: 11420 | Total: 14,620 |
| Magnetite | 6,095 | 10,590 | (a) Reserves: 286 | (a) Reserves: 58 | (a) Reserves: 58 |
| | | | (b) Remaining Resources: 10,396 | (b) Remaining Resources: 10,550 | (b) Remaining Resources : 10,550 |
| | | | Total: 10,682 | Total: 10,608 | Total: 10,608 |
| Total | 17,564 | 22,787 | (a) Reserves: 6,311 | (a) Reserves: 6,058 | (a) Reserves: 7,058 |
| | | | (b) Remaining Resources: 17,277 | (b) Remaining Resources: 15950 | (b) Remaining Resources: 18170 |
| | | | Total: 23,588 | Total: 22008 | Total: 25,228 |

## UNFC Code

The UNFC classifications code for mineral evaluation is guided by three major dynamic axes where each of the axes has further been subdivided into active subgroups, exception being the geological axis.

In three digits code based system, Economic viability axis representing the first digit, the feasibility axis the second digit and the geological axis the third digit. Each of the axes, have three sub-codes, 1 2 3 in decreasing order. Thus, the highest category of resources under UNFC system will have the code (111) and the lowest category of code will be (334). Now, each of the subgroups is guided by the specific sets of activities and coding is strictly to be made on evaluation of degree and intensity and achievements against each of the activities.

Exploration is one the major activities in evaluating the mineral RESERVES AND RESOURCES. UNFC guide line on exploration on iron ore comprises:

- ☆ Topographical survey and mapping in 1: 1000 scale
- ☆ Geological study comprising structural and lithological mapping, structural analysis, control of mineralization, ore body configuration, ore body-host rock relation
- ☆ Trenching, pitting and sampling
- ☆ Drilling at closer intervals, say 100mX 50m
- ☆ Characterisation of deposit through detailed petro-mineralogical studies and laboratory testing
- ☆ Geostatistical data analysis and ore body modeling

Mineral reserve has been defined by UNFC under two heads, namely "Proved Mineral Reserves (111)" and "Probable Mineral Reserves (121) and 122)." The "Remaining Resources" is equivalent to "Possible Reserves" as followed earlier.

For implementing any mining project where huge financial liabilities are involved, the prime consideration will be the availability of "PROVED RESERVES" in the prospect. The "PROBABLE RESERVES" needs to be upgraded to PROVED CATEGORY.

## Facts and Fallacy

The mine operators; private and public, along with SMEs and FIMI came heavily on steel mills' concerns on the future availability of iron ore to support the enhanced steel production capacity in the country. Indian Council for Research on International Economic Relation (ICRER) also expressed similar view on the abundance of iron ore reserves. They have agreed that estimated resources can easily be enhanced, even without undertaking serious exploration campaign by

- ☆ Reducing the cut-off grade from a level of 55 per cent Fe to 45 per cent Fe
- ☆ Increasing the depth continuity of the ore body
- ☆ Carry out exploration for proving resources

In this context, it is worth mentioning that cut off grades for iron ore deposits are based on certain technological requirements and economic considerations. Of the estimated reserves, even with present Fe cut off grade, only a limited part of the same will meet the desired quality specification for iron making.

Also, the iron ore deposit in India is controlled by complex and multiple structural elements. This will be clearly evident from some of the field photographs of structural features still preserved in Jamda-Koira iron ore belt.

In such a structurally disturbed belt, there is no reason to believe that depth continuity of the ore at a point source will continue over the total prospect. So, before increasing the resource base on consideration cut off grade reduction and depth continuity; it will be prudent to consider the geology and milieu of ore deposit in totality.

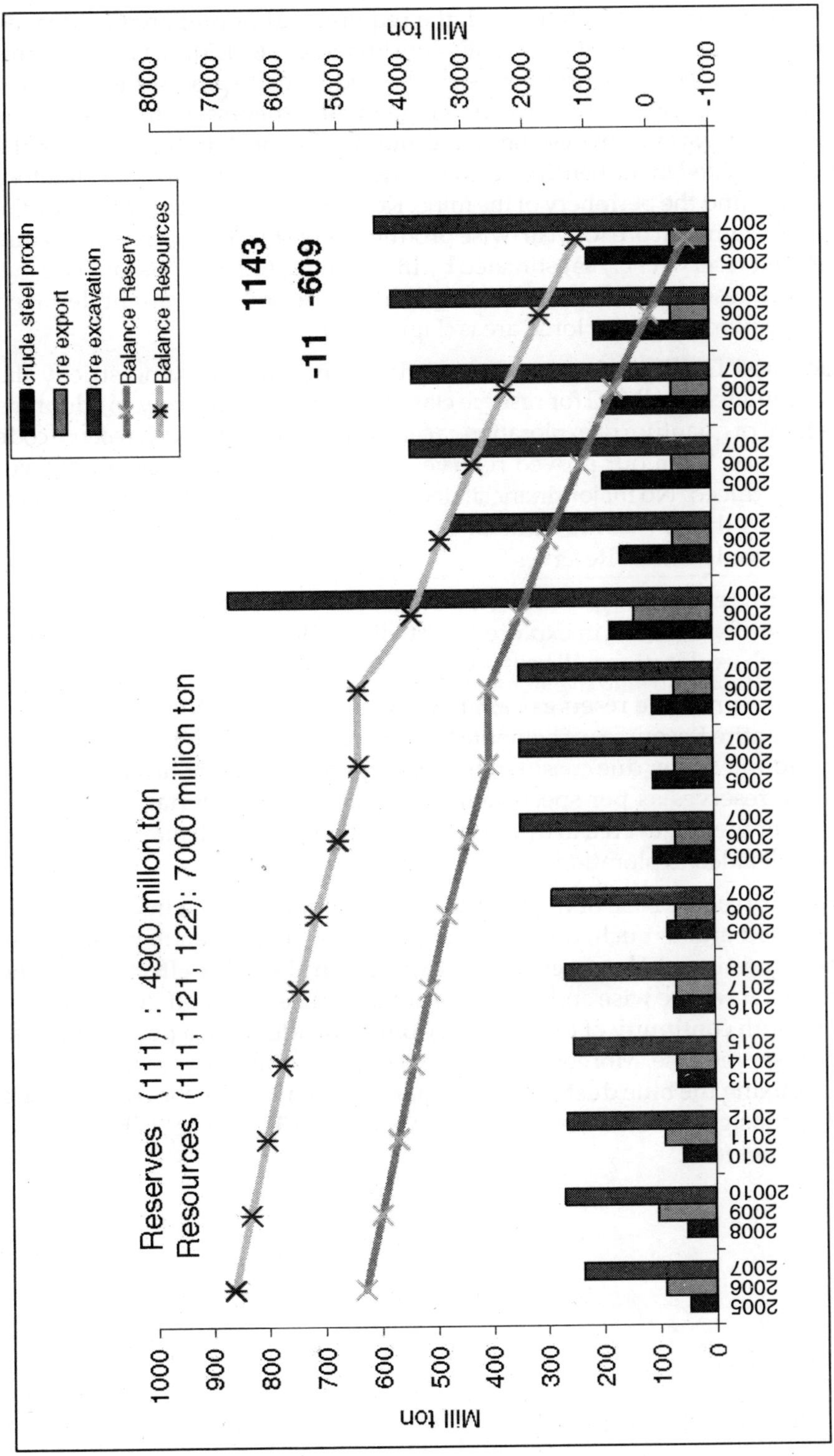


**Figure 9.6: Steel Production vs Ore Availability**

For production of 1 ton of hot metal, the requirement of prepared oxide feed (sized lump ore, sinter, pellets etc) is usually considered at 1.6/1.5 ton. However, this factor increases with decrease of iron content in the feed. Thus, to process the excavated rom for producing usable feed for iron making, it will be necessary to consider the losses against excavation, processing, handling & transportation as well as the deposits that are locked in the bench slopes and within the zone required for statutory requirements around the periphery of the mine. Keeping all these factors in mind, the requirements of rom iron ore for year-wise production of steel has been worked out. With this proved reserve (111) as estimated by IBM in 2005, *there will be shortfall of iron ore from 2019*, unless systematic explorations with all seriousness are undertaken both in the unexplored and explored areas (Figure 9.6).

IBM adopted UNFC code for reserve estimation. But, following strictly the guidelines stipulated in UNFC for reserve classifications, it is unlikely to adopt the same in the light of quantum of exploration carried out in India. If UNFC reserve code is strictly followed, even our proved reserves as reported by IBM since 1990 will drastically be reduced. No major financial decision is likely to be taken on "Mineral Reserves" unless the "Probable Mineral Reserves (121,122)" are brought under category of "Proved Mineral Reserves"

To support the envisaged growth of steel capacity, it will be necessary to undertake the detailed exploration both in explored, partially explored and virgin areas. The objectives of such exploration will broadly comprise:

Upgrade the probable reserves base to proved category (UNFC classification 111). Bring the entire Resources of hematite to Reserve category. UNFC classification code may be adopted after due consideration of economic and metallurgical vectors. Categories the reserves as per specifications of end users. Undertake systematic exploration over the virgin area to discover newer deposits, which may be followed by systematic detailed exploration.

Finally, our reserve base of high grade iron ore, suited for the iron making, is extremely limited and as such, due considerations are to be given to preserve the reserves for domestic use. However, limited exports can always be effected from the selected sectors. It will be wise and advisable not to reduce Fe cut off grade, and/or increase the depth continuity of the iron ore, from an incidence in a point source, to increase the reserves base. Moreover, our reserves of the blue dust are very limited and as such, mixing the blue dust with low grade fines to increase the overall grade of exportable consignment may be restricted. About 25 to 30 per cent of blue dust is now used in sinter feed.

# Chapter 10

# The Future of Iron Ore and Steel Industry

The future growth and success of iron ore mining on a sustainable basis shall depend on a variety of factors. Some of these are being discussed here. The foremost amongst is the *regulatory challenge* which involves land acquisition. At present our steel consumption is low, and very minimal as compared to the industrialized nations. The production does not meet the domestic demand. At present the private participation is low, but it may increase in the coming years.

Another difficulty is in long delays in granting of prospecting license and mining lease, the time taken for this is ranging between 3 to 7 years, although this could generally happen in a few months time. When prospecting permission is delayed, subsequent weeks or exploration, assessment all get affected (Table 10.1).

On the logistics–there is a deficiency in infrastructure such as a good railway network in the mining areas and evacuation of ore to the mills. One may be disappointed that present only around 3,800 MT of dedicated wagon of iron ore are available, as compared to 20,000 MT wagons in Australia and 40,000 MT in Brazil. There is thus need and scope for growth. Similarly the road not work, especially in Jharkhand-Orissa state border region need attention.

Overall, we need more infrastructure development at ports, and support at social as well as administrative level.

Global steel production has been mainly driven by China. Chinese steel production during 2005–2009 grew at a CAGR (Compound Annual Growth Rate) of 12.4 per cent. Non-Chinese steel demand has reached at a CAGR of 4.5 per cent. Import of basic input materials such as iron ore by China has increased from 275.3

Million Tonnes in 2005 to 628.3 Million Tonnes in 2010. India exports major share of iron ore to China (average 7.5 per cent yoy growth in the last decades) and huge demand of natural resources to meet the development of its economy, is offering a vast market for the Indian iron ore as can be seen in Tables 10.2, 10.3 and 10.4

**Table 10.1: Status of Mining Leases and Mines in India (Iron ore)**

| *State* | *No. of Mining Leases* | *No. of Reporting Mines* |
|---|---|---|
| Andhra Pradesh | 31 | 23 |
| Chhattisgarh | 13 | 11 |
| Goa | 187 | 72 |
| Jharkhand | 48 | 20 |
| Karnataka | 158 | 90 |
| Madhya Pradesh | 11 | 07 |
| Maharashtra | 24 | 11 |
| Orissa | 9Q | 81 |
| Rajasthan | 15 | 01 |
| India | 577 | 316 |

*Source*: Indian Bureau of Mines.

**Table 10.2: Major Steel-Producing Countries 2008 and 2009 (Million Tonnes)**

| *Country* | *2008* | *Rank* | *2009* | *Rank* |
|---|---|---|---|---|
| China | 500.3 | 1 | 567.8 | 1 |
| Japan | 118.7 | 2 | 87.5 | 2 |
| India | 57.8 | 5 | 62.8 | 3 |
| Russia | 68.5 | 4 | 60.0 | 4 |
| United States | 91.4 | 3 | 58.2 | 5 |
| South Korea | 53.6 | 6 | 48.6 | 6 |
| Germany | 45.8 | 7 | 32.7 | 7 |
| Ukraine | 37.3 | 8 | 29.9 | 8 |
| Brazil | 33.7 | 9 | 26.5 | 9 |
| Turkey | 26.8 | 11 | 25.3 | 10 |
| Italy | 30.6 | 10 | 19.8 | 11 |
| Taiwan, China | 19.9 | 12 | 15.9 | 12 |
| World | 1,329.0 | | 1,226.5 | |

*Source*: World Steel Association.

India accounts for around 5 per cent of the global steel consumption. Almost 70 per cent of the total steel used is for kitchenware. The scope for raising the total consumption of steel is huge, given that per capita steel consumption is only 40 kg–

compared to 150 kg average across the world and 250 kg in China. Freight advantage ($ 15/MT) for supplies to eastern hemisphere (Japan/China) compared to Brazil (Freight $ 26/MT) (Table 10.5).

**Table 10.3: World Crude Steel Production 1970 to 2009 (Million Tonnes)**

| *Year* | *World* | *Year* | *World* |
|---|---|---|---|
| 1970 | 595 | 2000 | 849 |
| 1975 | 644 | 2001 | 851 |
| 1980 | 717 | 2002 | 904 |
| 1985 | 719 | 2003 | 970 |
| 1990 | 770 | 2004 | 1,072 |
| 1995 | 752 | 2005 | 1,144 |
| 1996 | 750 | 2006 | 1,247 |
| 1997 | 799 | 2007 | 1,346 |
| 1998 | 778 | 2008 | 1,329 |
| 1999 | 789 | 2009 | 1,227 |

*Source*: World Steel Association.

**Table 10.4: Grade-wise Iron Ore Resources as on 1-4-2005 (provisional) (Unit: Million Tonnes)**

| *Ore Type* | *Grade* | *Resources as on 01-04-2005 (Provisional)* |
|---|---|---|
| Iron ore (Hematite) | (+) 65% Fe | 2132 |
| | (+) 62% to 65% | 6694 |
| | Below 62% Fe (including all Other grades) 5804 | |
| | Total | 14630 |
| Iron ore (Magnetite) | Metallurgical | 2186 |
| | Coal washery | 8 |
| | Foundry | 1 |
| | Others | 25 |
| | Unclassified | 8113 |
| | Not Known | 287 |
| | Total | 10620 |

*Source*: Indian Bureau of Mines, Nagpur.

**Table 10.5: Top Ten World Steel Member Companies'2009, Crude Steel Production over 3 (Million Tonnes)**

| *Rank* | *Company* | *Mmt* |
|---|---|---|
| 1 | ArcelorMittal | 77.5 |
| 2 | Baosteel | 31.3 |
| 3 | POSCO | 31.1 |
| 4 | Nippon Steel (1) | 26.5 |
| 5 | JFE | 25.8 |
| 6 | Jiangsu Shagang (2) | 20.5 |
| 7 | Tata Steel (3) | 20.5 |
| 8 | Ansteel | 20.1 |
| 9 | Severstal | 16.7 |
| 10 | Evraz | 15.3 |

1. Does not include share of Usiminas production (1.6 mmt)

2. Does not include Yonglian (4.4 mmt) and Xixing (1.4 mmt)

3. Includes Corus and NatSteel

*Source*: International Steel University.

In India Iron ore and Steel industry is second largest industry after Coal industry. There are 25 billion tonnes of iron ore resources. Most of the reserves are economically exploitable. The three states of Orissa, Chhattisgarh and Jharkhand account for almost half of India's iron ore reserves. Steel Authority of India Limited and National Mineral Development Corporation are major producers of Iron ore. Based on the physical size, Iron ore is divided into lumps and fines. In India most of the Iron ore is used for making of steel. Our steel sector consumes mostly lumps and we export fines to other countries due to lack of advanced technology. Domestic consumption in India is mostly in construction, infrastructure and automobile. China and Japan are the major Indian iron ore importing countries. Iron ore and steel industry faces logistic challenges in the form of regulatory, infrastructure and social/political aspects. Government should concentrate on the issues like granting of mining leases, and license, land acquisition, environmental and financial approvals. decreasing the freight charges both in rail and roadways, revise the Mining and Mineral Taxation Laws, encourage the private and foreign investments in infrastructure areas like Railways, Roadways and Ports, control the illegal mining activities, and provide security for safe mining from extremist activities laying the separate rail lines and road ways from Iron ore mining areas to ports like Brazil and Australia, encourage the R & D activities to invent the new technologies for industrialization and using iron ore fines efficiently. The opportunities in iron ore and steel industry in India are vast. India will emerge as the strongest market in the world between 2010 and 2015, when demand will grow annually at 7.7 per cent. This year, steel consumption in India is expected to grow by a hefty 10 per cent (last year, the country had to import about 4.7 million tonnes of steel). The steel scenario in India will continue to remain buoyant over the next few years, as the hunger for the metal keeps rising, thanks to vibrant end-user demand.

Industry being one of the core sectors in any economy, consumption of steel is usually a good indicator of the economic development of any country. The end use patterns of steel means that the steel demand has strong positive correlation with economic growth of any country. The demand of steel with respect to GDP (Gross Domestic Product) in most of developing countries is generally more than 1. For China it has been estimated at 1.15 and for India at 0.95. The demand intensity of steel with respect to GDP per capita varies depending upon the state of development of economy rising in initial stages and then falling off in advanced stages of economic development. We analyse China and India economies today, the demand elasticity and intensity of Steel with respect to the GDP is expected to fall in China in next 4–5 years. Whereas, in India it is likely to be on the rising trend for the next 10–15 years. There is so much of backlog to be covered in India (Krishnamurthy, 2009).

In India based on the current GDP, the planners believe that the steel demand growth is likely to mirror the GDP growth till about 2025 and will be in the range of 135–165 million tonnes by the year 2025 and by 2050 in the range of 465–540 million tonnes. According to Goldman Sachs report released in the month of October 2003, The Global Economic Paper called 'Dreaming with BRICs: The Path to 2050', Going by analysis and projections of this report, the size of the Indian Economy in 2050 will be $27.8 Trillion and it will be the 3$^{rd}$ largest economy after China and The US. According to an estimate, with the growing need for oil and gas transportation infrastructure, a US$ 118 billion opportunity is waiting to be tapped by steel manufacturers in the next five years. Indian steel companies are likely to get 19 per cent of the total global demand in the years to come. A host of steel companies have lined up with major investment proposals. Indian steel industry is likely to receive huge domestic and foreign investments.

The domestic steel sector has attracted a staggering investment of about US$ 236 billion, this consists of nearly 222 MoUs signed between the investors and various state governments mostly in the states of Orissa, Jharkhand. Chhattisgarh and West Bengal. According to the Investment Commission of India, investments of over US$ 30 billion in steel are in the pipeline over the next 5 years. Tata Steel itself plans to invest over $15 billion in these three minerals-rich eastern states, adding 23 million tonnes to its existing capacity of 5 million tonnes.

The National Steel Policy has envisaged steel production to reach 110 million tonnes by 2019–20. However, based on the assessment of the current ongoing projects, both in green field and brown field, Ministry of Steel has projected that the steel capacity in the county is likely to be 124.06 million tonnes by 2011–12. Further, based on the status of MOUs signed by the private producers with the various State Governments, it is expected that India's steel capacity would be nearly 293 million tonne by 2020.

The Indian government plans to invest over US$ 350 billion in industries related to infrastructure and construction. In such a scenario, the Indian steel industry has a long way to go. Rising demand from the automotive and capital goods segments are other drivers for consumption of the commodity. Passenger car sales during the first four months of FY11 have increased by 29.6 per cent yoy, while commercial vehicle sales have increased by 64.8 per cent . We forecast the construction and infrastructure spending by the government to continue unabated. This is likely to help maintain strong steel demand over the next 2–3 years.

# References


ACHARYA, S. (1964) Stratigraphy of the banded iron formations of Daitari-Tomka area, Cuttack district, Orissa, India. *Intern. Geol. Cong. Sec* 10, pp.13-21.

ACHARYA, S. (1983) A study on wad with structure, its relation with manganese deposit and associated rocks of Orissa. Research Project- Min. Dev. Board.

ACHARYA, S. (2000) Some observations on parts of the Banded Iron-Formations of Eastern India. Pres. Address, 87th session, Ind. Sc. Cong. Ass., pp. 1-34.

ACHARYA, S. (2004a) The Daitari-Tomka basin –its structural and stratigraphic evolution and genesis of associated iron ore. *Ind. Jour. Geol.* vol. 74. pp. 49-81.

ACHARYA, S. (2004b) Iron ore deposit of Orissa. Supra-or-Infra to BIFs. *SGAT* v.5, No.2, pp.39-41.

ACHARYA, S. (2005a) Field characterization of BIF for futuristic mining. *Vista Geol. Res.* v.5, pp.121-125.

ACHARYA, S. (2005b) Genetic modeling of iron and manganese ore deposits of the Joda- Koira iron ore basin (BIF-3), India- Its application to exploration. Int. Sem.VMD-2020, *SGAT*, pp. 44-66.

ACHARYA, S. (2008) Genesis of banded iron formation and associated iron and manganese deposits of Orissa–Jharkhand region, India and its role as exploration grade. *SGAT Sem. On Iron Ores*, p. 1–31.

ALAXENDROV, E.A. (1973) Precambrian banded iron formation of the Soviet Union. *Econ. Geol.*, 68: 1035–1068.

AUG´E, T., COCHERIE, A., GENNA, A, ARMSTRONG, R., GUERROT, C., MUKHERJEE, M. M., and PATRA, R.N. (2003) Age of the Baula PGE mineralization (Orissa India) and its implications concerning the Singhbhum Archaean Nucleus. *Precambrian Res.*, v.121, p. 85–101.

BANERJI, A.K. (1977) On the Precambrian banded iron formations and the manganese ores of the Singhbhum region, eastern India: *Econ. Geol.*, v. 72, p. 90-98.

BEUKES, N. J. (1973) Precambrian Banded Iron-Formation of South Africa. *Econ. Geol.*, v. 68, pp. 960-1004.

BEUKES, N. J., GUTZMER, J., and MUKHOPADHYAY, J., 2003, The geology and genesis of high-grade hematite iron ore deposits: Applied Earth Science, Transactions of the Institute of Mining and Metallurgy, Section B, v. 112, p. 18-25.

BEUKES, N. J., MUKHOPADHYAY, J. and GUTZMER, J., Genesis of high-grade iron ores of the Archean Iron Ore Group around Noamundi, India. *Econ. Geol.*, v. 103, p. 365-386.

BEUKES, N.J. (1973) Precambrian iron formations of Southern Africa. *Econ. Geol.*, 68: 960-1004.

BEUKES, N.J. (1984) Sedimentology of the Kuruman and Griquatown iron-formation, Transvaal Supergroup, Griqualand west, south Africa. *Proc. Res.*, vol.24, pp. 47-84.

BEURA, D. and SINGH, P. (2005a) Geological setting and mineral deposits of Archaean schist belt- A case study around Badampahar belt, north Orissa, India, Int. Sem.Khon Ken Uni. Thailand, pp.326-329

BEURA, D. and SINGH, P. (2005b) Environmental deposition of iron formation of greenstone belt of north Orissa, India Vistas in Geol Research, U.U. Spl. Pub. In: Geol No.4 pp. 246-255.

BEURA, D. and SINGH, P. (2006) Tectonic and structural control characterization of iron ore deposits of Badampahar-Gorumahisani-Suleipat Belt, north Orissa, India, Nat. Sem. On EMRI, Andhra Uni. Abs.

BEURA, D. and SINGH, P. (2008) Tectonically hypothecated genetic model of precambrian iron ore deposits of Badampahar-Gorumahisani-Suleipat belt, Orissa, India. *SGAT Sem.*, p. 32–40.

BEURA, D., SINGH, P. and ACHARYA, S. (2007) BIF and iron ore: an academic perspective and commercial vision. Vistas in Geol. Res, Spl. Pub. No.6, pp. 71-73.

BORCHERT, H. (1960) Genesis of marine sedimentary iron ores. *Trans. Inst. of Mining, Metal*, 69: B261-B279.

CHAKRABORTY, K. I. and MAJUMDER, T. (1986) Geological aspects of the Banded Iron- Formation of Bihar and Orissa. *Geol. Soc. India*, 28, pp.109-133.

CHAKRABORTY, K. L., CHAKRABORTY, T. L. and MAJUMDER, T., (1980) Stratigraphy and structure of the Precambrian banded iron formations and chromite-bearing ultramafic rocks of the Sukinda Valley, Orissa. *J. Geol. Soc. India*, 21, p. 398404.

CHANVEL, J.J. and DIMORTH, E. (1974) Facets types and depositional environments of the Sokomanu iron formation. Labrator Trough. Quebec Canada. *J. Sed. Palm.*, 44: 299–377.

CHATTERJEE, A.K. and MUKHERJEE, P., (1981), The structural set up of a part of the Malangtoli iron ore deposits, Orissa. *Journal Geological Society of India*, v. 22, p. 121–130.

CLOUD, P. (1972) A working model of the primitive earth. *Amer. J. Sci.*, 272: 537-548.

CLOUDE, P.E. Jr. (1973) Palaeoecological significance of the banded iron formation. *Econ. Geol.*, 68: 1135-1143.

DEARNLEY, R. (1965) Orogenic fold belts and continental drift. *Nature*, 206: 1083-1087, 1284-1290.

DEVARAJU, T.C. and SADASHIVAIAH, M.S. (1966) Pyroxene quartz magnetite rock from Satnur-Halagut and Mysore State. *J. Geol. Soc. India*, 7: 70-85

DIMROTH, E. (1977) Facies models. 5. Diagnostic facies of iron formation. *Geoscience* Canada, 4: 83-88.

DIMROTH, E. (1986) Depositional Environments and Tectonic Settings of the Cherty Iron-Formations of the Canadian Shield. *Jour. Geol. Soc. India*, pp. 239-250.

DIMROTH, E. and CHAUVEL, J.J. (1973) Petrography of the Sokoman Iron Formation in part of central Laborato Trough. *Quebec Canada. Gen. Soc. Env. Bill.*, 84: 111–134.

DORR, II, J.V.N. (1973) Iron formation and associated manganese in Brazil. In: Proc. Kiev Symp. UNESCO, Earth Sci., 9: 105-113.

DORR, J.V.N. (1964) Supergene iron ores of Minas Gerais, Brazil. *Econ. Geol.*, 59: 1203-1241.

DORR, J.V.N. (1973) Iron formation in South America. *Econ. Geol.*, 68: 1005-1022.

DREVER, J.I. (1974) Geochemical model for the origin of Precambrian banded iron formations. *Bull. Geol. Soc. America*, 85: 1099-1106.

DRURY, S.A. (1984) A Proteozoic intractratonic basin, dyke swarns and thermal evaluation in south India. *J. Geol. Soc. India*, 25: 437-449.

DUNN, J.A. (1937) Mineral deposits of Eastern Singhbhum and surrounding areas. *Mem. Geol. Surv. India*, No 69, 1,

DUNN, J.A. (1940) Stratigraphy of the south Singhbum. *Mem. Geol. Surv. India*, 63: 303-369.

DUNN, J.A. (1940) The stratigraphy of south Singhbhum. *Mem. Geol. Surv. India*, No. 63, p. 303-309.

DUNN, J.A. (1941) The origin of the banded hematite ores in India. *Econ. Geol.*, v. 36, p. 355-370.

DUNN, J.A. and DEY, A.K. (1942) Geology and petrology of Eastern Singhbhum and surrounding areas. *Memo. Geol. Surv. India*, v. 69, pt. 2.

EICHLOR, J. (1976) Origin of the Precambrian banded iron-formation. Chapter 4, pp. 157-201. In: Handbook of strata-bound and stratiform ore deposits. Part II. Regional studies and specific deposits. Elsevier.

FIROZ, A.S. (2008) Mineral Policy Issues in the Context of Export and Domestic Use of Iron Ore in India, Working Paper – 207, ICRER, Delhi.

FRENCH, B.M. (1973) Mineral Assemblages in Diagenetic and Low-grade Metamorphic Iron-Formation. *Econ. Geol.*, v. 68, pp. 1063-1074.

FRENCH, V.M. (1973) Mineral assemblages in diagene and low grade metamorphic iron-formations. *Econ. Geol.*, 68: 1063-1074.

FRYER, B.J. (1977a) Trace element geochemistry of the Sokomon Iron Formata. *Canadian J. Earth Sci.*, 14: 1598-1610.

FRYER, B.J. (1977b) Rare earth evidence in iron formation for changing Precambrian oxidation state. *Geochem. Cosmochem Acta*, 41: 361-367.

FRYER, B.J. (1983) Rare earth elements in iron formation. In: A.F. Trendall and R.C. Morris (Eds.) *Iron Formation: Facts and Problem*. Elsevier, pp. 345-357.

GAAL, G. (1989) Tectonic evolution of Fenno-Scandian (Baltic) Shield: Comparison of Archaean and Proterozoic Geology with emphasis of granite-greenstone terrains. *(Abs). 28th Int. Geol. Cong.* Washington D. C., v.1, p.521.

GABRIELSE, H. (1972) Younger Precambrian of the Canadian Cordillera. *Am. J. Sci.*, 272: 521-536.

GAIR, J.E. (1973) Iron deposits of Michigan (United States of America). In: *Genesis of Precambrian Iron and Manganese Deposits*. UNESCO, p. 365-375.

GARRLES, R.M. and CHRIST C.L. (1965) *Solutions, Minerals and Equilibria*. Harper & Row, pp. 450.

GASTIL, G. and KNOWLES, D.M. (1960) Geology of the Wabush Lake, South Water Labradow and eastern. Quebec Canada, *Bull. Geol. Amer.*, 71: 1243-1254.

GHOSH, G. and MUKHOPADHYAY, J. (2007) Reappraisal of the structure of the Western Iron Ore Group, Singhbhum craton, eastern India: Implications for the exploration of BIF-hosted iron ore deposits: *Gondwana Research*, v. 12, p. 525-532.

GHOSH, K.P. (2006) Dichotomy in iron ore reserves and supply for projected growth of steel capacity in India: *Procd. National Seminar on Emerging Technology in Iron and Steel Making*, Ranchi, 28-29th January 2006.

GHOSH, K.P. (2006) Dichotomy in iron ore reserves and supply for projected growth of steel capacity in India. Proc. Nat. Sem. Emerging Tech. in Iron Ore Steel Making. Ranchi, 28-29 Jan. 2006.

GHOSH, K.P. (2006) Raw materials' quality – It's impact on iron making - Indian Scenario China – India: Iron Ore Summit, Proceedings, China, 13-14 April, 2006.

GHOSH, K.P. (2008) Iron ores: Issues and controversies. *SGAT Sem. On Iron Ores*, p. 131–140.

GHOSH, K.P., PAL, D., CHAKRABARTY, S. and SEN, A. (1996) Global pellet situation – an overview: Proc. National Seminar on Indian Iron and Steel Industry: Vision 2012, V. II, PP. 777-785, 28-30 October, Goa.

GHOSH, K.P., SENGUPTA, N.and SENGUPTA, A. (2000) Raw materials for Iron and Steel Industry – Indian Scenario: Steel Scenario, Vol. 10/Q1, July-September.

GOLDISCH, S.S. (1973) Ages of Precambrian banded iron formation. *Econ. Geol.*, 68: 1126-1134.

GOODWIN, A.M. (1973) Archaean Iron-Formation and Tectonic Basins of the Canadian Shield. *Econ. Geol.*, 68, pp. 915-933.

GOODWIN, A.M. (1977) Archean basin-craton complexes and growth of Precambrian shield. *Canadian J. Earth Sci.*, 114: 2737-2759.

GOODWIN, A.M. and RIDLER, R.H. (1970) The Apitibi Orogenic belt. *Geol. Surv., Canada*, Paper 40, 1-30.

GOSWAMI, J.N., MISRA, S., WIEDENBACK, M., RAY, S. L., and SAHA, A.K. (1995) 3.55 Ga old zircon from Singhbhum-Orissa Iron Ore craton, eastern India. *Current Science*, v. 69, p. 1008-1011.

GOVETT, G.S. (1966) Origin of banded iron formations. *Bull Geol. Soc. Amer.*, 77: 1191-1212.

GROGS (1980) A classification of iron foundation based on depreidone environments. *Canadian Mineral*, 18: 215–222.

GROSS, G.A. (1970) Nature and occurrence of iron ore deposits. In: *Survey of World Iron Ore Resources*. UN Pub. ST/ECA/113. pp. 13-31.

GROSS, G.A. (1980) A classification of iron formation based on depositional environments. *Canadian Min.*, 18: 215-222.

GROSS, G.A. 1965. Geology of iron deposits in Canada. Vol. 1: General geology and evaluation of ore deposits. Canada Geol. Surv. *Econ. Geol.* Rept., 27: 181 pp.

GUNDERSON, J.N and SCHWARTZ, G.M. (1962) The geology of the metamorphosed Biwabik iron-formation. Eastern Mesabi district, Minnesota. *Bull. Minn. Geol.* Surv.., 43, 139.

GUTZMER, J., MUKHOPADHYAY, J., BEUKES, N.J., PACK, A., HAYASHI, K., and SHARP, Z.D. (2006) Oxygen isotope composition of hematite and genesis of high-grade BIF-hosted iron ores, in Ohmoto, H., Kesler, S.E. (eds.), Evolution of Earth's Atmosphere, Hydrosphere, and Biosphere – Constraints from Ore Deposits: Geological Society of America, Memoir 198, pp. 257-268.

HUBER, N. K. (1958) The environmental control of sedimentary iron minerals. *Econ Geol.*, v. 58, p.123-140.

HUBER, N. K. and GARRELS, W.H. (1953) Relation of pH and oxidation potential to sedimentary iron mineral formation: *Econ. Geol.*, v. 48, pp. 337-357.

IYENGAR, S.V.P, and MURTY, N.G.K. (1982). The evolution of the Archean-Proteozoic crust in parts of Bihar and Orissa, Eastern India. *Rec. Geol. Surv. India*, v.112, pp. 1-5

IYENGER, S. V. P. and ALWAR, A. M. A., 1965, The Dhanjori Eugeosyncline and its bearing on the stratigraphy of Singhbhum, Keonjhar and Mayurbhanja Districts, *DN Wadia Comm Vol, Min. Met. Inst. India*, Calcutta, pp. 138-162

JAMES, H.L. (1906) Chemistry of the iron rich sedimentary rocks. US 95 Proc. Paper 440-61 pp.

JAMES, H.L. (1954) Sedimentary facies of iron-formation. *Econ. Geol.*, 19, pp. 235-291.

JAMES, H.L. (1983) Distribution of Banded Iron-Formation in space and time. Iron-Formation: Facts and Problems. Elsevier, pp. 471-490.

JAYARAM, B. (1917) Preliminary note on the iron bearing and associated rocks in neighbourhood of Madder and Kunigal. *Rec. Mysore Geol. Deptt.* No. 12.

JONES, H. C. (1934) The iron ore deposits of Bihar and Orissa. *Geol. Surv. India Mem.*, v.63 pt. 2, p.167-302.

KENNEDY, W.Q. (1964) The structural differentiation of Africa in the Pan-African (± 500mg) tectonic episode. 8th Ann. Rep. Sci., Results Leeds, 1964.

KLEIN, C. (1973) Change in mineral assemblage will metamorphum of some Precambrian iron formation. *Econ. Geol.*, 68: 1075–1088.

KLEIN, C. (1973) Regional metamorphic of Proterozoic iron formation. Labrador, Trough. Canada. *Amer Min.* 63: 898-912.

KLEIN, C. (1974) Greenalite, stilpnomelne, minnestotatie, crucidolite and carbonocilli in a very low grade metamorphic Precambrian iron formation. *Canada Min.*, 17: 475–498.

KLEIN, C. and BEUKES, N.J. (1989) Geochemistry and Sedimentology of a facies Transition from Limestone to Iron-Formation Deposition in the early Proterozoic Transvaal Supergroup, South Africa. *Eco. Geol.*, 84, pp. 1733-1742.

KLEIN, C. and GOLE, M.J. (1981) Minerology and petrology of parts of Marra-Mamta iron formation, Hamersley Basin, Western Australia. *Amer. Mineral.*, 66: 517-525.

KLEIN, C. Jr. (1973) Changes in mineral assemblage with metamorphism of some banded Precambrian iron-formations. *Econ. Geol.*, 68: 1075-1088.

KOKALE, P.J. (1978) Iron ore: Energy, labour and capital changes with technology. *Science*, 202: 1151-1157.

KRAUSKOPF, K. B. and BIRD, D. K. (1995) *Introduction to Geochemistry*. Ed. 3, McGraw-Hill, Inc.

KRISHNAN, M. S. (1954) Iron ore, Iron and Steel. Bull. Geol. Surv. India, *Econ. Geol.* Series, 9, 264p.

KRISHNAN, M.S. (1982) *Geology of India and Burma*, 6th edn. CBS Pub., Delhi, 536 pp.

KRUMBEIN, W.C. and GARRELS, R.M. (1952) Origin and classification of chemical sediments in terms of pH and oxidation-reduction potentials. *J. Geol.*, 60: 1-33.

KRUMBEIN, W.C. and GARRLES, R.M. (1952) Origin and classificate of chemical sediments in term of pH and oxidation-reduction potentials. *J. Geol.* 60: 1-33.

LA BERGE, G.L. (1964) Development of magnetite in iron formations of the Lake Superior region: *Econ. Geol.*, 59, pp. 1313-1342.

LAAJOKI, K. (1975) Rare earth elements in Precambrian iron formations in Vayrylankyla, South Puolanka area, Finland. *Bull. Geol. Surv., Finland*, 47: 93-107.

LAAJOKI, K. and LAVIKARINOU, S. (1977) Rare earth elements in the prcheau iron formation and associated sults in Ukkoknavaara, Ilomantsi, Se. Finland. *Bull. Geol. Surv., Finland*, 49: 105-123.

LAAJOKI, K. and SAIKKONEN, R. (1977) On the geology and geochemistry of the Precambrian iron-formations inf Vayrylankyla, South Poulanka area, Finland. *Bull. Geol. Surv., Finland*, 292, 137 pp.

LAHIRI, J.K. (2002) Geochemistry and genesis of banded iron formation and iron ores of Gandhamardan area, Orissa. *Indian Journal of Geology*, v. 74, p. 83-98.

LEPP, H. and GOLDICH, S.S. (1964) Origin of Precambrian iron formations. *Econ. Geol.*, 59: 1025-1060.

LEPP. H. and GOLDRICH S.S. (1964) Origin of Precambrian Iron-formation EC. GI.,v. 68, pp-1098-1109. MENGEL J.T. (1973) Physical sedimentation in Precambrian. cherty iron formation of lake superior type Ed. Anstudy and Bepenard, Ores in sediments Ind. *Uni. Geol. Sc. Srs.*A. No3 pp-179-193.

MAHABALESWAR, B. (1986) Mineral chemistry of the silicate minerals phaws of banded iron formations of high grade region, Karnataka. *J. Geol. Soc., India*, 28: 965-975.

MAHABALESWAR, B., BASAVANNA, M. and MAASKANT, P. (1987) Iron formations of archean high grade region, Karnataka, India. 487-511. In: Precambrian Formations (Ed.) P.W.V. Apped and G.L. Le Berge. Theophrastus Pub., 674 pp.

MAJUMDAR, T. and CHAKRABORTY, K.L. (1977) Primary sedimentary structure in the banded iron formations of Orissa, India. Sed. Geol., 19: 297-300.

MAYNARD, J.B. (1983) *Geochemistry of sedimentary ore deposits*. Springer-Verlag, New York, 305 p.

MAZUMDAR, T., WHITE, J.E. and CHAKRABORTY, K.L. (1984) Rare earth elements in the India and banded iron formation. *Chem. Geol.*, 45: 203-211.

MELNIK, Y.P. (1982) Precambrian banded iron-formation. Elsevier, 310.

MISRA, S. (2006) Precambrian chronostratigraphic growth of Singhbhum-Orissa craton, eastern Indian shield: an alternative model. *Jour. Geol. Soc. India*, v. 67, p. 356-378.

MISRA, S., DEOMURARI, M. P., WIEDENBECK, M., GOSWAMI, J. N., RAY, S., and SAHA, A. K. (1999) $^{207}Pb/^{206}Pb$ zircon ages and the evolution of the Singhbhum craton, eastern India: an ion microprobe study. *Precambrian Res.*, v. 93, p.139-151.

MONDAL, S. K., FEI, R., and RIPLEY, E.M. (2007) Os isotope systematics of Mesoarchean chromitite-PGE deposits in the Singhbhum Craton (India):

Implications for the evolution of lithospheric mantle. *Chem. Geol.*, v. 244, p. 391-408.

MONDAL, S. K., RIPLEY E., M., LI, C., and FREI, R. (2006) The genesis of Archaean chromitites from the Nausahi and Sukinda massifs in the Singhbhum Craton, India. *Precambrian Res.* v.148, p. 45–66.

MOOKHERJEE, A. (1998) *Ore Genesis – A Holistic Approach.* Prentice Hall. Calcutta.

MOOKHERJEE, A. (2000) Crustal Fluids and Formation of Mineral Deposits. Foundation Lecture at The Earth System Science Section. 87th Ses. Ind.Sc.Cong.Pune. p. 1-19.

MORRIS, R.C. (1980) A textural and mineralogical study of the relationship of iron ore to banded iron formations in the Hamersley iron province of Western Australia. *Econ. Geol.*, 75: 184-209.

MORRIS, R.C. (1986) The cycling redox state of iron in the genesis of Banded Iron-Formations and their associated enrichment iron ores. *Jour. Geol. Soc., India*, v.28, pp. 227-236.

MORRIS, R.C. and HORWITZ, R.C. (1983) The origin of the iron formation-rich Hamersley Group of Western Australia deposition on a platform. *Precambrian Res.*, vol. 21, pp. 273-297.

MÜCKE, A. and ANNOR, A. (1993) Examples and genetic significance of the formation of iron oxides in the Nigerian banded iron-formations. *Mineral. Deposita.* 28, 136-145.

MUKHOPADHYAY, D. (1986) Structural pattern in the Dharwar Craton. *J. Geol.*, 94: 167-186.

MUKHOPADHYAY, J. GUTZMER, J., BEUKES, N. J., and BHATTACHARYA, H. N., (2008) Geology and Genesis of BIF-hosted high-grade iron ore deposits of India. *In:*, Hagemann, S., Rosiere, C. A., Beukes, N. J., and Gutzmer, J. Eds., Geology and Genesis of BIF-hosted high-grade iron ore deposits of the world., *Reviews in Economic Geology, Society of Economic Geology (SEG)*, USA, v. 15, p. 291-316.

MUKHOPADHYAY, J., BEUKES, N. J., and GUTZMER, J. (2002) Petrographic evidence of Hydrothermal Origin of BIF-Hosted High-Grade Iron Ores from Eastern and Central India [Abs.]: International Sedimentological Congress, 16th, Johannesburg, Abstract Volume 2002, p. 271-272.

MUKHOPADHYAY, J., BEUKES, N. J., and GUTZMER, J. (2004) Deep-Seated Hydrothermal Magnetite Ore from Gorumahishani, Archean Iron Ore Group, Singhbhum Craton, India: *32nd IGC, Florence Italy*, Aug-20-28.

MUKHOPADHYAY, J., BEUKES, N. J., ARMSTRONG, R. A., ZIMMERMANN, U., GHOSH, G., and MEDDA, R.A. (2008) Dating the Oldest Greenstone in India: A 3.51-Ga Precise U-Pb SHRIMP Zircon Age for Dacitic Lava of the Southern Iron Ore Group, Singhbhum Craton. *Journal of Geology*, 116, p. 449-461.

MUKHOPADHYAY, J., GHOSH, G. BEUKES, N.J. AND GUTZMEN, J. (2008) Eastern India high grade iron ores: Genetic models and implication for exploration. *SGAT Sem. On Iron Ores*, p. 51–56.

MUKHOPADHYAY, J., GHOSH, G., BEUKES, N. J., and GUTZMER, J. (2007) Precambrian colluvial iron ores in the Singhbhum craton: implications for origin, age of BIF-hosted high-grade iron ores and stratigraphy of the Iron Ore Group: *Journal of the Geological Society of India*, 70, p. 34-42.

MUKHOPADHYAY, J., GHOSH, G., NANDY, A., and CHAUDHURI, A.K. (2006) Depositional setting of the Kolhan Group: its implications for the development of a Meso to Neoproterozoic deep-water basin on the South Indian craton. *South African Journal of Geology*, 109, p. 183-192.

NAYANNA, C. and MAHABALESHWAR, B. (1976) Iron formations associated with granulites of Karnataka. *Proc. Symp. Geol. of ferrous and ferro-alloy minerals*, p. 7-14.

O'ROURKE, J.F. (1961) Paleozoic banded iron formation. *Econ. Geol.*, 56: 331-361.

PANIGRAHI, A.B. and MURTHY, A.N. (2008) Genesis and exploration scenario of north Goa iron ore. *SGAT Sem. On Iron Ores*, p. 41–50.

PARRY, E.C. and AHMAD, S.N. (1981) Oxygen and carbon isotype geochemistry of Kriroy Rog iron formation. Ukranian SSR. *Lithos*, 14: 83-92.

PAUL, D. K., MUKHOPADHYAY, D., PYNE, T. K., and BISHUI, P.K. (1991) Rb-Sr age of granitoid in the Deo River section, Singhbhum and its relevance to the age of iron formation. *Indian Minerals*, 45, p. 726-728.

PFLUG, R. (1987) Die Prekambrisch Miogeosynklinle der Espinkaco-Kordillerse. Mmas, Gerais Brasillien, *Geol. Rundsch.*, 56: 825-844.

PITCHAMATHU, C.S. and SRINIVASAN, R. (1984) The Dharwar craton. *India Nat. Sci. Acad.* Golden Jubilee, Pub. 34 pp.

PRASAD RAO, G.H. S. V., MURTHY, Y.G.K. and DEEKSHITULU, M.N. (1964) Stratigraphic relation of Precambrian iron formations and associated sedimentary sequences in parts of Keonjhar, Cuttack, Dhenkanal and Sundargarh districts, Orissa, India. Proc. Int. Geol. Congress, 22nd Session, Part 10, pp. 72-87.

RADHAKRISHNA, B.P. (1983) Archaean granite-greenstone terrain of the South Indian Shield. *Memo. Geol. Soc. India*, 4, pp. 1-46.

RADHAKRISHNA, B.P. and NAQVI, S.M. (1983) Archean granite greenstone terrain of the South Indian Shield. In: S.M. Naqvi and J.J.W. Rogers (Ed.) *Precambrian of South India. Mem. Geol. Soc. India*, 4: 1-46.

RADHAKRISHNA, B.P., DEVARAJU, T.C. and MAHABALESWAR, B. (1986) Banded Iron Formation of India. *Jour. Geol.Soc. India*, 28, pp. 71-91.

RUNEORN, S.K. (1962) Paleomagnetic evidence in continental drift and its geological cause. Continental Drift I. Academic Press.

SAHA, A.K. (1994) Crustal evolution of Singhbhum-North Orissa, eastern India. *Geol. Soc. Ind. Mem.* 27, pp. 341

SAMPAT IYENGER, P. (1920) The acid rocks of Mysore (South India). *Bull. Mysore Geol.* Deptt. No. 18.

SARKAR, S.C. (2000) Crustal evolution and metallogeny in the eastern Indian craton: *Geological Survey of India Special Publication* 55, p. 169-194.

SARKAR, S.C. (2002) Crustal Evolution and metallogeny in South Singhbhum and the adjacent parts of Orissa: results of some recent studies and their possible significance. *Indian Jour. Geol.*, 74, p. 27-36.

SARKAR, S.C. and GUPTA, A. (2005) Nature and origin of the iron ores of eastern India: a subject of scientific interest and industrial concern: Mining, Geological, Metallurgical Institute of India, Seminar on Mineral and Energy Resources of Eastern India, Kolkata, Proceedings, p. 79-101.

SARKAR, S.N. and SAHA, A.K. (1962) A revision of the Precambrian stratigraphy and tectonic of Singhbhum and adjacent region. *Quart. J. Geol. Mining, Mefall, Soc. India*, 34: 91-136.

SARKAR, S.N. and SAHA, A.K. (1983) Structure and tectonics of the Singhbhum-Orissa Iron Ore craton, eastern India. In Rec. Res. Geol., 10, (*Structure and Tectonics of the Precambrian rocks*). Hindustan Pub. Corp. India, Delhi, pp. 1-25.

SAWKINS, F. J. (1990). *Metal deposits in relation to plate tectonics*. Springer-Verlag, Berlin. p. 461.

SEMENENKU, V.P. (1973) Iron-chart formation of the Ukrainian shield. In: *Genesis of Precambrian Irion and Manganese Reports*, UNESCO, 135-142.

SMEETH, N.F. (1916) Outline of the geological history of Mysore. *Bull. Mysore Geol.* Deptt. No. 6.

SPENCER, E., and PERCIVAL, F.G. (1952) The structure and origin of the banded hematite jasper of Singhbhum, India. *Econ. Geol.*, 67, p. 365-385.

SWAMINATH, J. and RAMAKRISHNA, M. (1981) Early Precambrian supranatrual of Southern Karnataka. *Mem. Geol. Surv., India*, 112: 350 pp.

TRENDALL, A.F. (1973a) Precambrian iron formation of Australia. *Econ. Geol.*, 68: 1023-1024.

WEDOPOHL, K.H. (1969 Ed.) *Handbook of Geochemistry*. Springer-Verlag.

# Author Index

# Subject Index